GUIDE TO THE MANAGEMENT GURUS

THE BEST GUIDE TO BUSINESS THINKERS

CAROL KENNEDY

BUSINESS
BOOKS

Published by Random House Business Books in 2007

3 5 7 9 10 8 6 4 2

First published by Century in 1991.

Random House Business Books
The Random House Group Limited
20 Vauxhall Bridge Road, London SW1V 2SA

Addresses for companies within The Random House Group Limited can be found at:
www.randomhouse.co.uk/offices.htm

The Random House Group Limited Reg. No. 954009

www.randomhouse.co.uk

A CIP catalogue record for this book
is available from the British Library

The Random House Group makes every effort to ensure that the papers used in its books
are made from trees that have been legally sourced from well-managed and credibly certified forests.
Our paper procurement policy can be found at:
www.randomhouse.co.uk/paper.htm

ISBN 9781905211029

Typeset by Palimpsest Book Production Limited, Grangemouth, Stirlingshire

Printed and bound in Great Britain by
Mackays of Chatham plc, Chatham, Kent

GUIDE TO THE MANAGEMENT
GURUS

THE BEST GUIDE TO
BUSINESS THINKERS

CONTENTS

PREFACE TO THE
FIFTH EDITION

In the boom times of the 1990s, management theory exploded into a series of fads, a phenomenon that had a lot in common with the latest fashionable diet. If the current big idea didn't work, the next one surely would, and there was always another just round the corner. Both management fashions and diets shifted huge numbers of books and made fortunes for their progenitors. They did so by selling optimism and hope, and usually worked just well enough to keep the faithful hooked and to ensure that no theory or diet was ever entirely supplanted by its successor. Many companies today are still wedded to business process re-engineering, total quality management or the error-free discipline known as Six Sigma – the three great fads of the 1990s – just as individuals can be found still adhering to the F-Plan, the Hay Diet or the Atkins Diet, despite the regular appearance of newer formulae offering everything from radical detoxification to a longer lifespan.

These days, the procession of diets still marches on, but the business world has grown more sceptical. After the dotcom crash, widespread equity meltdown, the impact of global terrorism and a rash of corporate scandals – at least one company, Enron, having once been a management fad for its supposed culture of innovation – there is less enthusiasm for the silver-bullet solution or ten-steps-to-heaven approach peddled by those promising instant management wisdom. The gurus of the conference circuit are still there, but their messages are less magnetic. It is time to cast a more critical eye on what works and what doesn't, and to review the core values in management theory, hence this new edition of a book that has been constantly in print since 1991 and updated three times.

Management theory is not served well by fads. It is a constant work in progress, sending out new shoots and capable of being re-interpreted for a changed business environment. In 1999, the late Peter Drucker, the greatest business thinker of the 20th century, said that even if all the big management ideas had already been conceived, management theory was 'an unfinished business always in need of constant repairs and rejuvenation'.

Though the power of the management guru has waned since its peak in the 1990s, theories continue to be important if only because, as the British management writer Simon Caulkin has observed, they tend to become self-fulfilling. If managers believe in Douglas McGregor's famous Theory X – that workers will only respond to stick and carrot treatment – and design the running of their companies accordingly, that is what will happen. The reverse is also true, as McGregor proved when he designed a plant for Procter & Gamble in Atlanta in the 1950s run on a Theory Y system of self-managed, responsible teams: it was so productive that the company kept it a trade secret for 40 years.

Caulkin quotes Professor Jeffrey Pfeffer of Stanford, an eminent thinker on human relations in industry and one of the new additions to this book, as saying that the conventional view is that theories win because they are better at explaining behaviour, whereas the truth is that they win because they affect behaviour, fulfilling their own influence.

Pfeffer is not alone among business academics in taking a jaundiced view of the effect that management theory can have on practice. Shortly before his untimely death in 2004, Professor Sumantra Ghoshal of London Business School attacked what he saw as bad management theories destroying good management practice. He argued that the disasters uncovered by the Enron and WorldCom scandals had a connection with some of the ideas loudly promoted by business schools before the crash – ideas which assumed a negative view of people as self-interested and motivated principally by incentives, reducing the ethical or moral content of management.

Pfeffer says: 'There is growing evidence that self-interested behaviour is learned behaviour – and people learn it by studying business and economics.' He goes so far as to say that such courses are 'hazards to your moral health'.* The eminent Canadian management thinker Henry Mintzberg has also become a severe critic of the way management is taught in business courses such as the MBA to people he feels are often too young. Students without prior management experience have no means of testing what they are taught against the realities of the workplace.

But management, as Drucker always believed, has a role that far exceeds the running of business corporations. From family to government, from charity to orchestra or ballet company, managing people to produce a desired result is one of the greatest human skills, and the newest management thinking is beginning to reflect this, along with more of a social conscience than in the past century.

Most of the fresh entries in this book have made their reputations along these lines. Karen Stephenson and Jeffrey Pfeffer study how human beings interact together in working relationships. Fons Trompenaars is an expert on managing diversity in different national cultures. The importance of trust as a motivating glue within the organization is one of the themes explored by W. Chan Kim and Renée Mauborgne of INSEAD. James MacGregor Burns, a seminal leadership theorist of the 1960s, worked primarily in the political sphere, but his concepts of 'transactional' and 'transformational' leaders apply in all types of organization.

Corporate social responsibility (CSR), a concept hardly known in the freebooting 1990s, is now a leading item on boardroom agendas. For most companies it means enhancing their respect in society through establishing good governance procedures and ethical practices such as regulating the treatment of employees in low-cost producer countries. Nike suffered serious reputation loss for a time through 'sweat-shop' behaviour by some of its suppliers.

C. K. Prahalad, a notable new entry in this book, has taken CSR into a whole new dimension. His bold vision of helping

---

* The *Observer*, 2 October 2005.

the world's poorest consumers through innovative marketing strategies by multinationals represents a truly original strand of management thinking. The practical examples he cites from his native India support his belief that the untapped 'bottom of the pyramid' market can furnish genuine business opportunities as well as a moral good.

As the business environment grows tougher and more competitive, innovation generally is becoming a dominant theme in management thinking, from sheer corporate survival to the international productivity league. (US success in the latter is largely attributable to a better innovation record than European countries.) The mechanics and processes of innovation distinguish the work of another new entry, Harvard professor Clayton Christensen, whose books explore the ways in which businesses can lose out or triumph against competitors through 'disruptive technologies'. Innovation by locating hitherto uncharted markets is also a key theme of Professors Kim and Mauborgne in their 'blue ocean' strategy.

The last three new entries are classic names who should have qualified for earlier editions but now find their rightful place: the time-and-motion study pioneers, Frank and Lillian Gilbreth, a unique married partnership of engineers in the early 20th century; Henry Gantt, whose work-flow chart still governs much industrial practice today, and the 1970s futurologist Alvin Toffler, whose influential books were far more right than wrong in foretelling the shape of our society and business organizations.

Carol Kennedy, London, May 2006

INTRODUCTION

The age of the guru

There is a limit to the number of original ideas in any field of human activity, and management is no exception. After all, it is said that there are no more than seven basic plots throughout the whole world of fiction and drama. Some of the most enduring themes of management were conceived centuries before commercial or industrial management was born, let alone the concept of the management guru with his or her prescriptives for performance.

Machiavelli's *The Prince*, written at the height of the Renaissance in Florence, is still a classic text on leadership and the uses of power (and inspired a popular management book of the 1960s by Antony Jay). The translator of its bestselling Penguin edition, the late George Bull, observed that *The Prince*'s precepts are 'perfectly applicable to the actions of captains of industry or budding entrepreneurs', citing as just one example Machiavelli's advice that when a ruler seizes a state (or a new chief executive moves into a company), he must do the hardest things first. 'The new ruler must determine all the injuries that he will need to inflict. He must inflict them once and for all, and not have to renew them every day. In that way he will be able to set men's minds at rest, and win them over to him when he confers benefits.' Every takeover king has instinctively practised that.

Further back in history, the basic human responses to work and responsibility were articulated by Plato and Aristotle in their differing views of man; the former believing that authoritarian direction was needed if anything of value was to be accomplished, the latter that man as a 'social' or 'political' animal required a sense of participation in his own destiny. In the 1960s, Douglas McGregor dressed up the concepts with sociological research into industrial practice and presented them as Theory X and Theory Y – authoritarian versus democratic management. It became one of the great management theories of all time.

Digging even deeper into antiquity, management writers have adapted the wisdom of Taoism to the modern executive office. There is even a book on management in Shakespeare and jokey exercises on Genghis Khan and Attila the Hun as business tacticians. No doubt the Roman emperors will one day yield a book on leadership strategy.

Variations on ideas, of course, are infinite or can be made to seem so. It is this which accounts for the vast numbers of management books that pour annually from publishing houses on both sides of the Atlantic, and for the lucrative packaged wisdom that brings handsome incomes – indeed, millionaire status – to the leading management gurus. The explosion of management advice has been phenomenal; from 771 business books published in the UK in 1975 to 3,749 in 2002, the last year for which figures are available. In the US, birthplace of the management guru, business publishing and consultancy is a multi-billion-dollar industry.

The management guru whose precepts are bought as the key to success is essentially a phenomenon of the last 50 years. Before World War II, when, as Peter Drucker has recalled, 'all the books on management filled no more than a modest shelf' – perhaps 70 in all languages except Japanese – the thinkers on management who won the admiration of their peers could be numbered on the fingers of one hand.

Several were career businessmen whose management wisdom was distilled into books long after they had learned it on the job; notably Alfred P. Sloan of General Motors, who built the world's largest corporation out of a medium-sized, ailing automobile manufacturer, and Chester Barnard of AT&T, who wrote what remained for many years the definitive text on the functions of the executive. Sloan's memoir, *My Years With General Motors*, is still revered, more than 40 years after publication and some 80 years after the events it chronicled, as the classic exposition of how to create a great business enterprise by applying the principles of total marketing and decentralization.

In Britain, the lone management theorist in the 1930s was Lyndall Urwick, who had been converted to 'scientific management' as an officer in the Flanders trenches by reading the works of Frederick W. Taylor, the progenitor of time-and-motion study. In 1934, Urwick set up Britain's first management consultancy, Urwick Orr and Partners.

Others who worked away in the interwar years, reacting against Taylor's mechanistic approach by studying the human element in organizations and the springs of motivation – including Elton Mayo with his experiments at Western Electric's Hawthorne plant in Chicago – did not publish their findings until the 1950s and 1960s. Then, backed by distinguished academic appointments in North American universities, they became almost instant gurus.

Management gurus are overwhelmingly a US phenomenon, bred out of the great business schools such as Harvard, Stanford and the Sloan School of Management at Massachusetts Institute of Technology (MIT). The UK can boast only one guru of world class, the philosophical Charles Handy, who is withdrawing from the study of business organizations to focus on wider questions of capitalism and society, though the ideas of earlier, underrated thinkers such as Reg Revans, the originator of action learning, continue to resonate.

As with inventions, Britain has given birth to several key management theories and seen them developed elsewhere. The principle of separating value-adding from non-value-adding activities, which lies behind re-engineering, the value chain and much else, was first developed by an obscure ICI work-study researcher, while several of today's dominant management themes, including group working and the impact of technology on employees, were pioneered by the Tavistock Institute in London's Bloomsbury.

Hugely but quietly influential over the 50 years of its existence, the Tavistock, a hybrid research establishment which was set up to help postwar organizational reconstruction, has never possessed the flair of the US business schools in marketing ideas. 'Socio-technical systems', in Tavistock-speak, does not have the ring of 're-engineering', though it took a more humanistic approach to technology-driven processes; something re-engineering's Michael Hammer and his disciples have adopted only belatedly. Professor Enid Mumford, a Tavistock council member, has described re-engineering as 'the poor man's version of socio-technical systems – restructuring without any human element'. Elements of Tavistock research also paved the way for teamworking and empowerment and contributed to Japanese quality circles and to the admired group work practices at Saab and Volvo.

In mainland Europe, the concept of the management guru is almost unknown, except for a cluster of high-powered thinkers at INSEAD, the international business school at Fontainebleau, near Paris. Here, some significant theories are being developed in the field of strategic management by a Korean-born academic, W. Chan Kim, and a fellow professor of strategy, Renée Mauborgne, who are new entries in this edition. Their concepts of innovation thinking and of fair process – capturing the loyalty and creativity of employees through transparent management decision-making – provoked international interest after their publication in *Harvard Business Review*.

INSEAD also has its own leadership guru, Dutch-born Manfred Kets de Vries. He is unusual in taking a psychoanalyst's approach to the subject and has published a popular book on leadership and stress, *Life and Death in the Executive Fast Lane*. Yves Doz is another INSEAD heavyweight thinker who has linked up with the ubiquitous Gary Hamel of California but has yet to establish his solo guru credentials with a major book.

Hamel is a former Stanford professor who had been lecturing unobtrusively on strategy at London Business School for a decade before shooting to virtually overnight guru status after the publication of *Competing for the Future* in 1994. This identified the concept of core competencies and strategic intent, which have become his trademark subjects. Now he ranks almost in the Peters–Porter league as a highly paid management speaker, in demand all over the world and on video-conference link-ups, although his star faded after the collapse in 2001 of Enron, the energy company he had praised as a new kind of business model, but whose success turned out to be built on fraudulent accounting.

Hamel's co-author on *Competing for the Future*, Indian-born

C. K. Prahalad of the University of Michigan Business School, has taken some ten years to achieve his proper recognition as a management guru but is now acknowledged as an original thinker, especially in helping the world's poorest regions through applications of business innovation. He has his own entry in this new edition.

The guru phenomenon is also curiously absent from Japan and the other erstwhile 'tiger' economies of the Pacific Rim. These appear, until recently, to have generated world-beating success in business without benefit of home-grown gurus, unless one counts the heads of Honda, Sony and Matsushita, who have achieved a certain guru status through the way they run their companies. (Japan's one great obeisance to management gurus remains its homage to Americans W. Edwards Deming and Joseph Juran, who, in the 1950s, converted the Japanese to the principles of quality control.) Since the word 'guru' (a Sanskrit derivation meaning weighty and extended to mean a Hindu priest) originated in the East, one may ask why Eastern businesses have been able to manage pretty well without them.

The inescapable conclusion is that, in the West, everything has to be marketed before it is taken seriously, and that goes for the whole management-improvement business. Not surprisingly, a number of leading US academics who enjoy high guru status dislike being tagged with the word, though nearly all have highly commercial consultancies and are no strangers to marketing their own skills.

How are gurus born or created? Many a management writer and professor of business studies has laboured towards the elusive goal without ever coming close to it, while others seem to be elevated to guru status without even trying. You can be a highly successful author, invent a genre of books, such as Kenneth Blanchard's *The One-Minute Manager*, and still not approach gurudom, however much in demand you are on the lecture or after-dinner circuit.

You can be a captain of industry with a brilliant track record at turning companies around and a gift for the bestselling memoir, like Sir John Harvey-Jones, Lee Iacocca or the late Harold Geneen, and spend a lucrative retirement passing on high-priced pearls of wisdom to business or TV audiences, yet still not rank as a true guru. An exception may be made for Jack Welch, because over the course of 20 years at the helm of General Electric, he initiated genuinely innovative management practices which have since been adopted by companies around the world.

Gurus have to be measured against the hard problems of here and now: Charles Handy may seem to be an exception now that he has adopted the mantle of a social philosopher, but his reputation was made as an expert on the culture and structure of business organizations. Likewise, the futurologist Alvin Toffler, a new entry here, has had an influence on the development of business practices well beyond his visions of social change.

The three leading gurus of our time are Peter Drucker, Tom Peters and Michael Porter. Drucker, who died in 2005, has been the acknowledged master of management principles for half a century. He defined the art – and to him it was an art rather than a science, with the emphasis on human relations – in the 1950s, and originated most of the theories that became fashionable under later thinkers: Management by Objectives, customer focus, performance measurement, privatization and all the ramifications of the information economy, whose coming he foresaw as early as 1969.

Tom Peters, a generation younger and a former McKinsey consultant, is the supreme showman among management gurus, an evangelist of business ideas whose lectures are theatrical entertainments exuding megawatts of energy. His books, eccentrically designed and spattered with schoolboy expressions such as 'Yikes!', carry this hyped-up style into print.

Michael Porter, recently described as the world's leading business intellectual, is lower-key in style but has a brilliant ability to package heavyweight ideas and complex models for a non-academic audience. His seminars and conference events are laced with humour and are much more accessible than his books.

Packaging is more than half the art of becoming a modern guru. Ten years after Porter's first book, *Competitive Strategy* (1980), *Business Week* reported that some US academics regarded his concepts as gimmicky, but they acknowledged that he was a master at packaging and marketing ideas. In those ten years, four books alone made him more than $2m and he is now the highest-earning management academic in the world. Porter himself talks about the importance of the Michael Porter 'brand', and for ultimate fame as a guru it is essential to become as identified with a business theory as Porter is with competitive strategy. The underlying truths may be as old as trading itself, but Porter has branded them, and thus made them saleable commodities.

Gurudom can start with one stunningly successful book, a book that every executive must have read. The prime example here is, of course, Peters' and Waterman's *In Search of Excellence*, still reprinting in its original format 25 years after first publication, despite the fact that two-thirds of its excellent companies have since faded from glory and that Peters himself opened his second book, *Thriving on Chaos* (1987), with the cheeky statement 'There are no excellent companies.' He has since light-heartedly admitted to the journal *Fast Company* that they faked some of the research data behind *Excellence*; a typical piece of Peters chutzpah.

Of the two authors, however, only Peters has chosen to haul himself up to the top rung of international gurus; his temperamentally opposite co-author Robert Waterman, a quiet, reflective Californian, prefers a less stressful, time-pressured existence. Waterman's first solo book, *The Renewal Factor* (1987), is regarded by some management teachers as a far deeper, more intellectually rigorous work than Peters' bestselling *Thriving on Chaos*, but it is Peters who commands the global branding factor and the huge fees that go with it.

Of course, branding, packaging and a flair for show business are only part of the answer. What marks out the real guru – the one who will be read in business schools and boardrooms – from the business-hero-turned-media-celebrity, or the author who hits on a jokey formula such as *The One-Minute Manager* or the business strategy of Genghis Khan, is the ability to generate original, durable thinking on the hard matter of managing people and resources.

All the gurus whose ideas are summarized in this book (and no summaries can do full justice to a lifetime of thinking: their key books should be read) meet this requirement, even out-of-date theorists such as F. W. Taylor and Max Weber. Their ideas were not only important in their time; they have been adapted and built on for generations, even if they have been partly destroyed in order to use the bricks again. And in some quarters they have not been wholly destroyed: Robert Waterman muses that many more managers are Taylorists at heart than would ever admit it.

Gurus broadly divide into those with one big idea – Edward de Bono's lateral thinking being the perfect example, out of which he has spun a sparkling web of books, international seminars and blue-chip consultancy – and those, like Peter Drucker and Charles Handy, whose fizzing intellects spray ideas in all directions; about the future of work and society, new designs for organizations, geo-political shifts and managing change. Michael Porter's emphasis on competitive strategy puts him largely in the first category (a big idea can have endless spin-offs), while Tom Peters shows signs of developing into a multi-ideas guru.

All have one thing in common: they build on each other's ideas and on their own. There is nothing remotely discreditable or plagiaristic in this: it is only what historians and philosophers have done down the ages. The Californian professor of management William Ouchi had a tremendous success with his 1981 book *Theory Z*, which used the terminology of Douglas McGregor's Theory X and Theory Y, going a step beyond Theory Y to describe, with case studies, the kind of consensus-seeking management which has succeeded so brilliantly in Japan. McGregor himself had begun to formulate a Theory Z, but did not have time to develop it in depth before he died. Richard Pascale, in *Managing on the Edge* (1990), says McGregor's last theory was quickly forgotten, and it was reborn independently as the archetype of Japanese business practice.

Another typical piece of guru language (gurus being also identified by their ability to invent terms that become part of the management vocabulary, such as Theory X, re-engineering, the psychological contract or lateral thinking) that has gone through many retreads is adhocracy. The term, meaning, roughly, the opposite of bureaucracy, a sort of flexible task force that crosses the frontiers within organizations, first surfaced in Warren Bennis' *The Temporary Society* in 1968, gained wider currency in Alvin Toffler's *Future Shock* in 1970, emerged independently in Henry Mintzberg's *The Structuring of Organizations* in 1979 and, most recently, formed the subject of an entire short book by Robert Waterman, *Adhocracy: The Power to Change*. Charles Handy has also explored the implications of the term. 'We all build on each other's work,' smiled Waterman when asked about the genesis of his title.

Everybody, for two generations of gurudom, has drawn somewhere on Drucker, that monumental quarry of management wisdom and original thought. Even Theories X and Y, as McGregor acknowledged, synthesized the ideas of others, including some which Drucker had presented in three early books – *Concept of the Corporation* (1946), *The New Society* (1951) and *The Practice of Management* (1954). Peters and Waterman, too, said that much of what they discovered in identifying their principles of excellence had first been aired by Drucker 30 years earlier.

There are few great themes of management, just as there are few great plots in fiction. Probably the richest vein, and the one that has attracted most theorists over the years, involves the human side of management, understanding what motivates men and women to work and to strive for better performance. Frederick Taylor thought that efficiency was all, and that it could be measured and mastered by a stopwatch: later gurus tackled more complex, deeper themes.

The first area to be explored in management writing, by the French mining manager Henri Fayol at the turn of the 20th century, was the function of management itself; still a fertile field as the early 21st century continues to be obsessed with how to manage change and discontinuity. Another early and long-lived theme is organizational theory, including hierarchies and the need or otherwise for them, and the now fashionable 'flatter management structures', which are supposed to empower the employee further down the line. 'Empowerment' is a new subdivision of this genre (or maybe a new word for an old concept) and the formidable Rosabeth Moss Kanter, who formerly edited the *Harvard Business Review*, along with teaching, consultancy and writing influential books, has explored all that this implies for releasing the forces of change and innovation within organizations.

In the late 1990s, the growing emphasis on intellectual capital – the sum of employee talent and accumulated knowledge in a company – created a new theory of 'knowledge management'. No single guru has yet been identified with the field, though the business school at the University of California in Berkeley has created the first chair of knowledge management, held in 1997 by the Japanese professor Ikujiro Nonaka. The subject, a natural for the information age and 'knowledge workers' (a term first coined by Peter Drucker in 1969), was business-led, most notably by Skandia, the Swedish financial services company, and its potential as management theory was initially spotted by a *Fortune* magazine writer, Thomas A. Stewart, in the first of several 1997 books with the same title, *Intellectual Capital*. It has since been the subject of a spate of conferences, seminars and heavy management reports, and a number of US companies have followed Skandia in appointing chief knowledge officers or the equivalent.

The search for better organizational performance is an almost inexhaustible field, with spin-offs ranging from strategy to marketing to company culture to the art of the mission state-ment. In Britain, the Strategic Management Centre, set up by Ashridge Management College in Berkhamsted, Hertfordshire, is breeding a stable of potential gurus in strategy and corporate missions, headed by Andrew Campbell and Michael Goold. If anything is likely to hinder their progress to guru status it is probably their prolific output of books, and the changing permu-tations of authors. Gurus rarely come in pairs, and even more rarely stay in pairs: Anthony Athos, who co-authored *The Art of Japanese Management* with Richard Pascale in 1981, has vanished from view, and it took nine years for Pascale to appear in print again – most successfully – with *Managing on the Edge*. He is now firmly established as a solo guru of fast-growing influence. One recent exception to this rule seems to be Kim and Mauborgne of INSEAD, who are always firmly linked in their writings.

Leadership is a field that has attracted surprisingly few gurus, perhaps because its mystique, like that of monarchy, suffers from exposure to daylight; leadership, ultimately, may be in the eye of the beholder. The US leadership guru James MacGregor Burns, a political scientist who worked for President John F. Kennedy and a new entry in this book, described leadership as one of the most observed and least understood phenomena on earth. Burns was the first to identify the distinction between transactional and transformational leadership, explaining that the first is a tacit agreement to exchange one benefit for another (i.e. jobs for votes) while a leader of the second type engages in a deeper relationship with his followers. 'The transforming leader looks for potential motives in followers, seeks to satisfy higher needs . . .'

Sometimes, however, excellent work just fails to turn its progenitors into gurus, especially when there are established stars in the field. The pairing of Harvard professor Christopher Bartlett and INSEAD professor Sumantra Ghoshal produced, in 1989, a book called *Managing Across Borders* that was of much more practical value to managers in multinationals than Kenichi Ohmae's later, more abstract work, *The Borderless World* (1990). Yet Ohmae still has major guru status, and his book, though undermined in its thesis that nationalism is on the wane by the savage warring in former Yugoslavia, rides on a reputation created by his earlier, 1980s works, *The Mind of the Strategist* and *Triad Power*.

Bartlett and Ghoshal delved into case studies just as fascinating in their application to global-marketing companies as the Japanese and US companies featured in *The Art of Japanese Management*. As the enlarged and progressively integrated single market in Europe becomes a reality and a challenge, they, too, may find their hour, as did Pascale and Athos in the 1980s, when US industrialists were running scared of the Japanese threat and desperate to learn how to defeat it. Timing is of the essence in achieving gurudom.

Until his untimely death in 2004, Sumantra Ghoshal was emerging as a significant management thinker in his own right. By then a professor of strategy and international management at London Business School, he was increasingly concerned with the changing relationship between employer and employee as the era of career security and the 'psychological contract' faded into history.

Timing, originality, forcefulness, a gift for self-promotion and, perhaps above all else, the ability to encapsulate memorably what others immediately recognize as true – these are the marks of the modern management guru. Peters and Waterman created the first mass-selling management book – the one everyone needed to read – by packaging some fundamental truths in snappy slogans such as 'stick to the knitting'. Beneath the glossy paintwork, however, was a solidly built motor that, while not entirely original in every part, would probably last as long as the heavy-duty classics of Chandler, Barnard and Mayo – indeed, was partly cannibalized from those very vehicles.

One thing is certain: in an age of incessant searching for a holy grail of business and personal success that recedes as surely as Gatsby's green light into the distance, of the making of management gurus there is no foreseeable end.

Since this book was first published in 1991, a number of quasi-business gurus have made their names in the field of personal development. The best-known is Stephen Covey, a Mormon entrepreneur who has built a multi-billion-dollar industry on the basis of his book *The Seven Habits of Highly Effective People* (1989), and whose nine children all work in the Utah-based business. President Bill Clinton and members of his administration bought into the Covey prescriptives, which are based on character-building exercises not so far removed from those associated with the Victorian ur-guru of self-help Samuel Smiles.

In the 1990s, before the collapse of so many Internet businesses and the world-changing arrival of mass terrorism on 11 September 2001, management fads and fashions flared across the horizon so fast that it was difficult to tell which would burn out and which, if any, would survive. Hugh Macdonald, a former academic at MIT and Cranfield School of Management, once calculated the lifespan of a management fad at 11–12 years, from its first germination in academic papers through publication in the *Harvard Business Review*, bestselling book, lectures, conferences and a lucrative consultancy. (Oddly, the average lifespan of companies has been put at a similar age, around 13 years.) By 1995, however, fads had reached such a velocity that Adrian Wooldridge and John Micklethwait, authors of *The Witch Doctors*, a witty dissection of the management-guru industry, were putting the survival of some at no more than a year.

Inevitably, the curve of interest dips and the theory then has to be replaced by an advanced or different model. Some theories just fade slightly, leaving ghosts of themselves, like Peters' and Waterman's eight rules of excellence, in which 'stick to the knitting' was reborn a decade later as 'core competencies', having never really been abandoned; others, like re-engineering, having been tested to destruction in the real world of management, need to be relaunched.

By Macdonald's system, re-engineering has already run its course: born at MIT and the neighbouring consultancy CSC

Index in the early 1980s, it appeared in an *HBR* article in 1990 and achieved bestsellerdom in 1993. Disillusionment set in around 1995, with a 70 per cent failure rate and a fatal association in people's minds with cost-cutting and downsizing. But the principle does work well in certain types of organization, and its 'godfather', Mike Hammer, has had a Damascene conversion to understanding that it is people, not processes alone, that make change work.

In today's more sceptical business climate, the power of the gurus has waned and the stream of big-idea books has slowed, though the private and public sectors of industry still spend inordinate amounts of money on consultants. The tendency now is towards practical, see-what-works measures, successful execution of strategy and back-to-basics management. Business leaders who have themselves produced outstanding corporate results, such as Larry Bossidy of AlliedSignal and Honeywell, are selling more books than the academic theorists: Bossidy's *Execution* was a notable success in 2004. The most admired business book of recent years – and the one most read by senior managers – has been Jim Collins' *Good to Great* (2001), a thorough, research-based analysis of what companies can achieve through decades of low-profile good management.

Ultimately, time and experience sort the wheat from the chaff. The theories that have best stood this test are those of the behavioural scientists such as Elton Mayo, Abraham Maslow, Douglas McGregor and Frederick Herzberg, whose work lit the way to a deeper understanding of what makes people function best in office, shop or factory. Their ideas gave rise to empowerment, self-managed teams and the sort of relationship between employer and employee that could survive in a very different world of work from that of the 1950s or 1960s.

One human resources director in the late 1990s, Colin Ions of UK brewing giant Courage, stated that he still drew immense support from the big ideas of Maslow and McGregor: the latter's work, he believed, was all about trust. In the 2000s, trust is a key buzzword, while Maslow's 'hierarchy of needs' underpinning employee motivation is as valid as ever.

Maslow's and McGregor's books may be out of print, but their theories shifted the management landscape and are rooted in timeless truths about human nature. Will the same be said a generation hence about re-engineering, performance measurement or the 'virtual' corporation?

The most enduring theories of today are also likely to be about 'people issues'; ideas that redefine our approach to human aspirations in the workplace, to the development of talent, trust, creativity and loyalty, without which a business is nothing but hardware, software and the fickleness of markets. If one were to place a bet on the survival of recent management theories, the safe money is likely to be on the learning organization, if only because it is all about the interdependence of the individual and the whole; it is capable of infinite interpretations; and (cynically) it is virtually impossible to disprove as the template for tomorrow's company.

JOHN ADAIR

(b. 1934)

Action-Centred Leadership:
how task, team and individual overlap

Pioneering British thinker in the theory and practice of leadership, and the first to occupy a chair in leadership studies in the UK (at the University of Surrey, 1979–1983). Since 1991 he has been visiting professor in leadership studies at the University of Exeter, which established the world's first diploma and master's degree in leadership in 1993. A centre for leadership studies was set up at Exeter in 1997.

Cambridge graduate Adair, whose quiet and business-like demeanour is belied by a colourful career including service in a Bedouin regiment under Glubb Pasha; working as a deckhand on an Arctic trawler; and lecturing at the Royal Military Academy, Sandhurst, has written nearly 50 books on leadership and management development. He now works as an international management consultant and the Adair Leadership Foundation gives workshops and seminars under the aegis of Falconbury, an executive training consultancy in London (www.falconbury.co.uk).

Before his appointment to the leadership chair at Surrey, Adair was visiting fellow at the Oxford Centre for Management Studies and assistant director of the Industrial Society, where he headed the leadership department.

Adair believes his contribution to management thinking is threefold. He can claim to have been the first to demonstrate that people can be trained for leadership as a transferable skill rather than a matter of inborn aptitude. Second, he has helped alter the concept of management to include the larger element of leadership, with which he associated the neighbouring skills of decision-making, communication and ability to manage time. Finally, he has defined leadership in terms of three overlapping circles – task, team and individual – distilled into his teaching concept, Action-Centred Leadership (ACL).

Without undue modesty, Adair suggests that the ACL model is 'emerging in management studies, in effect, as something akin to Einstein's General Theory of Relativity'. It does, he maintains, 'identify the main forces at work in working groups and organizations, and it charts ... their main interrelationships with a degree of predictive accuracy'.

ACL encompasses much of the teaching on individual human needs first charted by Abraham Maslow (qv) and Frederick Herzberg (qv). It was developed by Adair first at Sandhurst and later at the Industrial Society.

Adair has written 48 books on leadership, the best known of which are *Effective Leadership*, *Not Bosses But Leaders* and *Great Leaders*, a study of leadership qualities in historical figures. He claims his 'mission' is to be 'in the forefront of long-term management thinking' and to integrate management concepts to better effect.

John Adair goes to etymological roots to explain the crucial difference between 'leading' and 'managing'. In an interview in *Director* magazine (November 1988), he explained it neatly:

Leadership is about a sense of direction. The word 'lead' comes from an Anglo-Saxon word, common to north European languages, which means a road, a way, the path of a ship at sea. It's knowing what the next step is . . . Managing is a different image. It's from the Latin *manus*, a hand. It's handling a sword, a ship, a horse. It tends to be closely linked with the idea of machines. Managing had its origins in the 19th century with engineers and accountants coming in to run entrepreneurial outfits. They tended to think of them as systems.

But there are valuable ingredients in the concept of management that are not present in leadership. Managing is very strong on the idea of controlling, particularly financial control, and administration. Leaders are not necessarily good at administration or managing resources.

What leaders are – or should be – good at, he elaborated in the same interview, is inspiring others. 'That's tied in with the leader's own enthusiasm and commitment and with the ability to communicate and share that enthusiasm with others and to enthuse them. It's not quite the same as motivation, which is something that's learned about in the business schools, a rather mechanical thing.

'And leadership is about teamwork, creating teams. Teams tend to have leaders, leaders tend to create teams.

'Finally, you can be appointed a manager, but you're not a leader until your appointment is "ratified" in the hearts and minds of those who work for you. There's got to be a degree of acceptance of you by followers that is not necessary if you're just holding an appointment.'

The ethos of the team is at the heart of Adair's leadership theories and his Action-Centred Leadership model. He believes that working groups share three areas of common needs: the need to accomplish a common task, the need to be maintained as a cohesive social unit or team and the sum of the group's individual needs. These form his overlapping 'three-circle' model: failure in one area affects the other two. For example, failure to achieve the task (or lack of a task altogether) will both disrupt the sense of teamship and lower the level of individual satisfaction. The approach can best be understood by drawing three interlocking circles labelled Task, Team and Individual and placing a coin over any one of them. Segments of the other two are immediately blotted out. The overlapping circles, maintains Adair, illustrate 'the essential unity of leadership; a single action can be multifunctional in that it touches all areas'.

In *Understanding Motivation* (1990), Adair lists the functions of leadership as originally worked out at Sandhurst:

- Planning (seeking all available information; defining group tasks or goals; making a workable plan)
- Initiating (briefing the group; allocating tasks; setting group standards)
- Controlling (maintaining group standards; ensuring progress towards objectives; 'prodding' actions and decisions)
- Supporting (expressing acceptance of individual contributions; encouraging and disciplining; creating team spirit; relieving tension with humour; reconciling disagreements)
- Informing (clarifying task and plan; keeping group informed; receiving information from the group; summarizing ideas and suggestions)
- Evaluating (checking feasibility of ideas; testing consequences; evaluating group performance; helping group to evaluate itself)

The functions of leadership are a key element in Adair's integrated ACL theory, in which the three-circle model plays a central role without being the whole concept. The originality of ACL, he points out, lies not in its parts – 'none of which were actually brought into their first existence by me' – but in their integration into a whole and the application of that whole to training.

'By being brought into a new relation with one another, those parts have undergone varying degrees of transformation, which is inevitable in any creative work.'

Among the constituents borrowed and re-evaluated from earlier gurus are Maslow's 'hierarchy of needs' model and Henri Fayol's classic definitions of management functions. In *Understanding Motivation*, Adair also expounds his 'Fifty–Fifty Rule', a variation on the Pareto Principle, in which he contends that half an individual's motivation comes from within himself or herself, the other half from external factors, including leadership. This theory contradicts most of the motivation gurus, led by Maslow and Herzberg, who stressed that motivation lies pre-eminently within the individual.

Adair has applied his Fifty-Fifty Rule in other contexts, for example in *Effective Teambuilding* (Gower, 1986), where he suggests that 50 per cent of success depends on the team and 50 per cent on the leader. The Fifty-Fifty Rule has the benefit, he says, of challenging each party to get its performance right before criticizing the quality or contribution of the other. 'It is the ultimate cure for the "Us and Them" disease of organizations.'

The prolific Adair's most recent book, *How to Grow Leaders*, has won five-star plaudits among Amazon's reader-reviewers for its three-level analysis of leadership roles – strategic, operational and teamworking. It describes the skills a leader has to master: qualities (what a leader has to be), the situational approach (what a leader has to know) and the group or functional approach (what a leader has to do). A section on the manager as leader also reflects the development of Adair's earlier thinking on the divide between those roles.

KEY WRITINGS

Adair, J. (1983) *Effective Leadership*, Aldershot: Gower.

Adair, J. (1986) *Effective Teambuilding*, Aldershot: Gower.

Adair, J. (1988) *Not Bosses But Leaders*, Guildford: Talbot Adair Press; (2002) with Reed, P. (ed.) London: Kogan Page.

Adair, J. (1988) *Developing Leaders*, Guildford: Talbot Adair Press.

Adair, J. (1989) *Great Leaders*, Guildford: Talbot Adair Press.

Adair, J. (1990) *Understanding Motivation*, Guildford: Talbot Adair Press.

Adair, J. (1996) *Effective Leadership Masterclass*, London: Pan.

Adair, J. (1997) *Effective Communication*, London: Pan.

Adair, J. (1997) *Effective Innovation*, London: Pan.

Adair, J. (1998) Thomas, Neil (ed.) *The John Adair Management and Leadership Handbook*, London: Thorogood.

Adair, J. (2002) *Effective Strategic Leadership*, London: Pan.

Adair, J. (2003) *The Inspirational Leader*, London: Kogan Page.

Adair, J. with Thomas, Neil (ed.) (2004) *The Concise Adair on Teambuilding and Motivation*, London: Thorogood.

Adair, J. (2004) *The John Adair Handbook of Management and Leadership*, London: Thorogood.

Adair, J. (2005) *How to Grow Leaders: the Seven Key Principles of Effective Leadership Development*, London: Kogan Page.

2

H. IGOR ANSOFF

(1918–2002)

The theory and practice of strategic planning

Russian-born pioneer of strategic management and corporate planning, whose 1965 book *Corporate Strategy* was described by Henry Mintzberg as 'the most elaborate model of strategic planning in the literature'. Professor Bernard Taylor of Henley Management College, a leading British authority on strategic planning, describes Ansoff as 'the guru's guru' in the field, which he effectively founded in 1963, the year he left Lockheed to teach strategy at Carnegie Institute of Technology. Until that time, Taylor recalls, 'business policy was regarded as a "capstone course" in general management which had no theory to speak of and therefore must be taught entirely by the case method.'

From *Corporate Strategy* (republished in 1988 as *The New Corporate Strategy*) onwards, Ansoff's major books have been milestones in the development of strategic management: *Business Strategy* (1969), *From Strategic Planning to Strategic Management* (1976), *Strategic Management* (1979) and *Implementing Strategic Management* (1984, 1990). The last two, representing a shift from a focus on strategy to the 'bottom line' success of strategic behaviour, have consolidated his leadership in a field that remained underrated, in the UK at least, until the mid-1980s.

Born in Vladivostock of a Russian mother and an

American diplomat father, Ansoff spent his first 16 years
in newly Sovietized Russia. The family then returned
to New York, where Ansoff studied mechanical engineering and physics. After service in World War II he
took a doctorate in applied mathematics under a government sponsorship scheme for ex-servicemen.

In 1948 Ansoff joined the Rand Foundation, an influential think-tank of the postwar years specializing in
military problems. Here he worked on strategic problems for NATO, and the methodology he developed for
strategic problem-solving was later to prove a powerful
influence on his development of theory and practical
technology for business.

Joining the Lockheed aerospace company as a long-
range planner gave him a practical outlet when he was
appointed to be responsible for Lockheed's diversification. He has said that this job gave him the opportunity
to learn how business works and how to identify the
key variables and relationships in complex problems.
He was promoted to vice-president and general manager
in Lockheed Electronics Company where he was faced
with the human traumas involved in reducing a division with 17 high-technology businesses down to three,
requiring the layoff of 100 engineers. Thus he learned
at first hand the difficult part of management, which
is managing other people's lives.

Managing a large corporation did not, however, fulfil
Ansoff's own long-term career strategy. He became a
professor at Carnegie School of Industrial Administration,
and shortly after joining Carnegie published his seminal
Corporate Strategy.

His next move was to become founding dean of the
Graduate School of Management at Vanderbilt University
in Nashville, Tennessee, where he created a pioneering
new business school, based on the concept of strategic
management, to train 'change agents'.

Although *Corporate Strategy* received worldwide acceptance, the prescription for strategic planning contained in
the book produced mixed results in practice. In some firms
it produced significant improvement in performance and

became a way of life, but in many others, strategic planning became a phenomenon which Ansoff called 'paralysis by analysis'.

Ansoff decided to find an explanation of this anomaly, a decision which led to 20 years of theoretical and empirical research on successful strategic behaviours. An early step was a four-year research study of success and failure of mergers and acquisitions strategies, the outcome of which was *Acquisition Behaviour of US Manufacturing Firms 1946–1965*, published in 1971. In the following year Ansoff published an article, 'The Concept of Strategic Management', which argued that explanation of the planning failure must be sought through studying the firm's overall process of strategic management and not just the planning component. Ansoff organized the first international multidisciplinary conference on strategic management, sponsored by IBM and General Electric, at Vanderbilt in 1973. An outcome of this conference was *From Strategic Planning to Strategic Management,* published in 1976.

Ansoff spent the next six years at the Brussels-based European Institute of Advanced Studies in Management, where he led a number of pan-European projects on strategic management and societal strategy and continued his research on strategic management, in particular on the identification of the kinds of strategic behaviour that lead to success in organizations in turbulent environments.

Out of this research came *Strategic Management* (1979), which offered a comprehensive theory of strategic behaviour, and *Implanting Strategic Management* (1984, 1990), which presents a comprehensive practical approach to optimizing strategic behaviour.

Ansoff returned to the US in 1983 to become Distinguished Professor of Strategic Management at US International University, where he created master's- and doctoral-level programmes in strategic management. He also formed his own consultancy in San Diego, California. He retired from USIU in 2000 as emeritus professor.

Ansoff's achievement was to establish strategic planning as a management activity in its own right, but for many years in the 1960s and 1970s his theories were more accepted in Europe and Japan than in the US, where they were regarded as too complex until the business environment itself became turbulent and unpredictable. Every two years an award in his name is presented to an individual who has made a significant contribution to strategic management thinking.

Igor Ansoff's *Corporate Strategy*, as the author wrote in his preface, seeks 'to develop a practically useful series of concepts and procedures which managers can use to manage . . . a practical method of strategic decision-making within a business firm'.

The book accomplishes this with a methodology of processes and checklists so detailed and rigorous that the former ICI chairman Sir John Harvey-Jones, introducing the 1986 edition in Sidgwick and Jackson's Library of Management Classics, observed that using it, 'superficially at least, the corporate strategy could be drawn up by an unintelligent computer . . .' Harvey-Jones went on to rank the book as 'one of the best business books of all time'.

Professor Bernard Taylor of Henley Management College describes it as 'a brilliant, original contribution, and still an essential introduction to the concept of strategy'. Since the 1970s, however, Ansoff has moved away from the prescriptive approach of the book, which, according to a leading member of Britain's Strategic Planning Society, tended to be interpreted by some of Ansoff's followers in too deterministic a manner ('he preached rigour, not rigidity'). Ansoff's most recent works focus on the necessity of building flexibility and adaptation to change into the planning process.

Corporate Strategy begins by analysing the three main types of decision-making – strategic, administrative and operating – and how they interact. It then explains the specific questions addressed in the strategic category:

- What are the firm's objectives and goals?
- Should the firm seek to diversify, in what areas, and how vigorously?
- How should the firm develop and exploit its present product–market position?

Ansoff explains that most strategic decisions have to be made within the practical framework of a limited total resource, involving a choice of alternative commitments among resources. Thus, emphasis on current business activity will preclude diversification; over-emphasis on diversification will lead to neglect of present products. 'The object is to produce a resource-allocation pattern which will offer the best potential for meeting the firm's objectives.'

Ansoff next examines how those objectives, both economic and social, can be defined by individual firms according to their own circumstances; moves on to devise a practical method of setting objectives within varying time horizons and of building in enough flexibility to cope with unforeseen calamities or catastrophic change.

'Objectives,' Ansoff writes, 'are a management tool with many potential uses. In the operating problem they can be used for establishing performance standards and objectives for all organizational levels, for appraisal of performance and for control decisions. In the administrative problem they can be used to diagnose deficiencies in the organizational structure. In our main area of interest, the strategic problem, objectives are used as yardsticks for decisions on change, deletions and additions to the firm's product-market posture.'

The book then moves into denser thickets of analysis, evolving its own mathematical formulae to demonstrate the meaning of synergy as a component in strategy, applied to acquisitions, start–ups and diversifications. Ansoff follows this by developing a 'concept of strategy' from which a firm can (1) identify the business it should be in, (2) use specific guidelines to search for strategic opportunities and (3) be given decision rules to narrow that selection process down to the most attractive options.

Ansoff preceded Harvard's Michael Porter (qv) by nearly two decades in identifying 'competitive advantage' as a key element

in strategic planning. He observed that identifying a competitive advantage requires 'uncommon skills in anticipating trends'
to ensure really successful results, and that, because of the need
for knowledge of the industries involved, the concentric forms
of diversification (linked related products and markets) is likely
to be more successful than conglomerate diversification.

Corporate Strategy concludes by analysing the pros and cons
of 'make or buy' new product-markets, e.g. whether to plump
for organic growth or acquisition.

In summary, *Corporate Strategy* provides both the concepts
and practice of strategic decision-making, starting with the
philosophical issues that underlie company objectives and
progressing to the point at which the firm commits itself to a
specific product-market strategy. It finally develops a procedure
for appraising and monitoring a strategic project and explains
how strategy fits as a management tool into the overall peri-
odic planning process of a firm.

Ansoff's work in Brussels on strategic behaviour patterns
and their results on organizations, which was embodied in his
theoretical book *Strategic Management*, has been described by
him as 'the most important phase of my intellectual development . . . I begged, borrowed and stole concepts and theoretical insights from psychology, sociology and political science.
And I attempted to integrate them into a holistic explanation
of strategic behaviour.' The centrepiece of the theory presented
in that book was the 'strategic success' hypothesis.

While in Brussels he also wrote a series of three important
papers ('Strategic Issue Management' [1980], 'Managing
Strategic Surprise by Response to Weak Signals' [1976] and
'Dispersal Positioning in Strategic Portfolio Analysis' [with
Kirsch and Roventa, 1980]). These developed a set of practical
methods for adapting a firm to fast-changing and unpredictable
threats and opportunities.

Implanting Strategic Management, first published in 1984 and
updated in 1990, translated the theoretical concepts of the 1979
book into practical 'how to do it' technology. It represents the
distillation of Ansoff's 35 years' experience in management (as
manager, teacher and consultant) and a culmination of his 20
years' search for a comprehensive explanation of why the original strategic planning failed to work.

Ansoff explains that since the 1960s his thinking developed along three parallel paths: enlargement of his scientific perspective from unidisciplinary to multidisciplinary; the search for a theoretical explanation of strategic behaviour; and development of practical technology for strategic management in turbulent environments.

Implanting Strategic Management is built on the 'strategic success' formula (a practical translation of the strategic success hypothesis), which states that a firm's performance is optimized when its external strategy and internal capability are both matched to the turbulence of the firm's external environment.

The book reports that the strategic success formula has been 'empirically validated' in eight countries around the world, in different industries and in banks.

Implanting Strategic Management represents the most comprehensive exposition of concepts and practical techniques current in strategic management, and recommends processes for creating a dual system within a firm which can both manage strategic change and the daily profit-making activities.

Since his return to the US in 1983, Ansoff had been developing further his work on strategic behaviour, with particular emphasis on patterns that lead to success – most crucially, the ability to manage strategic responses to a turbulent external environment – and on helping firms to behave successfully in strategic terms. He claimed that the strategic success formula demonstrates that the days of simple, universal management prescriptions are over, and that each organization must work out its own best solution, whose complexity is neither higher nor lower than the complexity of the firm's environment. Ansoff offered *Implanting Strategic Management* as a tool for finding this solution.

Professor Taylor says Ansoff's work has 'educated and enthused a whole generation of practitioners, consultants and academics in the USA and around the world'. Throughout his distinguished academic career, 'he has kept his contact with practice, working with top management teams in leading multinational companies – always bringing new and original ideas, expressed with energy and enthusiasm.'

KEY WRITINGS

Ansoff, H. I. (1965) *Corporate Strategy*, New York: McGraw-Hill; (1986) London: Sidgwick and Jackson.

Ansoff, H. I. (1969) *Business Strategy*, London: Penguin Books.

Ansoff, H. I. (1971) *Behavior of US Manufacturing Firms 1946–65* (with R. J. Brandenburg, F. E. Portner, H. R. Radosevich), Nashville: Vanderbilt University Press.

Ansoff, H. I. (1976) *From Strategic Planning to Strategic Management* . (with R. Hays, R. Declerck), New York and London: John Wiley and Sons.

Ansoff, H. I. (1979) *Strategic Management*, London: Macmillan.

Ansoff, H. I. (1984, 1990) *Implanting Strategic Management*, New Jersey: Prentice-Hall.

Ansoff, H. I. (1988) *The New Corporate Strategy*, Chichester: John Wiley.

3

CHRIS ARGYRIS

(b. 1923)

Developing individual potential within the organization;
single and double-loop learning

US organizational psychologist born in Newark, New Jersey, whose special area is the personal development of individuals within organizations, and the defence mechanisms that managers often unwittingly use to resist change. Working with Donald A. Schon for the last 25 years, he has been developing a theory of individual and organizational learning in which human reasoning – not just behaviour – becomes the basis for diagnosis and action. His book *Knowledge for Action* (1993) analyses how organizations go wrong through the ways people think.

One of the squadron of eminent management thinkers associated with Harvard University, he has been James Bryant Conant Professor of Educational and Organizational Behaviour there since 1971. Before that he was Professor of Industrial Administration at rival Yale University.

Argyris has also worked as a consultant in industry, notably for IBM, Shell and Du Pont, as well as for various departments of the US government and for governments in Europe. He is a full board member of the UK consultancy Monitor, which Michael Porter (qv) helped to found.

Peter Drucker has called organization theorists like Argyris 'romantics' for hoping that by encouraging the principle of participation they can disprove the anarchist assertion that 'organization is alienation.'

Drucker himself had no such ideals. 'Authority is an essential dimension of work,' he wrote in *Management: Tasks, Responsibilities, Practices* (1973). 'It has little or nothing to do with ownership of the means of production, democracy at the workplace, worker representation or any other way of structuring the "system". It is inherent in the fact of organization.'

Argyris starts from the premise that each individual has a potential that can be developed – or stultified – by the organization and the particular group circumstances in which he or she works. Developing a person's full potential should be to the benefit of both the individual and the organization, his argument runs, but managers and even peer groups within the organization often lack the 'interpersonal confidence' to allow this to flourish. Managers in particular, he warns, may develop defensive mechanisms to protect their control over others.

In an article for *Harvard Business Review* in which Argyris studied six companies and observed 265 decision-making meetings, he concluded that executive behaviour often creates an atmosphere of distrust and inflexibility, despite the fact that the executives involved genuinely believe trust and innovation to be crucial to good decision-making.

Argyris observed that such discrepancies were not restricted to business organizations: he had obtained similar patterns of behaviour from leaders in education, research, the Church, trade unions and government.

His solution was for executives to try asking important 'feedback' questions, at quiet and non-risky times when the pressure was off, discussing tapes of their own meetings and actively entering a learning process about their own behaviour and that of their group.

He identified three basic values that affected his study groups:

• 'The significant human relationships are the ones which have to do with achieving the organization's objective.' In other words, executives concentrated their efforts on 'getting the job done', often using this as an excuse to avoid probing into workers' interpersonal factors and how groups were getting on together.

- 'Cognitive rationality is to be emphasized; feelings and emotions are to be played down.' Thus interpersonal relations are viewed as irrelevant, not real work.
- 'Human relationships are most effectively influenced through unilateral direction, coercion and control, as well as by rewards and penalties that sanction all three values.' Direction and control are accepted, Argyris found, as an inevitable, unquestioned part of the managerial chain of command.

The whole suppressed awareness of what senior management was doing was summed up by Argyris: 'During the study of the decision-making processes of the president and the nine vice-presidents of a firm with nearly 3,000 employees, I concluded that the members unknowingly behaved in such a way as not to encourage risk-taking, openness, expression of feelings and cohesive, trusting relationships.'

But in later interviews, the executives claimed that negative feelings were not expressed because 'we trust each other and respect each other.' The reasons why issues of conflict were ignored at meetings included such explanations as 'we should not air our dirty linen in front of people who may come in to make a presentation,' and 'when people are emotional, they are not rational.'

A similar pattern of misinterpreted signals emerged from studies of executives' relationships with middle managers, most of the latter feeling that they did not know where they stood with their bosses and that conflicts were very rarely tackled.

'One key to group and organizational effectiveness is to get this knowledge (that a group was decaying) out into the open and to discuss it thoroughly. The human "motors" of the group and the organization have to be checked periodically, just as does the motor of an automobile. Without proper maintenance, all will fail' (*Harvard Business Review*, 'Interpersonal Barriers to Decision-Making').

Argyris worked with Donald A. Schon on examining how organizations cope with the contradictory goals of maintaining a stable status quo and adapting to change (*Organizational Learning: A Theory of Action Perspective*). How, for example, do members of an organization reconcile such opposing messages in their culture as: take initiatives but keep to the rules; think ahead but remember that pay is linked to present performance; cooperate with others but be ready to compete with them?

Argyris and Schon developed what they call Model I to demonstrate how managers resolve these contradictions. What they do is to concentrate on setting goals as an individual; on being as self-contained as possible; on keeping negative feelings to themselves and on discouraging others from speaking their minds about matters that worry them. In this way they hope to protect their own positions and to deflect issues that could build up a head of steam in other people.

The primary aim of Model I managers is to defend themselves and their positions from change while imposing change where necessary on others. Where they fail, however, is in creating mistrust and repression. The process is self-perpetuating because they learn nothing except the importance of conforming. This is described by Argyris as 'single-loop' learning. The prescription he and Schon worked out for Model II management proposes 'double-loop' learning, which takes an opposite course: here the manager acts on information (once assured that it is valid), invites free discussion and choice and is prepared to change. Double-loop learning involves learning from others rather than from one's own self-perpetuating experience.

To switch managers from Model I to Model II thinking, Argyris advises a training programme for managers using interpersonal consultants.

He is fully aware of the difficulties involved in making the change. In *Strategy, Change and Defensive Routines*, he writes: 'Top management believes that to change defensive routines is the equivalent of changing the world, a belief that I share with them. They conclude that the most realistic solution is to bypass them . . .'

Argyris explains that organizations can perform well in spite of defensive routines operating within them: indeed, defensive managers are usually loyal, hard-working and dedicated. The best advice in tackling defensive routines, says Argyris, is 'to move slowly and iteratively. Let the organization learn from each experiment so it can make the next one even more successful and build up organizational intelligence on these change processes that can be disseminated throughout the organization.'

Defensive routines are one strong reason why changing the existing culture in organizations rarely lasts, however. In Argyris' view, 'defensive routines pollute the system and undermine it the same way air pollution undermines our lives.'

KEY WRITINGS

Argyris, C. (1957) *Personality and Organization*, New York: Harper and Row.

Argyris, C. (1965) *Organization and Innovation*, Toronto: Irwin.

Argyris, C. and Schon, D. A. (1978) *Organizational Learning: A Theory of Action Perspective*, Wokingham: Addison-Wesley.

Argyris, C. (1985) *Strategy, Change and Defensive Routines*, London: Pitman.

Argyris, C. (1991) 'Teaching Smart People How to Learn', Cambridge, Mass.: *Harvard Business Review* (May/June).

Argyris, C. (1993) *Knowledge for Action: a guide to overcoming barriers to organizational change*, San Francisco: Jossey-Bass.

Argyris, C. (1994) 'Good Communication That Blocks Learning', Cambridge, Mass.: *Harvard Business Review* (July/Aug).

Argyris, C. with Schon, D. (1996) *Organizational Learning II: Theory, Method and Practice*, Reading, Mass.: Addison-Wesley.

Argyris, C. (2000) *Flawed Advice and the Management Trap*, Oxford: OUP.

Argyris, C. (2003) *Overcoming Organizational Defences by Facilitating Organizational Learning*, London: Prentice-Hall.

4

CHESTER BARNARD

(1886–1961)

Managing the values of the organization

New England-born Chester Barnard was a rarity among management gurus in being a full-time business executive. He spent 40 years with the Bell Telephone Company and eventually became president of New Jersey Bell.

Barnard was one of the first to study the process of decision-making in organizations, the relationships between formal and informal organizations, and the role and function of the executive. His 1938 book *The Functions of the Executive* exerted tremendous influence in its time: in it, he identified what we now call 'organization man', stating that 'the most important single contribution required of the executive, certainly the most universal qualification, is loyalty, domination by the organization personality.'

Barnard saw business organizations as more effective instruments of social progress than either Church or State, partly because they were driven by the cooperation of individuals working to a common purpose rather than by authority.

Barnard's work also encompassed pioneering thinking on the nature of leadership, upon which others have built, and on corporate culture and value-shaping, a good 30 years before the rest of the management world woke up to their importance. The real role of the chief executive,

he suggested, was to manage the values of the organization, as well as to secure employee commitment. Peters and Waterman in their *In Search of Excellence* paid tribute to Barnard's work as 'probably the first balanced treatment of the management process'.

In the late 1930s, the work of Chester Barnard and Elton Mayo challenged the long-established theories of Max Weber (qv), who defined (and admired) the organization as bureaucracy, and F. W. Taylor (qv), who believed that management could be made an exact science, capable of being applied by a set of rules.

Barnard recognized that organizations are made up of individual human beings with individual motivations, and that every large formal organization carries within it a host of smaller, less formal groupings whose goals need to be harnessed to those of the parent body. This linkage Barnard saw as the responsibility of management. He made an important distinction between management effectiveness and management efficiency, and argued that to be effective, an organization's purpose or goals must be accepted by all the contributors to its system of effort. The willingness of all concerned to cooperate in a common purpose was essential, Barnard considered, to an organization's survival.

For a businessman of his time, Barnard was remarkably percipient in the message he constantly reiterated: that authority in an organization only exists insofar as the people in that organization are willing to accept it. Hence his emphasis on the value of communications, and his three basic principles for ensuring their effectiveness:

- Everyone should know what the channels of communication are.
- Everyone should have access to a formal channel of communication.
- Lines of communication should be as short and direct as possible.

The functions of managers, Barnard believed, were to establish and manage that system of communications; to motivate employees towards the organization's goals; and to formulate those goals in a clearly communicable way. *In Search of Excellence* pinpoints Barnard's contribution to the theory of corporate culture (then barely in its infancy) and the role of the executive within it. 'Barnard was . . . the first (we know of) to talk about the primary role of the chief executive as the shaper and manager of shared values in an organization,' wrote Peters and Waterman.

Barnard's emphasis on managing the corporate whole was still an unusual concept at the time Peters and Waterman were writing in the early 1980s. He was alone among his contemporaries in sensing 'the unconventional and critical role of executives in making it all happen', the *Excellence* authors observed. In the preface to *The Functions of the Executive*, Barnard stated that his primary aim was to provide a comprehensive theory of co-operative behaviour in formal organizations.

Barnard's contribution to leadership theory is bound up with this concept of the good manager as value-shaper. He contrasted this concept with that of the authoritarian, manipulative manager working strictly on a system of rewards and short-term efficiency. But his theories, as Peters and Waterman pointed out, lay virtually dormant for 30 years while most management thinking concentrated on structure and its relation to postwar growth.

The fact that his vision of an organization is essentially one of desired equilibrium – a state sought by all leading management theorists until comparatively recently – has led to a critical reassessment by those gurus like Richard Pascale (qv) of *Managing on the Edge*, who believe that the vital organization of today must welcome change, discontinuity and even conflict within itself, and manage those things creatively. Pascale points out that Barnard advocates 'coherence among such elements as values, informal social networks, formal systems and purposes. The better they are orchestrated, the better the organization performs.'

Some of Barnard's disciples, notably Jay Lorsch of Harvard, have filled this gap by evolving 'contingency theory'. But on the whole, Barnard's theories are deemed to be as relevant today as they were in the late 1930s.

Despite this, his work is largely neglected, perhaps because some of his books, especially *The Functions of the Executive*, are written in a fairly impenetrable style. Peters and Waterman call it 'virtually unreadable', but they have no doubt that it remains a monument in management theory.

KEY WRITINGS

Barnard, C. (1938) *The Functions of the Executive*, Cambridge, Mass.: Harvard University Press.
Barnard, C. (1948) *Organization and Management*, Cambridge, Mass.: Harvard University Press.

5

MEREDITH BELBIN

(b. 1926)

Complementary roles in team-building

Ex-psychologist and training expert whose system of selecting and building teams out of complementing and balancing the strengths and 'allowable weaknesses' of individuals has become an industry standard.

A rangy, energetic man still fizzing with ideas in his early seventies, Belbin first studied classics at Clare College, Cambridge, then switched in his final year to experimental psychology. His first – and abiding – interest in training was in the development and employment of older workers; his MA and PhD in 1952 were in gerontology, and later he worked as a consultant for OECD in Paris, developing the 'guided discovery' method of enabling older workers to learn new skills. It was put into operation in OECD-sponsored projects in the UK, US, Austria and Sweden and described in a book called *Problems in Adult Retraining* (1972), written with his wife, Eunice.

The Belbin team-selection system grew out of a research programme with Henley Management College in 1967 into the effectiveness of management teams. Finding that the more complementary their contributions or roles, the better the team performed, Belbin developed psychometric tests to assess the contributions which each individual could make. These tests are also now widely used in the selection of senior personnel.

Belbin's two key books in this field are *Management Teams: Why They Succeed or Fail* (1981), described by the *Financial Times* as one of the top 50 business books of all time, and *Team Roles at Work* (1993). The first explains the evolution of Belbin's 'team role' theory, based on findings that 'imperfect people can make perfect teams' through balancing weaknesses with strengths in the team makeup. The second offers a methodology for combining independent observer assessments with self-assessments. Properly applied, the system shows that effective people have learned to project themselves accurately and the way they see themselves corresponds with others' perceptions. The wider the gap between the two, the less effective people are in teams.

Belbin's energy and range of interests remain phenomenal. As well as his family-run consultancy Belbin Associates in Cambridge, he lectures by invitation in the UK and overseas, and is working with Brathay Hall Trust in the Lake District on various training programmes including a course for 'the elite prospective entrepreneur'. Like Henry Mintzberg (qv), he believes that business schools fail to teach the realities of management.

The onetime classical scholar is still fascinated by the workings of ancient societies and has recently extended his studies of collective organizations to the insect world. In *The Coming Shape of Organizations* (1996), he looks at what we can learn from ants, termites and bees and argues that, whereas the intellect of *Homo sapiens* works most brilliantly in individuals, that of insect societies grows in power collectively.

Belbin himself describes his myriad research projects as having a unifying thread of an 'experimental approach to problems in business and social affairs, the creation of new conceptual models and the development of the means by which they can be delivered'. His style of working is 'empirical and operational', and he describes the core of what he does as: 'Diversity is in our genes. It's how to capture this diversity in groups and use it to best advantage.'

Meredith Belbin's system of psychometric testing for the selection of senior staff and the construction of effective management teams has become such an integral tool of the human resources business that it is commonly referred to simply by its inventor's surname, as in, 'We use Belbin in our recruitment.'

Yet the recent rediscovery of the virtues of self-managed teams (pioneered by Douglas McGregor, qv, in the late 1950s) has not, curiously, caused the world to beat a bigger path to his door. Belbin thinks this is because self-managed teams tend to be approached in the wrong way; less genuine empowerment than a convenient way for managers to shift responsibility.

While working for the Industrial Training Unit at University College, London, in 1967, he was invited to Henley Management College to study competing 'company' teams on a computer-based business game called Executive Management Effectiveness that formed part of a management course. He found very different patterns of effectiveness, linked to the behaviour patterns of team members and the ways in which each contributed to the whole.

Complementary contributions produced better results than competing contributions and one key finding was that certain strengths in individuals were often associated with what Belbin termed 'allowable weaknesses'. Such weaknesses were not detrimental to effective teamwork because they could be underpinned by the strengths of others. Sharing this knowledge helped to build effectiveness, along with the realization that 'imperfect people can make perfect teams.'

Management Teams: Why They Succeed or Fail sets out the eight main roles which contribute to the ideal team – company worker, chairman, shaper, plant, resource investigator, monitor-evaluator, team worker and completer-finisher. Their basic characteristics are defined as:

Company worker: conservative, dutiful, predictable, with organizing ability, practical common sense, hardworking. Allowable weakness: lack of flexibility, unresponsiveness to unproven ideas.
Chairman: calm, self-confident, controlled, with a capacity for treating all potential contributors on their merits and a

strong sense of objectives. Allowable weakness: ordinary intellect and creative ability.

Shaper: highly strung, outgoing, dynamic, with drive and a readiness to challenge inertia, ineffectiveness, complacency or self-deception. Allowable weakness: prone to provocation, irritation, impatience.

Plant: individualistic, serious, unorthodox, with genius, imagination, intellect, knowledge. Allowable weakness: up in the clouds, inclined to disregard practical details or protocol.

Resource investigator: extroverted, enthusiastic, curious, communicative, with a capacity for contacting people and exploring anything new. An ability to respond to challenge. Allowable weakness: liable to lose interest once the initial fascination has passed.

Monitor-Evaluator: sober, unemotional, prudent, with judgement, discretion, hard-headedness. Allowable weakness: lacks inspiration or the ability to motivate others.

Team worker: socially orientated, rather mild, sensitive, with an ability to respond to people and situations, and to promote team spirit. Allowable weakness: indecisiveness at moments of crisis.

Completer-Finisher: painstaking, orderly, conscientious, anxious, with a capacity for follow-through. Perfectionism. Allowable weakness: a tendency to worry about small things, a reluctance to let go.

Characteristics were assessed in two ways: through questionnaires completed by the participants themselves and through outside observations by course members who were more interested in watching than in participating. There were seven observed categories of contributory behaviour: asking, informing, proposing, opposing, delegating, building and commenting.

The book went on to analyse the designing and leading of teams, ideal team sizes and how to foster creativity in a team. Interestingly, one type of 'company' team participating at Henley, composed of exceptionally clever individuals, actually finished last, and continued to perform poorly through repeated experiments. Nicknamed 'Apollo' companies, they were hard to manage, prone to destructive debate and showed difficulties in decision-making. Belbin concluded that 'high, critical faculties bring destructive tendencies to the fore.'

In his follow-up book, *Team Roles at Work*, Belbin says: 'A team is not a bunch of people with job titles, but a congregation of individuals, each of whom has a role that is understood by other members . . . Members of teams seek out certain roles and they perform most effectively in the ones that are most natural to them.'

Team Roles at Work further explores the original role concepts and sets out the 'construct' theory on which Belbin's team selection and building process works. The key to this is the integration of self-perception and perception by outside observers. When the two coincide, the result is an effective team performer: the wider the gap, the greater the chance of failure. For the computer-based management programme which integrates the feedback data, Belbin and his son and partner Nigel have developed software that filters and weights information fed into it so that it cannot be deceived or corrupted by false or misleading data. *Team Roles at Work* is described by Belbin as 'a halfway house to understanding the Belbin method', though he says it is often applied simplistically.

Belbin's belief in the value of teams extends to his views on leadership and chimes with the latest thinking of Warren Bennis (qv) on 'Great Groups'. Strategic leadership, Belbin asserts, is 'much safer vested in small strategic teams rather than in a single individual'.

His 1996 book *The Coming Shape of Organizations* examines how insect societies can form models for the large-scale human organization to reinvent itself as a series of small teams. He describes the concept in this way: 'Small interacting teams act without interference and rely on their superior capacity for generating and acting on complex information. They have no "appeal" systems, so cannot be disempowered . . . Concurrent teams, comprising small competing teams, produce better results in tackling complex problems than one large conferring group headed by a leader.

'A model of the future organization, and for career progression, is the progression helix. People have personal jobs but are also invited into teams. An internal labour market competes for the best team members and one person may be invited into positions that would otherwise be perceived as belonging to different parts of the hierarchy.'

In *Managing Without Power* (2001), Belbin offers a scientist's perspective on gender politics through the ages. He unravels the evolution of humanity's power structures, showing how an initial balance between the genders was lost as societies became dominated by the drive for territorial expansion. The book concludes by suggesting how a beneficial balance of power could be restored to business organizations and society at large.

KEY WRITINGS

Belbin, M. (1981) *Management Teams: Why They Succeed or Fail*, Oxford: Butterworth Heinemann.

Belbin, M. (1993) *Team Roles at Work*, Oxford: Butterworth Heinemann.

Belbin, M. (1996) *The Coming Shape of Organizations*, Oxford: Butterworth Heinemann.

Belbin, M. (1997) *Changing the Way We Work*, Oxford: Butterworth Heinemann.

Belbin, R. M. (2001) *Managing Without Power*, Oxford: Butterworth Heinemann.

Video films: Building the Perfect Team (Video Arts)
        Selecting the Perfect Team (Video Arts)

CD Rom: How to Build Successful Teams (1996).

6

WARREN BENNIS

(b. 1925)

'Managers do things right. Leaders do the right thing'

NewYork-born industrial psychologist and adviser to four US presidents, best known as a guru of leadership theory, though his earlier work was concerned with organizational development. He is famous for his aphorism 'Managers do things right. Leaders do the right thing.'

Like Abraham Maslow (qv) and Britain's Charles Handy (qv), Bennis was strongly influenced while at MIT's Sloan School of Management by Douglas McGregor (qv) and his Theory X and Theory Y. Like Maslow, he attempted to put Theory Y into action in a practical management setting – upgrading the run-down University of Buffalo in the late 1960s – and found that it would not work without a stiffening framework of structure, direction and controls.

His vision of the organization of the future in *The Temporary Society* (1968) identified the need for 'adhocracy' (free-moving project teams) – a principle espoused by Alvin Toffler in *Future Shock*, by Henry Mintzberg (qv) and most recently by Robert H. Waterman Jr.

From 1971 to 1977 Bennis was president of the University of Cincinnati, but he has worked internationally in France, Switzerland and India. He is now Distinguished Professor of Business Administration and founder of the Leadership Institute at the University of Southern California in San Diego.

In the bestselling *Leaders: the Strategies for Taking Charge*, which he wrote in 1985 with Burt Nanus and which established his reputation as a world authority on leadership, Bennis studied 90 individuals in different sections of US society, including astronaut Neil Armstrong, sports coaches and orchestra conductors as well as businessmen, and identified four factors or 'competencies' common to all – the ability to manage attention, meaning, trust and self.

Since the mid-1980s he has been moving away from the study of the leader as heroic individual towards that of group leadership, believing that the former model no longer works in today's much-altered organizations, except where deep culture change is required. In his 1997 work *Organizing Genius* he analyses what he calls 'Great Groups' – dynamic and dedicated teams for whom the project is all, from Walt Disney Studios to the scientists of the Manhattan Project who built the first atomic bomb – and reformulates his earlier four competencies into four 'new rules' of leadership. Without exception, he says, leaders of such groups:

- Provide direction and meaning, a sense of purpose
- Generate and sustain trust, creating authentic relationships
- Display a bias towards action, risk-taking and curiosity
- Are purveyors of hope, optimism and a psychological resilience that expects success

Bennis' own personal first encounter with such qualities came in 1944, when he was serving in the US army in Europe as a 19-year-old second lieutenant, one of the youngest infantry officers in the war, receiving the Purple Heart and Bronze Star for gallantry. He recalls his company commander, Captain Bessinger, as 'the kind of leader you read about in the Bible'. He listened to his men, taught them the skills of survival and conveyed the same inspiring belief in his subordinates that Bennis' later mentor, Douglas McGregor, developed into Theory Y.

Over the years Bennis has modified his thinking several times on whether leadership can be taught or only learned experientially. 'I don't yet know enough about human thinking to be sure that leadership can or cannot be taught,' he said in 1997. But after teaching an undergraduate class at USC for two years he tends to think that ideas do have the power to change mindsets and behaviour.

To Bennis, the paramount factor in developing leaders is developing the self. In his workbook *Learning to Lead* (1997) he emphasizes the need for an 'integrated self' before leadership qualities can emerge.

Despite his famous aphorism about managers and leaders, he doesn't believe there is a complete dichotomy between them. 'Some have said you can't be both. I don't agree; there are examples of both in one person. I believe in "possible selves" – the capacity to adapt and change.'

Bennis regards himself as more of a journalist than a guru (in his eighties he is fulfilling a student ambition to be a playwright) and has an eye for the memorable quote. He is fond of quoting a little-known aphorism by Winston Churchill: 'The emperor of the future will be the emperor of ideas.'

Warren Bennis sees the leader, the person who transforms an organization, as 'the social architect' – a concept anticipated before World War II by Chester Barnard. Tom Peters has acknowledged that, 25 years before *In Search of Excellence*, Bennis had perceived much of what Peters and Waterman identified as landmarks of the excellent company.

In *The Unconscious Conspiracy – Why Leaders Can't Lead*, Bennis pointed up the ability of leaders to bring about change by positive motivation: 'In a study of school teachers, it turned out that when they held high expectations of their students, that alone was enough to cause an increase of 25 points in the students' IQ scores.'

Leadership, says Bennis, is 'probably the most studied and least

understood of any management subject'. His favourite definition of the attribute is: 'The capacity to create a compelling
vision and translate it into action and sustain it.' The best leaders,
he says, are 'ideas people, conceptualists'. But he describes leadership as 'an endless subject and endlessly interesting because
you can never get your conceptual arms fully around it. I always
feel rather like a lepidopterist chasing a butterfly' (*Director* magazine, April, 1991).

The four key abilities identified in Bennis' 1985 study of 90
successful US public figures are: the management of attention,
the management of meaning (communications), the management of trust and the management of self. The first he attributes to a vision that others can believe in and adopt as their
own. Vision is about the long term; market imperatives are short
term. 'With a vision,' says Bennis, 'the leader provides the all-
important bridge from the present to the future of the organization.' Among examples he cites are Lee Iacocca at Chrysler,
President John F. Kennedy and civil rights leader Martin Luther
King. (Two of those three, of course, were assassinated; the great
and permanent risk of strong political leadership.)

Communicating vision and translating it into successful results
for the organization is the second of Bennis' required leadership
skills; the management of meaning. This, he explains, is why
Ronald Reagan was deemed a more successful president than
the better-informed, more thoughtful Jimmy Carter.

The mission credo of Johnson & Johnson translates vision
into practical daily guidelines. General Motors under chief executive Roger Smith placed a high value on getting the company's
long-term vision shared by all employees.

Trust, the third key factor to leadership skills, is described by
Bennis as 'the emotional glue that binds followers and leaders
together'. He believes leaders have to be consistent, and in the
late 1980s cited Margaret Thatcher as a prime example – 'focused,
constant and all of a piece'.

Self-management, the fourth quality, means persistence, self-
knowledge, willingness to take risks, commitment and challenge.
Above all, it means willingness to go on learning, and in particular to learn from adversity and failure. 'The learning person looks
forward to failures or mistakes. The worst problem in leadership
is basically early success.'

In *Leaders*, Bennis and Nanus concluded that the most impressive and memorable quality of the individuals they studied was 'the way they responded to failure . . . They simply don't think about failure, don't even use the word, relying on such synonyms as "mistake", "glitch", "bungle" or countless others.'

On Becoming a Leader (1989) and *Learning to Lead* (1997) both address how leadership can be developed in the field. The first tackles three practical questions: how people learn to lead, how an organization can encourage or unwittingly stifle leadership qualities, and how leadership can be taught. His case studies are of less familiar personalities than those in *Leaders: the Strategies for Taking Charge*, consisting of 29 American personalities from feminists to film-makers. *Learning to Lead* is a practical workbook, previously available only on the US college circuit, which addresses itself primarily to developing personal character and qualities as a basis for leadership.

Organizing Genius, Bennis' 1997 study of how dynamic project groups are formed and led, written with Patricia Ward Biederman, is in many ways his most interesting book, the fruit of 40 years' fascination with the workings of 'creative collaboration' under the pressure of make-or-break deadlines and intense competition. The projects studied range from the race against Nazi Germany to perfect the first atomic weapon and Lockheed's development of advanced military aircraft such as the U2 spy plane and the Stealth bomber through Walt Disney's brilliant animated films to the Xerox and Apple teams that developed the first personal computers.

Although the book skirts around the central question of how organizations can sustain the dedicated creativity of such groups once projects come to an end, it is highly relevant to knowledge industries and to the coming era when, Bennis believes, team leadership rather than the charismatic individual leader will be the model for global business. In the 1980s, *On Becoming a Leader* bestowed almost iconic status on the individual achiever, but by 1997 Bennis had come to think that the heroic 'great man' model was not going to work in the very different organizations of the 1990s and the 21st century, except in circumstances where one inspirational person was needed to change an entire culture. He now believes that the 'Hollywood' model will increasingly take over, where a group of individuals come together to work on a particular project in an organization, much as a film is made. Afterwards, the group will dissolve and re-group when a new task is presented.

Geeks and Geezers, his oddly titled latest work, contrasts the experiences that have formed leaders aged over 70 (the Depression and World War II) and those in their thirties, and finds common ground in the personal crucibles each went through before emerging to lead others.

On a personal note, he told *Director* magazine in 1991 that true leaders needed the humility to learn from the people they led. 'My heroes are the people who are continuous learners, who have their eyebrows always raised in curiosity and who can say to themselves: "The more vulnerable I am to my people, the more I can influence them."'

While Bennis remains the acknowledged world guru on leadership theory, contenders are staking out their own areas of the field, such as Harvard's John P. Kotter (qv), who concentrates principally on the leadership of organizations and leader/manager differentials, and a European authority, Dutch-born Manfred Kets de Vries (qv) of INSEAD, the international business school near Paris, who writes from a psychological perspective. In Britain, John Adair developed an approach learned from his experience as a lecturer at Sandhurst military academy and now holds Europe's only chair of leadership, at Exeter University.

KEY WRITINGS

Bennis, W. (1968) *The Temporary Society*, New York: Harper and Row.

Bennis, W. (1976) *The Unconscious Conspiracy*, New York: Amacon Press.

Bennis, W. and Nanus, B. (1985) *Leaders: the Strategies for Taking Charge*, New York: Harper and Row.

Bennis, W. (1989) *On Becoming a Leader*, London: Business Books.

Bennis, W. (1993) *An Invented Life: Reflections on Leadership and Change*, New York: Addison-Wesley.

Bennis, W. and Townsend, R. (1995) *Reinventing Leadership:*

Strategies to Empower the Organization, London: Piatkus.

Bennis, W. and Biederman, P. (1997) *Organizing Genius*, New York: Addison-Wesley, Longman Inc.; London: Nicholas Brealey.

Bennis, W. and Goldsmith, J. (1997) *Learning to Lead*, New York: Addison-Wesley, Longman Inc.; London: Nicholas Brealey.

Bennis, W. (ed.) (2001) *The Future of Leadership*, San Francisco: Jossey-Bass.

Bennis, W. (2002) *Geeks and Geezers*, Cambridge, Mass.: Harvard Business School Press.

7

EDWARD DE BONO

(b. 1933)

Lateral thinking: 'the generation of new ideas and the escape from old ones'

Malta-born, Oxford-educated psychology and medical graduate who invented the concept of lateral thinking, now entered in the *Oxford English Dictionary* as 'seeking to solve problems by unorthodox or apparently illogical methods'.

De Bono is the foremost example of a guru who has built a reputation out of one 'big idea'. Describing himself as 'a thinker about thinking', he has generated nearly 70 books out of his brainwave, along with a highly lucrative career in teaching, lecturing and consultancy.

His central argument, derived from his medical experience, is that humans are quite good at processing with mathematics, statistics and computers, but have done very little about perception and creativity (functions that computers are unable to carry out). It was also from medicine that he derived his ideas of the patterning behaviour of self-organizing systems. His book *The Mechanism of Mind*, published in 1969, was about 20 years ahead of its time.

Among the world-class companies to whom he has acted as consultant are Shell, IBM, Exxon, 3M, Apple, Citibank, General Foods, Procter & Gamble and Unilever. His International Creative Forum brings together leading corporations in different fields to focus on the introduction of 'serious creativity' into their organizations. He has also been retained by governments and non-business organizations such as police forces and he runs the world's largest curriculum programme for the direct teaching of thinking in schools.

De Bono has taught at Oxford, Cambridge, London and Harvard universities and is the founder-director (since 1971) of the Cognitive Research Trust in Cambridge and the Centre for the Study of Thinking. He now spends much of his time working for the Supranational Independent Thinking Organization in The Hague, and is also chairman of the Council of Young Enterprise Europe, whose members set up mini-businesses while still at school. There are currently around 1.5m members across Europe, Israel and Russia.

His books have been translated into 25 languages and his work is academically respected in countries as different as Venezuela and the former Soviet Union.

'The purpose of lateral thinking,' says Edward de Bono in *Lateral Thinking for Management* (1971), 'is the generation of new ideas and the escape from old ones.' He likens the process to developing a cross-reference technique for a filing system set up to store data in a particular way. Creativity, he says, 'involves breaking out of established patterns in order to look at things in a different way', and creativity, he points out, comes into every aspect of managing a business – not only innovation but information systems, communications, finance, marketing, advertising and promotion, labour relations, problem-solving, planning, design, R&D and public relations.

De Bono differentiates lateral thinking from 'vertical' or traditional logical thinking, which proceeds step by step 'directly from one state of information to another state . . . One of the characteristic features of vertical thinking is continuity. One of the characteristic features of lateral thinking is discontinuity.'

The two systems do not cancel each other out, but are complementary. Where vertical thinking operates on a 'Yes/No' progression of alternatives, seeking always the solution that is right, lateral thinking proceeds by provocative leaps in unlikely directions, seeking what can be used in an idea rather than accepting or rejecting the whole idea outright. Quite often both systems come up with the same solution, says de Bono, but one can increase the chances of success by developing skills in lateral thinking.

In practice, he suggests, one could use lateral thinking for 5 per cent of the time and vertical thinking for the other 95 per cent, operating the systems alternately: 'lateral thinking turns up an idea, vertical thinking develops it.' Vertical thinking comes into its own in testing the creative ideas turned up by lateral thinking, and for transforming them into a plan of action. Lateral thinking, says its inventor, is not a method for decision-making.

De Bono's books on lateral thinking offer a system for teaching oneself the skill. High among his training 'tools' is the 'operational', nonsense-word PO, which acts like a railway signal to switch thinking patterns on to new tracks. In one of de Bono's examples, considering the problem of how to reduce traffic congestion in cities, use of PO triggers the 'intermediate impossible' solution of square wheels for cars. The underlying truth of that is how to make driving difficult or unpleasant and thereby discourage use of cars: more practical solutions could be a tax on road use or physical ridges in the road.

Other 'discontinuity' techniques include the use of analogy and 'random word' association to break the chain of vertical thinking. *Lateral Thinking for Management* also provides guidelines for formal brainstorming sessions and group practices for executives. De Bono summarizes the lateral-thinking process in five steps:

- Escape from clichés and fixed patterns
- Challenge assumptions
- Generate alternatives
- Jump to new ideas and then see what happens
- Find new entry points from which to move forward

In applying its uses to management, de Bono also looks to a future when the 'concept manager' will have an established role in a corporation, managing the 'concept capital' of the organization – creativity, new ideas, adapting to change, defining objectives. Until that time arrives, he suggests, the organization of lateral thinking as a management tool may fall to the training officer, the OR department, the planning department or R&D. It should not, he stresses, be the special preserve of any one department.

De Bono himself considers his most significant book to be *I Am Right,You Are Wrong* (Viking/Penguin, 1990), which he claims challenges the whole basis of the West's thinking culture. It explains the difference between 'rock' and 'water' logic, why rock logic has restricted the full potential of thinking, and how water logic arises from a fuller understanding of how the brain works.

The oddly titled *Six Thinking Hats* (1985) provides a system for escaping from traditional argument and confrontational thinking to better exploration of a subject and a more creative outcome in solving problems. It has been adopted by major corporations such as IBM, Prudential and Du Pont. J P Morgan found that using the *Six Thinking Hats* technique cut their meeting times by 80 per cent. De Bono is extending this system (in which imaginary 'hats' in different colours are donned to encourage specific mental functions: e.g. white for information, red for feeling and intuition, black for caution, yellow for bene-fits, green for creative thinking, blue for the organization of thinking) with a sequel called *Six Action Shoes*, which separates routine from emergency action.

De Bono believes that the usual approach to fostering creativity – relying on inspiration and release from inhibitions – is far too weak, and that the brain, not being naturally creative, requires the exercise of deliberate techniques to stimulate it. Although inevitably overlapping to some extent, his books and courses on thinking represent a genre he has made his own. A basic de Bono library is listed here.

KEY WRITINGS

De Bono, E. (1967) *The Use of Lateral Thinking*, Maidenhead: McGraw-Hill; London: Penguin.
De Bono, E. (1968) *The Five-Day Course in Thinking*, Maidenhead: McGraw-Hill; London: Penguin.

De Bono, E. (1969) *The Mechanism of Mind*, Maidenhead: McGraw-Hill; London: Penguin.

De Bono, E. (1971) *Lateral Thinking for Management*, Maidenhead: McGraw-Hill; London: Penguin.

De Bono, E. (1982) *De Bono's Course in Thinking*, Maidenhead: McGraw-Hill; London: Penguin.

De Bono, E. (1985) *Conflicts: A Better Way to Resolve Them*, Maidenhead: McGraw-Hill; London: Penguin.

De Bono, E. (1985) *Tactics: The Art and Science of Success*, Maidenhead: McGraw-Hill; London: Penguin.

De Bono, E. (1985) *Six Thinking Hats*, London: Penguin.

De Bono, E. (1990) *I Am Right, You Are Wrong*, London: Viking.

De Bono, E. (1991) *Handbook for a Positive Revolution*, London: Penguin.

De Bono, E. (1991) *Practical Thinking*, London: Penguin.

De Bono, E. (1993) *Water Logic*, London: Penguin.

De Bono, E. (1993) *Serious Creativity: Using the Power of Lateral Thinking to Create New Ideas*, London: HarperBusiness (also available on CD Rom).

De Bono, E. (1994) *Parallel Thinking*, London: Penguin.

De Bono, E. (1995) *Teach Yourself to Think*, London: Penguin.

De Bono, E. (1996) *The Edward de Bono Book of Wisdom*, London: Penguin.

8

JAMES MacGREGOR BURNS

(b. 1918)

Leaders who transform and empower their followers

US political scientist and pioneer of leadership studies, best known for his distinction between 'transformational' leadership, which changes the values of its followers through a shared vision, and 'transactional' leadership, which operates more managerially, through perceived goals and rewards. Burns' 1978 book, *Leadership*, powerfully argued the case for wider formal education in the subject, and since its publication there has been an explosion of leadership programmes in US business schools, as well as some 400 doctoral dissertations based on Burns' ideas. One academic at the University of Richmond, Virginia, has said: 'Burns is to leadership studies as Peter F. Drucker is to management and Sigmund Freud is to psychology.'

A native of Massachusetts, Burns began work as a congressional intern in Washington just before World War II, in which he served in the Pacific. He found his métier as a combat historian and was decorated for his part in the invasions of Saipan, Guam and Okinawa. After the war, he took a master's and a PhD in government from Harvard and taught at his alma mater, Williams College in Williamstown, Virginia, where he is still an emeritus professor. He lives nearby in a converted 18th-century barn, writing his books in longhand and only rarely resorting to an old-fashioned typewriter.

An unsuccessful candidate for Congress in 1958, Burns was later an adviser to President John F. Kennedy, of whom he wrote the first biography. He lists Kennedy, Lyndon Johnson and Franklin D. Roosevelt as the greatest presidents of the 20th century. His second biography of Roosevelt, on the president's wartime role, was awarded a Pulitzer Prize and became a seminal influence on US leadership studies.

Working on this and other presidential biographies fostered a deep fascination with the characteristics that great leaders had in common. Identifying the differences between transformational and transactional leadership was a key step, but Burns has also distinguished between transformational leaders such as Adolf Hitler, who are driven by a lust for power, and those who, like the great founders of religion, are motivated by vision and values. As a pre-eminent modern example of the latter, Burns has named Eleanor Roosevelt for her moral leadership and compassion.

In 1997, the University of Maryland, where Burns used to teach, renamed its Academy of Leadership in his honour. Established in 1981 to train women for positions in government, its website describes it as 'a contemporary think-tank on leadership and provider of custom-designed leadership development programs'.

James MacGregor Burns' theories of leadership derived from his work as an historian and biographer of political figures, unlike those later developed by Warren Bennis (qv), whose first major book, *Leaders: the Strategies for Taking Charge* (1985), studied such contemporary figures in US society as sports coaches, astronauts, businessmen and orchestra conductors. Many of these, in Burns' perspective, would be classified as 'transactional' leaders, with the skill to manage projects within a fairly limited time-frame. His fascination is with the rarer transformational ability to inspire hearts and minds over time, even to change followers in fundamental ways – as did Jesus, the Prophet Mohammed, Gandhi and, in a deeply perverted way, Adolf Hitler.

Although historically this ability has been exercised for good or ill by great religious or political leaders, it can be found in business. One of the first studies of Jack Welch's reign at General Electric, along with other US industrial change masters such as Chrysler's Lee Iacocca, was *The Transformational Leader*, by Noel Tichy and Mary Anne Devanna (1986), which pointed out that, in a business context, 'once transformational leaders create a vision and use it to mobilize individuals in the organization, they must turn their attention to designing new organizational structures and processes so that the vision can be achieved.'

This 'social architecture', as Tichy and Devanna described it, was well exemplified by Burns in his ground-breaking 1978 study *Leadership*, in which he draws many lessons from the founding fathers of the US Constitution. He notes especially the 'creative leadership' of James Madison, who designed the intricate system of political checks and balances to ensure that human ambition in the government of the young republic would have its wings clipped and be deprived of overweening power.

Of transformational leadership itself, Burns writes in *Leadership* that its essence 'is the capacity to adapt means to ends – to shape and reshape institutions and structures to achieve broad human purposes and moral aspirations. The dynamics of such leadership is recognizing expressed and unexpressed wants among potential followers, bringing them into fuller consciousness of their needs, and converting consciousness of needs into hopes and expectations . . . The secret of transforming leadership is the capacity of leaders to have their goals clearly and firmly in mind, to fashion new institutions relevant to those goals, to stand back from immediate events and day-to-day routines and understand the potential and consequences of change.'

Despite the inevitable critics who claim that leadership cannot be taught in the classroom, Burns' desired legacy is 'to provide people studying or practising leadership with a general guide or orientation – a set of principles that are universal to leadership which can then be adapted to different situations. We're intent on making it an intellectually responsible discipline.'

He continues to publish books on the presidency and, in 1999, his study of the Clinton–Gore administration concluded that their centre-ground strategy made real leadership impossible because truly transformational leaders pursue their vision regardless of public opinion or political difficulties. In 2003, he reworked his seminal book *Leadership* into *Transforming Leadership: The Pursuit of Happiness*, examining how leaders can become agents of social change by empowering their followers. The book studies leaders in history from Cleopatra to Mao Tse-tung, rating each as transactional or transformative. Surprisingly, Queen Elizabeth I is ranked only as transactional, though Winston Churchill, Gandhi, Nelson Mandela, Martin Luther King and Mao all rate as transformative.

The new work culminates in Burns' plan to encourage 'gifted leaders at the grass roots' – a sort of updated Peace Corps – to solve global poverty, which he believes is the greatest leadership challenge of the 21st century.

KEY WRITINGS

Burns, J. M. (1978) *Leadership*, New York: Harper Perennial.
Burns, J. M. (2003) *Transforming Leadership: The Pursuit of Happiness*, Boston Mass.: Atlantic Monthly Press; Grove Press.

9

ALFRED D. CHANDLER

(b. 1918)

Structure follows strategy in organizations

US economic historian, Straus Professor of Business History at Harvard University since 1971, whose work on organizations has been largely based on studies of major US companies between 1850 and 1920; the period, as he sees it, when modern capitalism was shaped and a new economic unit came into being. This was the business with a range of distinct operating units, each managed autonomously and completely different from its historical predecessor, the traditional single-unit firm, personally owned and managed.

Chandler believes that his work contributed to a nation-wide restructuring of corporations, with the multi-divisional form of organization becoming the standard for large industrial firms producing multiple products in multiple markets. He was one of the first management theorists to perceive the importance of creating a strategic plan for a business before framing its organizational structure.

His 1977 book *The Visible Hand*, challenging the classical market theories of Adam Smith, won the Pulitzer Prize. In it, Chandler argued that the management of great corporations had more influence on economic activity than Smith's self-actuating market mechanisms.

His most influential book, *Strategy and Structure*, was

used by AT&T executives in their restructuring exercise after the 1984 breakup of the telecommunications giant, and Chandler's theories were credited with helping to speed up the change of focus within AT&T from a service utility to an actively marketed sales organization.

Chandler's main contribution to management theory has been to explain the relationship in organizations between strategy and structure, from which he took the title of his best-known book, published in 1962. In *Strategy and Structure*, he demonstrates how the two are indissolubly linked in an organization, defining 'strategy' as the determination of long-term goals and objectives, courses of action and allocation of resources, and 'structure' as the way the organization is put together to administer the strategy, with all the hierarchies and lines of authority which that implies. Chandler is clear in his belief that structure follows strategy.

Like Weber, he believes that the managerial hierarchy system offers the best hope for long-term business prosperity, and he concentrates on the principle that the salaried manager's role is critical. 'The visible hand' of management, he observes in *Managerial Hierarchies*, replaced Adam Smith's 'invisible hand' of market forces by coordinating the flow of goods from producers to customers more efficiently and profitably than was achieved by simple market mechanisms. As managers receive power and authority through their official roles, so their careers became increasingly technical and professional.

Chandler was the first management writer to recognize the importance of the decentralization principle in a large corporation, which became the central tenet of so much business practice in the 1960s and 1970s. It had already contributed substantially to Alfred P. Sloan's restructuring of General Motors in the interwar years, but Sloan did not publish his own book until 1963.

Chandler was also an early advocate of the need to coordinate strategic planning from the centre to ensure long-term growth for the company, while allowing the individual units and their managers to get on with day-to-day tactics.

His guiding rule has always been that outside pressures dictate how firms evolve from Weber-style traditional, family-based businesses into large, hierarchical organizations – pressures born of the huge market expansions and technological changes of the late 19th and early 20th centuries. He traces the first managerial hierarchies to the rapid expansion of US railroads in the 1850s and 1860s, when a need emerged for centralized scheduling but local management of a variety of functions in geographic divisions that were responsible for up to 100 miles of track.

In his studies of four great US corporations – General Motors, Sears Roebuck, DuPont and Standard Oil – Chandler looks at how these companies responded to similar external pressures either by positive strategies such as seeking new markets or diversifying products, or by negative, defensive strategies such as vertical integration with suppliers to protect a market position.

Some were more successful than others: Standard Oil, in Chandler's view, was slow to respond with a decentralized structure in the 1920s because of a failure to understand how structure should follow strategy.

Chandler's analysis of corporate development in the different markets and economies of Europe as well as in the US has led him to conclude that 'only by comparing the evolution of large-scale multi-unit enterprises in different economies can organizational imperatives be identified and the impact of the cultural attitudes and values, ideologies, political systems and social structures that affect these imperatives be understood.'*

In each case, however, the structure of a management hierarchy followed the creation of the multi-unit business and enabled it to function through delegation of responsibility.

In 2001, after a long period of literary silence, he published a provocative study of the electronics and computer industries called *Inventing the Electronic Century*, again stressing the importance of scale and 'learned organizational abilities' over more entrepreneurial enterprises. Some critics felt this approach undervalued the impact of such phenomenal fast developers of the 'garage culture' as Microsoft and Sun Microsystems and the rich

* From *Managerial Hierarchies: Comparative Perspectives on the Rise of Modern Industrial Enterprises*, ed. by A. D. Chandler and H. Deams (Harvard University Press, 1980), quoted in *Organizational Theory*, ed D. S. Pugh (Penguin, 1990).

venture-capital sources in Silicon Valley that nurtured them. Although IBM was able in the nick of time to reinvent itself against upstart competitors, other giant corporations such as Honeywell and GE failed Chandler's big-is-best philosophy when it came to the PC revolution.

KEY WRITINGS

Chandler, A. D. (1962) *Strategy and Structure*, Massachusetts: MIT Press.
Chandler, A. D. (1977) *The Visible Hand: The Managerial Revolution in American Business*, Cambridge, Mass.: Harvard University Press.
Chandler, A. D. and Deams, H. (eds) (1980) *Managerial Hierarchies: Comparative Perspectives on the Rise of Modern Industrial Enterprises*, Cambridge, Mass.: Harvard University Press.
Chandler, A. D. and Tedlow, R. S. (1985) *The Coming of Managerial Capitalism*, Toronto: Irwin.
Chandler, A. D. (2001) *Inventing the Electronic Century*, New York: Free Press.

10

CLAYTON M. CHRISTENSEN

(b. 1952)

The power of disruptive innovation

The latest hot property from Harvard Business School to emerge on the international guru scene, this enormously tall (six feet eight inches) professor of business administration has established a reputation as the leading authority on 'disruptive innovations', the means by which companies create entirely new markets for products or services, with radical consequences for their competitors. They can do this by focusing on lower-end customers with the potential to become mass consumers: typical examples include the early personal computer and the advent of low-cost airlines. Christensen's research not only explains the positive side of this process for start-ups but also how well-established and well-run businesses can limit the damage when they are blindsided by such innovations.

Christensen, a devout Mormon and father of five who worked as a missionary in Korea during his student days and speaks fluent Korean, was born in Salt Lake City, Utah, and took an economics BA there in 1975 from Brigham Young University. He obtained a master's in applied econometrics from Oxford as a Rhodes Scholar, and a high-flying MBA from Harvard in 1979, returning there to take a DBA in 1992, when he became a member of the Harvard Business School faculty.

In the intervening years, he led a varied career in industry and as a project manager for Boston Consulting Group, helping to set up the firm's consultancy practice in manufacturing strategy. He took leave of absence from BCG in the early 1980s to become a White House Fellow and assistant to two secretaries of transportation, Drew Lewis and Elizabeth Dole. In 1984, along with some MIT professors, he co-founded a firm called Ceramics Process Systems Corporation, developing products and processes with high-technology materials such as silicon derivatives.

Christensen's teaching at Harvard covered technology and operations management, operations strategy and general management. He then developed a course on managing innovation and, by 2003, was teaching an elective called 'Building a Sustainably Successful Enterprise'. His first major book, *The Innovator's Dilemma*, won a global award for the best business book of 1997, and was followed by two other much-praised studies, *The Innovator's Solution* and *Seeing What's Next*, published in 2003 and 2004 respectively.

The concept of 'creative disruption' in economics can be traced back to an idea propounded by the Austrian Joseph Schumpeter in 1942, while that of breaking through into uncharted markets where competition does not exist is not new either. The latter galvanized the business world in 1994 when Gary Hamel and C. K. Prahalad (qv) published their phenomenally successful *Competing for the Future*. Currently the INSEAD team of W. Chan Kim and Renée Mauborgne (qv) are pursuing an associated theme in what they call 'blue ocean' strategy.

But Clayton Christensen, whom the *Financial Times* has called 'arguably the brightest star on Harvard Business School's star-studded faculty', has rapidly carved out a brilliant reputation for his work on 'disruptive innovation' and how companies can use this either to capture a whole new customer base or, if already well established in a market, guard against damage from a competitor practising such disruption.

Christensen was struck by his big idea while a doctoral student lodging in a motel outside San Jose, California. He still goes back there on sentimental visits. Starting from the premise that only about one in ten companies, however well managed, sustains a run of above-average returns for their shareholders, he reasoned that they fail precisely because they are so well managed. They succeed at what they do best, always improving and seeking higher-end, higher-margin customers. Yet pursuit of the high end leaves a vacuum at the low end where customers are ready for something cheaper that has less added-value but fits the needs of their lives. The PC was a perfect example; Dell's cutting out of dealerships was another; low-cost no-frills airlines a third; Toyota's challenge to General Motors a fourth, and so on. Eventually, these low-margin markets turn into profitable mass markets.

Christensen first expounded this theory in *The Innovator's Dilemma: When New Technologies Cause Great Firms to Fail* (Harvard Business School, 1997), which propelled him into the ranks of the most original minds in management. It also, to his eventual chagrin, turned him into an iconic figure for the dotcom revolution that was lurking round the corner with a rush of ill-thought-out business plans and inadequate financial resources.

An article in *Harvard Business Review* in March/April 2000 ('Meeting the Challenge of Disruptive Change') led in time to Christensen's second book, *The Innovator's Solution: Creating and Sustaining Successful Growth* (2003). This set out three ways by which established companies could combat the threat from disruptive upstarts; either by spinning off a new independent and properly resourced business, acquiring one with the appropriate processes in place or creating new organizational structures within the corporation where such processes could be developed. Each option had one non-negotiable component: the CEO's personal attention and oversight must be paramount.

Throughout his work, Christensen insists that studying successful companies (as 80 per cent of Harvard MBA cases do) is the worst way to learn about future success, because the data is all in the past. It is tempting for business books to list proven success factors as a model for the future but, as he told the magazine *Fast Company* in November 2003, 'that's just strapping on feathers hoping they'll make you fly'. The only solution, he advises, is to look into the future for 'signals of change', an area he explores in his third book, *Seeing What's Next: Using the Theories of Innovation to Predict Industry Change* (2004). Again he offers a three-part model, in practical terms, to identify situations where businesses 'can expect the future to be materially different from the past'. Quoting the old Chinese proverb about giving a man a fish and feeding him for a day or teaching him how to fish, thereby feeding him for life, he says: 'Our goal is to teach you how to fish.'

Potential consumers who are not currently catered for exist everywhere, the book maintains, and if presented with the right product at the right price, can form a lucrative new market. In the 1980s, Christensen points out, most people were non-consumers of mobile phones. Likewise, the University of Phoenix, Arizona, founded in 1976, targeted people who were unable to attend traditional institutions of learning, offering them degrees in work-related subjects such as accountancy or nursing/healthcare. When the Internet took off, so did the University of Phoenix.

Christensen applies his set of predictive tools to five industries not noted for low-end innovation – education, aviation, healthcare, telecommunications and semiconductors. Some of his insights are already recognizable: discount airlines could be reaching maturity, for instance, because the big players will always be driven to match their pricing, but there may be customer-driven opportunities in air taxi services operating regionally between smaller, local airports. In healthcare, nurse-practitioners in doctors' surgeries could provide more accessible primary care or take over some functions that previously required a hospital visit. In telecoms and microchips, more technical disruptive strategies are explored.

Christensen's view is that innovation management today is where quality management was about 20 years ago: on that analogy, it was only when the causal roots of quality deviation were tackled that the discipline was launched on its successful trajectory to the error-free Six Sigma model.

Most companies suffer disruptive attack at least once and some encounter it several times, such as IBM, Intel, Microsoft and Kodak. Christensen hopes to inspire a generation of 'serial disruptors' and is practising his own philosophy by setting up a consultancy called Innosight to take on big-league players such as McKinsey and

Bain. He told *Fast Company* in late 2003 that Innosight was developing a new low-end process for fostering growth that promised to be 'very disruptive to the big consulting firms'.

As an example of current possibilities for low-end disruption, he has cited voice-recognition technology; a process that IBM tried to apply to dictating documents but which proved too complex for most PC users and was only partially successful. Christensen suggests that a simpler version could work 'for kids in chat rooms'.

'Any given customer can only lead you in a certain direction,' he told an interviewer in February 2004.* 'So you need to listen to non-customers sometimes.' At the same time, he warns, a competitive strategy that rests on lower costs 'only works if there is a high-cost provider around'.

Christensen's three books each build incrementally on each other – in contrast to the non-incremental strategy he advocates in companies – and there is a good deal of overlap while he recapitulates the earlier development of his theories. But he is clearly in tune with a fast-moving zeitgeist and his ambition, he claims, is nothing less than 'to change the way people think'.

KEY WRITINGS

Christensen, C. M. (1997) *The Innovator's Dilemma: When New Technologies Cause Great Firms to Fail*, Boston, Mass.: Harvard Business School; London: HarperBusiness.
Christensen, C. M. and Overdorf, M. (2000) 'Meeting the Challenge of Disruptive Change', Boston, Mass.: *Harvard Business Review* (March/April), reprint no. 00202.
Christensen, C. M. and Raynor, M. E. (2003) *The Innovator's Solution: Creating and Sustaining Successful Growth*, Boston, Mass.: Harvard Business School Press.
Christensen, C. M., Anthony, Scott D. and Roth, Erik A. (2004) *Seeing What's Next: Using the Theories of Innovation to Predict Industry Change*, Boston, Mass.: Harvard Business School Press.

* Massachusetts Interactive Media Council, Fireside Chat, 11 February 2004.

11

W. EDWARDS DEMING

(1900–1993)

The key to quality: reducing variation

US statistician and founding father of the quality movement, who was responsible, with his fellow-American
Joseph Juran, for instilling the quality philosophy into
postwar Japanese industry. The message had been rejected
or ignored by American companies and was only re-
imported after Japanese manufacturing began its competitive march into American markets.

Deming and Juran remain icons of Japanese industry,
whose companies compete annually for a Deming Prize,
awarded since 1951 for major improvements in quality.
Both men were honoured by the Emperor with the Order
of the Sacred Treasure, second class, the highest Japanese
award ever given to foreigners.

Deming is regarded by the Japanese as the chief architect of their phenomenal industrial success, but his home
country only began to recognize him in 1980, as a result
of an NBC television documentary on Japanese industry
called *If Japan Can, Why Can't We?* Overnight, American
industry discovered his existence. Now he is revered
internationally for his simple yet revolutionary principle that all processes are vulnerable to loss of quality
through variation: if the levels of variation are managed,
they can be decreased and quality raised. Deming
conducted seminars across the US until well into his

nineties. A frugal man, he had no formal organization or consultancy but worked from a basement office in his Washington home.

After US industry finally woke up to Deming's theories, several large corporations suffering intractable problems came to credit Deming as the key to their revival; most notably Ford Motor Company in the early 1970s. Nashua Corporation in New Hampshire, a Fortune 500 company making computer disks, copiers and other office products, was one of the first Western companies to adopt Deming's principles. Nashua subsequently managed to cut its order-entry lead times from eight days to one hour and achieved a 70 per cent reduction in customer claims.

William E. Conway, Nashua's president and later chief executive officer, who 'discovered' Deming when the guru was 78, has called him 'the father of the Third Wave of the Industrial Revolution' for the way in which he developed statistical control of quality levels into a new way of managing business. 'The Japanese manufacturers utilizing the statistical control of quality are sweeping the world in the second half of the 20th century, just as American manufacturers utilizing mass production swept the world in the first half,' said Conway.

In the UK, Sir John Egan applied Deming principles to turning round the ailing fortunes of Jaguar Cars in the early 1980s. Egan wrote of Deming's 1986 book *Out of the Crisis* that it was 'required reading for every chief executive in British industry who is serious about ensuring the international competitiveness of his company' (*Director* magazine, September 1988). More recently, Bill Gates' Microsoft has acknowledged its debt to Deming's teachings.

Deming, an electrical engineer by training (University of Wyoming, 1921) and a PhD in mathematical physics from Yale, worked for a time in the 1920s at the Western Electric Hawthorne plant in Chicago where Elton Mayo carried out his famous experiments in communication and motivation. Here Deming discovered the work of Walter Shewhart, the pioneer of controlled and uncontrollable variables and the statistical control of processes. He later became a statistician for the US government, working on data for the national census of 1939/40. In 1942 he set up courses to teach Shewhart's methods to industrialists and engineers. After the war he was invited to Japan by General MacArthur to advise on the Japanese census. Contacts made then resulted in the watershed invitation of 1950 which was to have such reverberating effects.

Deming's approach to quality control is basically that of a statistician (his compatriot and fellow quality guru J. M. Juran has criticized him for it), but it is also firmly rooted in the belief that quality is about people, not products – an approach which made a particular impact on the Japanese. He also believed that 85 per cent of production faults are the responsibility of management, not workers. The famous Deming '14 Points' of management are at the heart of his philosophy.

Before his death in 1993, Deming set up the W. Edwards Deming Institute in Washington, DC, a non-profit organization which provides seminars, conferences and other educational events advancing his teachings.

In 1950, when W. Edwards Deming made his first visit to Japan, the country was still recovering from the atomic bombing raids of August 1945. The economy was struggling to stand upright, much less move ahead, and Japanese goods still suffered from their prewar reputation for shoddiness.

Deming embarked on an exhausting series of lectures to engineers, from 8am to 5pm day after day in punishing heat. 'I was dripping wet by 8.30am,' he recalled in the BBC2 television series *Nippon.* 'The Japanese appreciated it. They were sorely afraid that they had established a reputation for shoddy quality and that they could never undo it. I assured them that it would take only a short while to undo that reputation and develop a new one.

'I think I was the only man in Japan in 1950 who believed

my prediction – that within five years manufacturers the world over would be screaming for protection. It took four years.'

The core element in this apparent miracle was the 'management circle' – still known in Japan as the 'Deming circle' – of planning, implementation, check and action. Above all it rested on the belief in 'Management for Quality' (Deming uses this term where Juran 'brands' his approach as 'Company-Wide Quality').

Deming's basic management philosophy, as impressed on his eager Japanese audiences, was to regard the consumer as 'the most important part of the production line'. Developing this in *Out of the Crisis* (1986), he insisted that merely having a satisfied customer was not enough. 'Profit in business comes from repeat customers, customers that boast about your product and service, and that bring friends with them.'

Deming always taught the necessity of staying ahead of the customer, anticipating what his needs will be in years to come.

His 14 Points for management were developed over some 20 years and were still being refined and reworded by the master in the 1990s. Henry Neave, author of *The Deming Dimension* (SPC Press, Knoxville, 1990), explains that they are not instructions or techniques, but rather 'vehicles for opening up the mind to new thinking, to the possibility that there are radically different and better ways of organizing our businesses and working with people'.

These, as quoted in Neave's book and Deming's own words, are the basic 14 Points:

1. Create constancy of purpose for continual improvement of products and service.
2. Adopt the new philosophy created in Japan.
3. Cease dependence on mass inspection: build quality into the product in the first place.
4. End lowest-tender contracts; instead, require meaningful measures of quality along with price.
5. Improve constantly and forever every process for planning, production and service.
6. Institute modern methods of training on the job for all, including management.
7. Adopt and institute leadership aimed at helping people to do a better job.

8. Drive out fear, encourage effective two-way communication.
9. Break down barriers between departments and staff areas.
10. Eliminate exhortations for the workforce – they only create adversarial relationships.
11. Eliminate quotas and numerical targets. Substitute aid and helpful leadership.
12. Remove barriers to pride of workmanship, including annual appraisals and Management by Objectives.
13. Encourage education and self-improvement for everyone.
14. Define top management's permanent commitment to ever-improving quality and productivity, and their obligation to implement all these principles.

The 14 Points are comprehensively expounded, chapter by chapter, in *The Deming Dimension*, a fascinating exposition of the guru's work and its development since publication of *Out of the Crisis*.

Deming himself said: 'If I had to reduce my message for management to just a few words, I'd say it all had to do with reducing variation.'

KEY WRITINGS

Deming, W. E. (1982) *Quality, Productivity and Competitive Position*, Massachusetts: MIT, Center for Advanced Engineering Study.
Deming, W. E. (1986, 1988) *Out of the Crisis*, Massachusetts: MIT, Center for Advanced Engineering Study; Cambridge: Cambridge University Press.
Walton, Mary (1986, 1989) *The Deming Management Method*, New York: Dodd, Mead and Co.; London: Mercury Books.
Neave, H. R. (1990) *The Deming Dimension*, Knoxville, Tennessee: SPC Press; available in the UK through the British Deming Association, 2 Castle Street, Salisbury, Wilts SP1 1BB.

12

PETER DRUCKER

(1909–2005)

Originator of modern management thinking

The apparently indestructible Peter Drucker, who died a few days short of his 96th birthday in November 2005, is acknowledged as the greatest management thinker of the 20th century. Born in Vienna during the heyday of that city's pre-1914 culture, he once interviewed Adolf Hitler, and his first book, a study of Nazi Germany called *The End of Economic Man*, was admiringly reviewed by Winston Churchill in 1939. After World War II, Drucker went on to invent or prefigure most of the leading management theories of the next 50 years. These ranged from 'Management by Objectives' to privatization; from defining a business in terms of creating and satisfying customers to the role of chief executive in corporate strategy; from decentralization to the implications of the information age and the rise of the knowledge worker, a term he coined as early as 1969. In the infancy of modern management theory, when control-and-command and the mechanistic approach of Frederick W. Taylor (qv) and the efficiency experts still held sway, Drucker believed that management was a social art, dependent on good communication with others and regard for the people working in the organization.

His five basic principles of management, formulated in books published between 1954 and 1974, remain as valid as ever: setting objectives, organizing, motivating and communicating, establishing measurements of performance and developing people. His influence was felt far outside business, in areas as diverse as the public sector, voluntary organizations, churches and government, even President George W. Bush's White House, whose policy-makers revered Drucker's concept of Management by Objectives – setting long-term goals to be realized by managers in more immediate stages. In the 1990s, he founded the Peter F. Drucker Foundation to help non-profit organizations achieve excellence through good management.

Many big corporations were also totally transformed by his work. Invited to carry out a study of General Motors for his seminal book, *The Concept of the Corporation* (1946), Drucker propagated the decentralization principle introduced by GM's then chairman, Alfred P. Sloan (qv), and it spread around the world. Tom Peters, whose co-authored book *In Search of Excellence* developed many Drucker ideas, said the Viennese sage deserved much of the credit for moving 75 to 80 per cent of the Fortune 500 to radical decentralization, adding that no true discipline of management had existed before Drucker.

Probably by virtue of its many facets, and by being first in the field, his body of work has received less attention in the world's business schools than that of many later gurus who developed niche reputations in strategy, marketing, leadership, innovation and other aspects of management theory. Drucker himself always scorned the word 'guru', saying that it was only used because 'charlatan' was too long to fit in a headline, but in the overall study of management there was no one to touch him: he had formulated all the principles before many of the fashionable gurus of the late 20th century were even born.

The most admired business leaders of our time have all recorded their debt to Drucker. Jack Welch has said that when making his key decision that each General Electric business had to be No. 1 or No. 2 in the world or face closure, he learned to ask Drucker's question: 'If you weren't already in this business, would you enter it today?' Andy Grove of Intel claims him as 'a hero of mine', and Bill Gates ranks his work ahead of all other management books.

One of the latest PhD students of his work concludes that Drucker, a master synthesizer as well as creator of ideas, made a philosophy out of management by moving and extending its boundaries and making it an intellectual challenge.

From 1950 to 1971 Drucker taught management at New York University's Graduate Business School, and for the next 31 years he was Clarke Professor of Social Science at the modest institution of Claremont Graduate School, Claremont, California, where he lived. In his nineties he was still a star attraction at international conferences, speaking and answering questions by interactive video link, and he was still writing prolifically. The last of his 40 books, *The Effective Executive in Action*, was published posthumously in 2006. A blueprint for getting the right things done in organizations, and for effective self-management, it updated a book first written in 1966 for senior executives in the Eisenhower Administration.

His books divide almost equally between works on management theory and technique and works of economic, political and social analysis. Many of the latter are seminal works which mapped out whole landscapes of the future with much wider horizons than those bounded by management. Philip Sadler, vice-president and former director of Ashridge Management College (Berkhamsted, Hertfordshire), found his thinking entirely changed by Drucker's 1969 book *The Age of Discontinuity*, which for Sadler pointed clearly to the coming decline of Britain's manufacturing industry.

This book, still well worth study, prefigured many of the business bestsellers of the late 1980s and early 1990s on managing chaos and disruptive change. Drucker's books have anticipated those of Charles Handy (qv), Tom Peters (qv) and Richard Pascale (qv), to name only three. In some of its ideas, *The Age of Discontinuity* was 20 years ahead of John Naisbitt's *Megatrends* and Charles Handy's

The Age of Unreason. It also introduced for the first time in a management book the concept of the coming information economy and the 'knowledge worker', a term coined by Drucker.

It was in *The Age of Discontinuity*, incidentally, that Drucker introduced the concept of privatization, though he called it 'reprivatization'. He accurately forecast the disillusionment with government arising from the discovery that governments could not, after all, produce miracles. 'There is little doubt, for instance, that the British in adopting the National Health Service believed that medical care would cost nothing . . . Nurses, doctors, hospitals, drugs and so on have to be paid for by somebody. But everybody expected this "somebody" to be somebody else.'

Drucker advocated privatization on the grounds that the purpose of government was to govern, not to 'do', and that the two roles were incompatible. His vision, unlike the Conservative Party's realization of it, was for privatization to cover all institutions, not merely business ones – universities, for example.

In May 1970, a year or so after publication of *The Age of Discontinuity*, the word privatization made its first appearance in a Conservative Central Office pamphlet ('A New Style of Government'), which credited Drucker with the coinage.

In his nineties, Drucker's interests became more focused on changes in society and macro-economic matters, although he never lost his incisive ability to cut to the heart of business problems and put forward solutions in clear, clean-cut language that is a pleasure to read for its own sake. His towering reputation is unlikely to be challenged in the years ahead.

The son of an Austrian government official who helped found the Salzburg Festival, Drucker came to Britain in the late 1920s, and his first job was an apprentice clerk in a Bradford wool exporting firm, working with a quill pen in 80-pound/36-kilo-gram brass-bound ledgers chained to the desk. Between 1933 and 1936 he worked as an economist in a London merchant bank and then decided to throw in his lot with the United States. He emigrated to America in 1937, produced his first book two years later and, in 1942, took a consultant's job with General Motors, then the world's largest company.

Out of this experience came his influential 1946 book *Concept of the Corporation*, still one of the best and most perceptive analyses of the successful large organization. As well as General Motors, other companies studied in the book were General Electric, IBM and Sears Roebuck. Drucker identified their success with certain managerial characteristics, notably delegation and goal-setting (Management by Objectives) and certain structural characteristics, such as decentralization. Drucker believed that the ultimate key to success in all these companies was that 'they knew what businesses they were in, what their competencies were and how to keep their efforts focused on their goals' (*Organization Theory*, ed. D. S. Pugh). Nearly 40 years later Peters and Waterman reached much the same conclusion, set out in more populist style, in their bestseller *In Search of Excellence*. *Concept of the Corporation* also analysed the importance of marketing – at that time an almost universally neglected function – and the delicate balance which a company must seek to achieve between long-term strategy and short-term performance.

Drucker figures in more management-book indexes than any other individual by far. In *Makers of Management*, by David Clutterbuck and Stuart Crainer, he rates no fewer than 40 separate page references.

Peter Drucker's reputation as a management guru was established with *The Practice of Management* (1954), a work still regarded by later theorists as one of the best and clearest in the field. In this, he identified Management by Objectives as the first of seven primary tasks of management. MBO, dignified with capital letters, became a movement of its own, and Britain's John Humble (qv) made a speciality of developing its theory and practice.

Management by Objectives emerged out of Drucker's work with General Electric among his studies for *Concept of the Corporation*. Each GE manager was responsible for a profit centre and given targets to achieve – 7 per cent return on sales and 20 per cent return on investment. These were severely applied; you lost your job if you didn't meet them.

Drucker perceived that, since businesses survive or fall by the bottom line, corporate goals should be divided into objectives and clearly assigned to units and individuals. 'Management by Objectives,' as Richard Pascale observes in *Managing on the Edge*, 'ensures that each link in the chain of command does its part . . .'

A subsequent handbook, *Managing for Results* (1964) is, in Drucker's own words of introduction, a 'what to do' book. It was, he believed, 'the first attempt at an organized presentation of the economic tasks of the business executive and the first halting step towards a discipline of economic performance in business enterprise.' It sets out, in clear, no-nonsense prose, guidelines for understanding business realities and for analysing a company in terms of revenues, resources, prospects, cost centres, customer needs, building on strengths, finding potential, making key decisions and building strategies for the future. It is still one of the best practical vade-mecums for anyone running a business enterprise. Drucker believed that every three years or so a company should be put under the microscope and every product, process, technology, service or market subjected to a gruelling assessment.

Throughout his work, Drucker's emphasis has been on the effectiveness of managers – particularly in making good use of their human resources as the key to a productive and profitable organization. Management, said Drucker, is the job of organizing resources to achieve the satisfactory performance of an enterprise. Managers must in the end be measured by their economic performance, though this is not necessarily synonymous with maximum profits; rather, with sufficient profit to cover the risks that have been taken, and to avoid the enterprise making a loss. Management by Objectives is the key to this.

Drucker was sometimes criticized for neglecting theories of motivation, though he was one of the first to recognize and praise Douglas McGregor's Theory Y of consultative management as early as 1954.

Drucker's emphasis on objective-setting for management is most clearly set out in his mammoth compendium *Management: Tasks, Responsibilities, Practices* (1974). This represents an encyclopedia of his earlier writings and is recommended as the bedrock of any aspiring manager's reading list. Studded with illuminating case studies, the massive volume (weighing 3.5 pounds/1.6 kilograms in hardback) defines every aspect of managerial skills and pinpoints eight areas where clear objectives are vital: marketing, innovation, human organization, financial resources, physical resources, productivity, social responsibility and profit requirements. A thorough grounding in this vast work is virtually the equivalent of a do-it-yourself business-school course.

Shortly before this was published, Drucker had defined his broad view of management in *People and Performance* (1973): 'To fulfil the specific purpose and mission of the organization; to make work productive and the worker achieving; and to manage social impacts and social responsibility.'

In *Management: Tasks, Responsibilities, Practices*, he identified five basic operations in the work of the manager, which together result in the integration of resources into a viable growing organism. These summarize the essentials of management with more clarity than any other book before or since:

A manager, in the first place, sets objectives. He determines what the objectives should be. He determines what the goals in each area of objectives should be. He decides what has to be done to reach these objectives. He makes the objectives effective by communicating them to the people whose performance is needed to attain them.

Second, a manager organizes. He analyses the activities, decisions and relations needed. He classifies the work. He divides it into manageable activities and further divides the activities into manageable jobs. He groups these units and jobs into an organization structure. He selects people for the management of these units and for the jobs to be done.

Next, a manager motivates and communicates. He makes a team out of the people that are responsible for various jobs. He does that through the practices with which he works. He does it in his own relations to the men with whom he works. He does it through his 'people decisions' on pay, placement and promotion. And he does it through constant communication, to and from his subordinates, to and from his superior, and to and from his colleagues.

The fourth basic element in the work of the manager is

measurement. The manager establishes yardsticks – and few factors are as important to the performance of the organization and of every man in it. He sees to it that each man has measurements available to him which are focused on the performance of the whole organization and which, at the same time, focus on the work of the individual and help him do it. He analyses, appraises and interprets performance. As in all other areas of his work, he communicates the meaning of the measurements and their findings to his subordinates, to his superiors and to colleagues.

Finally, a manager develops people, including himself.

Taking an historical perspective, Drucker later identified seven key elements in postwar management development:

1. Scientific management of work as the key to productivity
2. Decentralization as a basic principle of organization
3. Personnel management as the orderly way of fitting people into organization structures
4. Manager development to provide for the needs of tomorrow
5. Managerial accounting – use of analysis and information as the foundation for firm decision–making
6. Marketing
7. Long-range planning

In recent years, Drucker's books have included *Innovation and Entrepreneurship* (1985), a typically wide-ranging study of growth sectors of the US economy in the early 1980s, including many businesses not normally considered as such: private health-care, for example, non-profit-making private schools and public/private partnerships in which government units contract out services to competitive private companies. *The New Realities* (1989) ranged over a global stage, anticipating the development of such contemporary phenomena as the transnational economy, the democratization of the Soviet republics, the changing ethos of the United States and the demands of a post-industrial, post-business society. *Post-Capitalist Society* (1992) examined among other phenomena the division of society into knowledge and service workers, and the economic and social challenges involved.

Drucker's breadth of vision and eclectic range of publications sprang from his belief that management is central to life, not merely to business. One of his recurring concepts was that of the chief executive as conductor of an orchestra. As he said: 'We are beginning to realize that management itself is the central institution of our present society, and that there are very few differences between managing a business, managing a diocese, managing a hospital, managing a university, managing a research lab, managing a labour union or managing a government agency. All along, this has been the main thrust of my work, and the one that distinguishes it from practically all my contemporaries working in the field.'

Rosabeth Moss Kanter (qv) views his goals as even more embracing. In an article in *New Management* (winter 1985), she wrote: 'Good management is also our best hope for world peace. In the Drucker perspective, imperatives for growth push organization beyond national borders in the search for new markets. The world becomes interconnected by a series of cross-cutting trade relationships in which the interests of managers in the survival of their multinational enterprises outweigh the interests of politicians. Quality of life, technological progress and world peace, then, are all the products of good management . . . At root, Drucker is a management utopian, descended as much from Robert Owen as Max Weber.'

To Drucker, the business organization, as any organization, was a human, a social, indeed a moral phenomenon. Customer service rather than profits should dominate management thinking, profit being the means of continued investment in innovation and improvement.

'Contrary to the approach to the study of political and social organization that has prevailed in the West since Machiavelli, I stressed all along that organization does not deal with power but with responsibility. This is the keynote of my work that has remained constant over more than 40 years.'

Drucker once summed up his own vast contribution to management thinking in these words, quoted in *Makers of Management* (Clutterbuck and Crainer): 'I was the first one to see that the purpose of a business lies outside of itself – that is, in creating and satisfying a customer. I was the first to see the decision process as central, the first to see that structure has to follow strategy, and the first one to see, or at least the first to say, that management has to be management by objectives and self-control.'

KEY WRITINGS

Drucker, P. F. (1946) *Concept of the Corporation*, New York: John Day.

Drucker, P. F. (1951) *The New Society*, London: Heinemann.

Drucker, P. F. (1954) *The Practice of Management*, New York: Harper and Row.

Drucker, P. F. (1964, 1989) *Managing for Results*, London: Heinemann.

Drucker, P. F. (1969) *The Age of Discontinuity*, London: Heinemann.

Drucker, P. F. (1974) *Management: Tasks, Responsibilities, Practices*, London: Heinemann; New York: Harper and Row.

Drucker, P. F. (1985) *Innovation and Entrepreneurship*, London: Heinemann.

Drucker, P. F. (1989, 1990) *The New Realities*, London: Heinemann Professional Publishing; Mandarin Paperback.

Drucker, P. F. (1992) *Post-Capitalist Society*, Oxford: Butterworth Heinemann.

Drucker, P. F. (1994) *Frontiers of Management*, Oxford: Butterworth Heinemann.

Drucker, P. F. (1997) *Drucker on Asia*, Oxford: Butterworth Heinemann.

Drucker, P. F. (1998) *On the Profession of Management*, Boston: Harvard Business School Press.

Drucker, P. F. (1999) *Management Challenges for the 21st Century*, London: HarperCollins.

Drucker, P. F. (2001) *The Essential Drucker*, Oxford: Butterworth Heinemann.

Drucker, P. F. and Maciarello, J. A. (2006) *The Effective Executive in Action*, London: HarperBusiness.

13

HENRI FAYOL

(1841–1925)

Five foundation stones of modern management

French mining engineer and manager, generally regarded as the first to ask 'what is management?', to analyse the nature of managerial activity and to formulate a complete theory of management, based on his own experience of running the mining and metallurgical combine Commentry-Fourchamboult-Decazeville.

Fayol was in his seventies before his ideas gained currency in print, and his classic work, *Administration Industrielle et Générale*, was not published in English (as *General and Industrial Management*) until 1949. His key definitions of managerial activity – to plan, to organize, to command, to coordinate and to control – remained accepted wisdom until Henry Mintzberg's revealing studies in the 1960s.

Henri Fayol was years ahead of his time in linking strategy and organizational theory and in emphasizing the need for management development and the qualities of leadership. Igor Ansoff in *Corporate Strategy* (1965) said that Fayol 'anticipated imaginatively and soundly most of the more recent analyses of modern business practice', although Peter Drucker in his great compendium

Management: Tasks, Responsibilities and Practices (1974), criticized the application of Fayol's functional approach to larger and more complex organizations than the one he knew and managed.

Fayol believed the same principles of management could be applied, regardless of size, to organizations of all kinds, whether industrial, commercial, governmental, political, or even religious. His five key elements of industrial management remain the foundation stones on which all later gurus, to a greater or lesser extent, have built.

These five elements are: to forecast and plan; to organize; to command; to coordinate; and to control. Fayol defined the first as 'examining the future and drawing up the plan of action'; the second as 'building up the structure, material and human, of the undertaking'; the third as 'maintaining activity among the personnel'; the fourth as 'binding together, unifying and harmonizing all activity and effort'; and the fifth as 'seeing that everything occurs in conformity with established rule and expressed command'.

An organization, therefore, begins with a strategic plan or definition of goals, progresses to a structure to put that plan into action, is carried forward by controlled activity between manager and workforce, has the work of its disparate departments harmonized by coordinated management and, finally, is subject to checks on the efficiency of its working, preferably by independent 'staff' departments separate from the functional departments.

Fayol believed that a manager obtained the best performance from his workforce by leadership qualities, by his knowledge of the business and his workers, and by the ability to instil a sense of mission. From his own long experience in industry, he distilled his 14 General Principles of Management:

1. Division of work with specialization allowing individuals to build up skills and become more productive. 'The object of division of work is to produce more and better work with the same effort.'
2. Authority, both official and personal, with matching responsibility. 'Generally speaking, responsibility is feared as much as authority is sought after, and fear of responsibility paralyses much initiative and destroys many good qualities. A good leader should possess and infuse into those around him courage to accept responsibility.

3. Discipline, 'in essence obedience, application, energy, behaviour and outward marks of respect observed in accordance with the standing agreements between the firm and its employees . . . When a defect in discipline is apparent or when relations between superiors and subordinates leave much to be desired . . . the ill mostly results from the ineptitude of the leaders.'

4. Unity of command: each man should have only one boss with no conflicting lines of command. 'In all human associations, in industry, commerce, army, home, State, dual command is a perpetual source of conflicts . . .'

5. Unity of direction: 'one head and one plan for a group of activities having the same objective. It is the condition essential to unity of action, coordination of strength and focusing of effort.'

6. Subordination of individual to general interest, reconciling conflicting interests where necessary: 'That represents one of the great difficulties of management.' Means of effecting it are (1) firmness and good example on the part of superiors, (2) agreements as fair as possible, (3) constant supervision.

7. Fair remuneration for effort. 'Every mode of payment likely to make the personnel more valuable and improve its lot in life, and also to inspire keenness on the part of employees at all levels, should be a matter for managers' constant attention.'

8. Centralization or decentralization, the choice to depend on the condition of the business and the culture of its staff. 'The finding of the measure which shall give the best overall yield; that is the problem of centralization or decentralization. Everything which goes to increase the importance of the subordinate's role is decentralization, everything which goes to reduce it is centralization.'

9. The scalar chain or hierarchical principle of management; a path 'dictated both by the need for some transmission and by the principle of unity of command, but it is not always the swiftest . . . It is an error to depart needlessly from the line of authority but an even greater one to keep to it when detriment to the business ensues . . . When an employee is obliged to choose between the two practices,

and it is impossible for him to take advice from his superiors, he should be courageous enough and feel free enough to adopt the line dictated by the general interest.'

10. Order, both material and social: 'Social order demands precise knowledge of the human requirements and resources of the concern and a constant balance between these.'

11. Equity in the treatment of employees: 'The head of the business should strive to instil a sense of equity throughout all levels of the scalar chain.'

12. Stability of tenure among personnel: 'Generally the managerial personnel of prosperous concerns is stable, that of unsuccessful ones is unstable. Instability of tenure is at one and the same time cause and effect of bad running. Nevertheless, changes of personnel are inevitable . . . Stability of tenure of personnel is also a question of proportion.'

13. Initiative: 'Thinking out a plan and ensuring its success is one of the keenest satisfactions for an intelligent man to experience. It is also one of the most powerful stimulants of human endeavour . . . The initiative of all, added to that of the manager and supplementing it if need be, represents a great source of strength for business . . . The manager must be able to sacrifice some personal vanity in order to grant this sort of satisfaction to subordinates.'

14. A sense of *esprit de corps*: essential for management to foster the morale of its workforce. 'Real talent is needed,' said Fayol, 'to coordinate effort, encourage keenness, use each person's abilities, and reward each one's merit without arousing possible jealousies and disturbing harmonious relations.'

KEY WRITINGS

Fayol, H., trans. Constance Storrs (1949) *General and Industrial Management*, London: Pitman.
Quotations taken from extract in *Organization Theory* (1990) ed. D. S. Pugh, London: Penguin Books.

14

MARY PARKER FOLLETT

(1868–1933)

'Responsibility is the great developer'

New England-born political scientist who became a pioneer of human relations in management in the 1920s, before Elton Mayo had even started his famous Hawthorne experiments in consultation. She was the first major figure to point out, at the height of fashion for F. W. Taylor's scientific management, that human considerations could not be separated from those of 'mechanical' efficiency.

Her Quaker background probably helped shape her beliefs on democratic participation in politics, society and business, and although overlooked for decades among management theorists, her work is now recognized as anticipating that of Rensis Likert (qv) and Douglas McGregor (qv) on participative leadership and self-managing teams, as well as much of today's thinking on the dynamics of groups.

Born in Quincy, Massachusetts, Follett attended the Society for the Collegiate Instruction of Women in Cambridge, Mass., later to become Radcliffe College and affiliated to Harvard. She also studied at Newnham College, Cambridge, England, and in Paris and published books on the processes of democratic politics before moving into the area of business management in 1924.

From her earliest writings she advocated greater participation and what is now called empowerment, stating firmly that 'responsibility is the great developer of men.' Sixty years before Richard Pascale (qv) she also perceived the creative possibilities of conflict – 'we should use it to work for us' – and her subtly thought-out principles for resolving adversarial disputes through behavioural understanding have become today's basic tools of negotiation strategy and tactics. She foresaw the need for re-engineering organizations away from hierarchies into something more like peer-group networks, with 'coordination from the bottom up and all along the line'.

Follett has been acknowledged by the visionary Peter Drucker as 'a prophet of management' and under this title a selection of her most powerful writings was published in 1995 along with commentaries from contemporary gurus and managers.

Mary Parker Follett's achievement, wrote her British biographer, Pauline Graham, was that 'she created a philosophy of management embedded in the full complexity of human nature. . . . So many others, from Taylor onwards, saw and still see management as a series of separate functions with one more important than the others, to which the others have to be subservient. Follett saw things differently.'

Another Follett devotee, the British industrialist Sir Peter Parker, wrote that 'she transformed the ideas of modern management into human proportions, into terms of community.' Her vision of business as an inextricable part of the society in which it operates is now mainstream thinking.

Her early work in the field of education in Boston, setting up vocational guidance centres in schools, and in the study of democratic political institutions, led to her interest in the dynamics of how people work together in groups and the potential creativity this could release. In 1918 she gained international stature with *The New State*, a book which advocated replacing bureaucratic government institutions by a true democracy of group networks in which people took part in decision-making and created their own authority.

In 1924 she moved the focus of her thinking on democracy into industry, which she saw as 'the most important field of human activity, and management is the fundamental element in industry'. As in the political process, she believed that the self-governing principle was the best way for individuals and groups in industry to fulfil themselves and attain their goals. Likewise, she thought that leadership should be a matter of knowledge and experience, 'no matter whether it is up the line or down the line', thus anticipating by 70 years the work on adaptive or non-authority leadership associated with Professor Ronald Heifetz of the John F. Kennedy School of Government at Harvard.

Her concept of 'power-with' rather than 'power-over' is as modern as the 21st century, though still too little practised. Like many prophets, however, she had more of a following abroad in her lifetime than in her home country; notably in Britain, where she delivered many lectures in the 1920s, and in Japan, which responded eagerly to her theories in the 1930s as it would 20 years later to those of the American quality-management guru W. E. Deming (qv).

Many of Follett's most lasting insights were published long after her death in collections of her lectures and writings entitled *Dynamic Administration* (1941) and *Freedom and Coordination* (1949). The most successful leader, she wrote, 'should make his co-workers see that it is not his purpose which is to be achieved, but a common purpose, born of the desires and the activities of the group'. She was an early advocate of management development, and believed the attributes of leadership could be taught. These involved 'the ability to grasp a total situation: facts, present and potential, aims and purposes, and men. The leader must see a whole. He must see the relation between all the different factors in a situation.'

She advocated horizontal rather than vertical authority in an organization; an advanced concept even today. Warren Bennis, the veteran guru of leadership studies, says: 'Just about everything written today about leadership and organizations comes from Mary Parker Follett's lectures and writings.'

Above all, she put people at the heart of business and industry. In a measured criticism of Taylorism, which was sweeping the industrialized world after World War I, she said: 'We should remember that we can never wholly separate the human from the mechanical side . . . If the industrial manager is to get the fruits of Scientific Management, he must understand first the intricate workings of a group' (*Dynamic Administration*).

Follett's other great contribution to industrial relations – indeed, to the management of human relationships as a whole – arose from her scientific eye on behavioural patterns and how these could interact to affect the management of conflict. In *Creative Experience* (1924) she outlined her theory of 'circular response' – that an individual's behaviour helps create the very situation to which that behaviour is responding. From that she evolved a theory of 'constructive conflict', in which the integration of both parties' desires would prove far superior to the domination of one by the other or even to compromise, in which both sides had to sacrifice something. Integration, she explained through simple anecdotal illustration, meant getting to the root of each party's aims so that both could be satisfied in some essential way.

The first rule for integration, she laid down, was to 'put your cards on the table, face the real issue, uncover the conflict, bring the whole thing into the open . . . Many conflicts could, I believe, be prevented from ending disastrously by getting the desires of each side into one field of vision where they could be viewed together and compared.'

Follett was, of course, developing this psychologically shrewd perception in the bitter aftermath of the 1919 Versailles conference in which Germany's humiliation by the victorious nations would fester until it bred another, even more destructive world war. Today her tactics are common in negotiation theory, where the aim is a 'win-win' resolution in which both parties walk away feeling in some measure satisfied with the outcome.

She also suggested that adult education courses could usefully teach 'the art of cooperative thinking'. Unfortunately for a world still afflicted by industrial disputes, adversarial politics and diplomatic stand-offs that all too often collapse disastrously into war, that piece of plain Bostonian common sense has yet to be widely adopted.

KEY WRITINGS

Follett, Mary Parker (1918) *The New State: Group Organization: the Solution of Popular Government*, London: Longman; reissued 1998 by the Pennsylvania State University Press.

Follett, Mary Parker (1924) *Creative Experience*, London: Longman.

Follett, Mary Parker (1941) *Dynamic Administration*, New York: Harper Brothers.

Follett, Mary Parker (1949) *Freedom and Co-ordination*, London: Pitman.

Graham, Pauline (ed.) (1995) *Mary Parker Follett – Prophet of Management: a Celebration of Writings from the 1920s*, Boston: Harvard Business School Press.

(This collection covers Follett's major contributions to management theory with commentaries by Peter Drucker, Rosabeth Moss Kanter, Henry Mintzberg and other leading thinkers.)

15

HENRY GANTT

(1861–1919)

The key tool for managing projects

Henry Laurence Gantt was the third leading figure in the scientific-management movement of the early 1900s in the United States, along with his mentor Frederick W. Taylor (qv) and close friend Frank Gilbreth (qv). He became driver of the movement on Taylor's death in 1915 but was to die prematurely himself four years later. Gantt was the first to plot both activity and time in pursuit of efficiency and his enduring legacy, still a staple tool of project management around the world, is the Gantt Chart, which enables projects to be monitored and completed on schedule.

Born in Maryland of a former slave-owning family (he liked to say that scientific management marked a great step forward from slave labour), Gantt graduated from Johns Hopkins University in Baltimore and worked as a teacher and draughtsman before turning to mechanical engineering as a profession.

In 1887, he joined Midvale Steel, where F. W. Taylor was chief engineer and beginning his stopwatch experiments to time the basic elements of manual tasks and speed up productivity. He became an eager disciple of Taylorism and worked with him until 1893. In 1901, Taylor described him as the best man he knew to introduce scientific management to the workplace: as a consultant, Gantt was to implement it in around 50 companies.

Gantt favoured the Taylor rather than the Gilbreth view of worker responsibility, once writing in a professional paper that it was hard to get workers to obey orders because 'a large percentage of men seem so constituted as to be apparently unable to do as they are told.' Nevertheless, Gantt and his wife Mary became personal friends of the Gilbreths and lived near them in Montclair, New Jersey.

Like Taylor and Gilbreth, Gantt died in his fifties, shortly after developing his bar chart that helped to speed up ship production during World War I. After his death, it was eagerly adopted by the young Soviet Union, along with other scientific-management tools, and also played a key part in such great US infrastructure projects as the Hoover Dam and the 1950s system of interstate highways.

Although most of the gurus in this book have left their mark one way or another on the evolution of management theory, no one else is remembered by such a practical, everyday tool as the Gantt Chart. Nearly 90 years after its invention, it remains indispensable to project managers, planners and system developers. It can be applied to simple or complex tasks, enables progress to be monitored at a glance and has been adapted to software packages for project management, being easily converted to spreadsheet format.

The Gantt Chart works on two planes: a vertical list of tasks or sub-projects and a horizontal scale broken down into time units for each task, measured in days, weeks or months. Horizontal bars, preferably hollow so that they can be filled in as the work progresses, show the time allocated to each task. These bars may run consecutively or overlap, to provide a bird's eye view of the project as a whole. For complex projects, sub-tasks can be moved on to their own charts and timelines. Apart from the obvious practical advantages of monitoring and measuring progress, there are motivational benefits for the project team in achieving and passing visible milestones.

Despite subscribing to Taylor's Theory X approach that workers largely needed to be controlled by instructions, Gantt was noted for his motivational schemes, believing that rewards for good work rather than penalties for poor work was the route to better perform-ance. He developed a pay incentive system which enabled those on fixed wages to achieve a minimum level of earnings and bonus payments, and he always emphasized the need for leadership and management skills.

He also felt that too much emphasis was put on the produc-tivity of workers compared to that of executives and that tasks should be set fairly at all levels in the organization, after which efficiency all down the line would be improved. After Taylor's death, he issued a call to arms in a lecture at Yale University for more democracy in industrial management. He saw a danger of the executives and financiers of the day becoming divorced from the shop floor, viewing them simply as 'buying at the cheapest rate and selling at the highest'. Such men, said Gantt, were not up to industrial leadership in the 20th century.

One of his keenest concerns after World War I was the threat from Russia's revolution and the risk that America's unbridled style of capitalist management would tip the country into 'following Europe into the economic confusion which seems to threaten the very existence of our civilization'. Ironically, it was Soviet Russia which provided the first mass adoption of the Gantt Chart. About 100,000 copies of it had been translated into Russian and circu-lated there by 1934, and the first Soviet Five-Year Plan was entirely calculated on Gantt bar charts.

Gantt's memorial, apart from his ubiquitous chart, is the Henry Laurence Gantt Medal, awarded since 1929 for distinguished achievement in management. In *The Practice of Management* (1954), Peter Drucker grouped Gantt along with Taylor, Henri Fayol (qv) and the Gilbreths as giving 'brilliant new insights into manage-ment ideas from 1890 until 1920'.

KEY WRITINGS

Gantt, H. L. (1911) *Work, Wages and Profits*.
Gantt, H. L. (1919) *Organizing for Work*.
Clark, W. (1942) *The Gantt Chart*.

16

SUMANTRA GHOSHAL

(1948–2004)

Transnational management and the 'new moral contract'

Professor of strategic and international management at London Business School and the first management academic (with Christopher Bartlett of Harvard) to analyse and define the attributes required of the modern global organization and its management. *Managing Across Borders* (1989) was ranked by the *Financial Times* of London as one of the 50 most influential management books of its time, identifying as it did a new form of 'transnational' corporation best fitted to compete in global markets. The pair's subsequent book, *The Individualized Corporation* (1998), identified the development of a new corporate relationship with employees, described as a 'new moral contract' that recognized their responsibility as value creators.

Ghoshal's sudden death in 2004 from a brain haemorrhage at the age of 55 deprived Britain's small band of international management gurus of a cerebral and charismatic communicator and a highly original mind who was beginning to question the whole basis of management theory and what he increasingly saw as its subversive effect on business practice through narrow and negative assumptions about human nature.

Born in India, Ghoshal epitomized a new breed of multicultural management academic whose background,

**mingling Asian, European and North American influ-
ences, gives them a truly global perspective on organizations and who seek to address deeper questions than
techniques of management. (C. K. Prahalad, qv, is
another.) Much of Ghoshal's later work focused on
evolving a 'new moral contract' between corporation and
employee, based on respect for the individual as a 'value
creator' for the company. He believed that business should
be 'a force for good in society', but that its potential
was being squandered.**

**Prior to joining LBS in 1994, Ghoshal was professor
of business policy at INSEAD, the international management college in France, and a visiting professor at the
prestigious Sloan School of Management, Massachusetts
Institute of Technology. While spending most of his
teaching time in London, Ghoshal was also founding
dean of the Indian School of Business in Hyderabad,
which was inaugurated in 2001 in partnership with LBS.**

Ghoshal and Bartlett caught the tide of globalization early,
analysing in detail the structure and strategy of organizations and
their management in the new borderless world of competition.
In *Managing Across Borders* they analysed the three historical
models of such organizations – the multinational or multi-
domestic, the global and the international – before outlining the
shape and character of a fourth, the 'transnational'.

The multinational was essentially a federation of multiple
national companies loosely connected across borders and managed
largely by expatriates sent out from the centre. The global model
was managed from the hub, benefiting from economies of scale
in manufacturing and distribution. The international resembled
the multinational but increasingly transferred its centrally produced
technology and marketing expertise to the local businesses.

The transnational, Ghoshal and Bartlett perceived, was a model
that combined local knowledge and quick market response with
global efficiency – more or less the famous philosophy of 'think
local, act global' preached in the 1990s by Percy Barnevik of

Asea Brown Boveri (ABB). They cited Procter & Gamble and Unilever as two companies that had restructured themselves away from over-centralized and rigidly managed multinational and international models into true transnationals.

In transnational corporations, knowledge transfer becomes more sophisticated, manufacturing and R&D are located in the most cost-effective places, and there is serious investment in local training and knowledge to exploit unfamiliar markets.

Management, in the Ghoshal and Bartlett view, lagged well behind strategy in creating the new model. It required, they wrote, 'a different set of motivations and assumptions about the role of the company's international operations. In the transnational view, the national subsidiaries become strategic partners whose knowledge and capabilities are vital to the corporation's ability to maintain a long-term global competitive advantage.'

To achieve the change to a transnational model, the corporate anatomy needed to be restructured, and managers' decision-making channels and responsibilities 'fine-tuned'. Organizational 'physiology', the information flow that governed decisions, also needed to be redirected, often through informal systems and forums. And finally, organizational 'psychology' had to be modified through behavioural tools to produce a transnational culture.

In their second book, *The Individualized Corporation* (1998), Ghoshal and Bartlett developed their organizational insights further and effectively relegated to history the decentralized corporation pioneered at General Motors by Alfred P. Sloan in the 1920s. Their new type of corporation and new generation of managers also banished the rigidities of employer–employee relationship that had produced 'organization man'. Immensely successful in the 1990s, corporations such as General Electric under Jack Welch and ABB, the Swedish–Swiss engineering conglomerate welded together by Percy Barnevik in 1988, were notable for the way they mobilized the ideas and initiative of their multinational workforces.

Welch wrote that GE had to 'redefine our relationship with our employees . . . to build a place where people have the freedom to be creative, where they feel a real sense of accomplishment – a place that brings out the best in everybody'. Barnevik observed in similar vein: 'We have to learn how to recognize and employ that untapped ability that each individual brings to work every day.'

GE and ABB were formerly traditional companies that managed a successful transition to the 'individualized corporation'. Others, such as Intel and IKEA, developed many of the new characteristics from scratch. Ghoshal and Bartlett analysed the techniques for creating them under three main headings: purpose, process and people. The book coined the phrase 'new moral contract' to replace the old 'psychological contract' between employee and employer as envisaged by Frederick Herzberg (qv) in an earlier era of career security. In this new version, each employee would take responsibility for his or her 'best-in-class' performance and continuous learning while the corporation undertook to provide the opportunity for that learning. This would protect and enhance the individual's job flexibility, not necessarily within that corporation but in the market as a whole. The corporation should also, the book argued, strive to create 'an exciting and invigorating work climate' to retain the best talents within it. The new moral contract embodied 'a fundamental change in management philosophy', the book stated. 'No longer are people seen as a corporate asset from which to appropriate value . . . they are a responsibility and a resource to add value.'

Since publication of *The Individualized Corporation*, Ghoshal's thinking had been focused more deeply on this theme, in the context of the individualistic Internet generation. His own experience at LBS in the late 1990s was a catalyst: of 140 students on his management course, only six were considering careers in large corporations. The others had been deterred by the experiences of their parents' generation, seeing them as stressed captives of the company, vulnerable in middle age to downsizing and redundancy notices. Ghoshal argued that corporations would have to examine more rigorously what they could offer the talented but footloose Generation X, whose skills, creativity and dynamism they badly needed. The new moral contract, he suggested, was already in place at the best-performing companies, based on respect for the individual as a value creator and in the absence of career assurance, accepting responsibility for helping individuals realize their best potential.

'The pattern of relationships in human lives has been fundamentally changing over a period of time – relationships of one individual to another, of the individual to the institution or organization and of the individual to society,' Ghoshal told the author in a 1999 interview. 'I believe we have not explored in any richness the implications at the individual–organizational level. I think the need for loyalty and commitment to an organization is very basic, but at the same time a profound sense of autonomy is rising, and this will pose a huge problem for big companies.'

Ghoshal subscribed to the idea of the 'third place', a concept of Richard Pascale's (qv), meaning a source of fulfilment and self-expression separate from both workplace and home, somewhere in which people find their own independence and identity as individuals rather than as employees or family members. Formerly, these tended to be places of relaxation and shared interests, such as social clubs, but for Generation Xers they might also be folded into work in some way.

In the same 1999 interview, Ghoshal cited his own adult children, multicultural and multilingual, equally at home in Asian, European or North American environments. Above all, he said, they seek work that excites them, 'where they can grow, where they can have fun'. It was possible, he felt, that team-based or project-based work of the right kind could help to import 'third place' satisfaction into the working environment.

KEY WRITINGS

Ghoshal, S. and Bartlett, C. (1989) *Managing Across Borders*, Boston, Mass.: Harvard Business School Press; London: Hutchinson Business Books.
Ghoshal, S. and Bartlett, C. (1998) *The Individualized Corporation*, London: William Heinemann, Random House.
Birkinshaw, J. and Piramal, G (eds) (2005) *Sumantra Ghoshal on Management*, London: Prentice-Hall.

17

FRANK AND LILLIAN GILBRETH

(1868–1924) (1878–1972)

Efficiency through studying time and motion

The husband-and-wife team of Frank and Lillian Gilbreth holds a unique place in the history of modern management. Not only was Frank the leading pioneer of time and motion study (which he called 'motion study'), developing independently of Frederick W. Taylor (qv) the concept of the 'one best way' to perform manual labour, but after his premature death his widow, Lillian, took up the torch of his work and became the first professionally recognized woman engineer in the US. In their strongly work-infused marriage they also produced 12 children, raising them on the principles of scientific management – a phenomenon captured hilariously on film in the 1950 comedy *Cheaper by the Dozen*, with Clifton Webb as Frank and Myrna Loy as Lillian.

Frank Bunker Gilbreth was born in Maine and chose to turn his mechanical talents to bricklaying rather than develop them academically at Massachusetts Institute of Technology. He worked for a building contractor for ten years before launching his own business in 1895, evolving through on-site experience his famous bricklaying system which minimized physical effort and fatigue while accelerating productivity.

Inventions and patents poured from him, such as the Gilbreth Scaffold with adjustable shelves to hold bricks and mortar at the same level as the rising wall. This eliminated stooping by the bricklayer and reduced the number of motions needed, resulting in a near-trebling of output from 1,000 bricks a day to 2,700. Another hugely successful invention was a portable gravity concrete mixer which preceded the rotary type and sold around the world, making Gilbreth's first fortune. By 1906, when his business boomed after the San Francisco earthquake, he was employing close to 10,000 men.

Gilbreth met Lillian Moller, from a wealthy west-coast family of German stock, in the Boston Public Library in 1903, when he was 35 and she was ten years younger. They married in 1904 and began a remarkable partnership in which it was understood that she would help in his life's work as well as produce his desired family of six sons and six daughters.

Her training as a psychologist complemented Gilbreth's own interest in the relationship between human beings and physical work. Unlike his sometime mentor and rival in scientific management, Frederick W. Taylor, Gilbreth was a natural union man, seeing more efficient labour from the perspective of the worker as well as of management. Among the Gilbreths' many innovations was the use of the fledgling motion-picture technology to study and break down the cycles of work. They used the term 'therbligs' (Gilbreth backwards, more or less) to describe their graphic notations of the fundamental elements in each cycle – always a constant 17 in number.

When they set up their management consultancy Gilbreth, Inc. in 1912, it was to seek the 'one best way' to perform everything in life from factory work to raising a family. The latter, as recounted by two of their children in *Cheaper by the Dozen*, included such time-and-motion devices as bathing with a set number of movements in less than three minutes, the time a phonograph in the bathroom took to play a French-language record; learning Morse code from a chart pinned to the lavatory door and a touch-typing system involving a paper keyboard with the keys coloured in blocks to match finger movements.

Gilbreth died suddenly in 1924, aged 56, while on his way to attend the world's first management conference in Prague. Lillian went in his place and began her long life's work of continuing to propagate his methods. She ran motion-study courses for industry at the family home in Montclair, New Jersey, devised appliances for the disabled and was elected the first woman member of the American Society of Mechanical Engineers in 1926. In 1935, she became the first woman to be appointed a professor of management, at Indiana's Purdue University.

She remained head of the family business until the age of 91 and died a year later, garlanded with honours, including more than a dozen degrees. When she was 66, her phenomenal skill at combining the management of work and family – what we would now call work–life balance – led to her being described in a California monthly magazine as 'a genius in the art of living'. About five of the Gilbreth children were surviving in 2005, according to the Gilbreth Network website.

Frank Gilbreth has never been accorded the place in management history enjoyed by Frederick W. Taylor, though both men were leading exponents of the new scientific management in the early years of the 20th century. Gilbreth developed his efficiency theories independently of Taylor, who was ten years his senior and had retired in 1890 from the Midvale Steel Works to become a consultant to industry. Taylor's stopwatch timing of labourers' movements at Midvale was originally intended to stop workers 'soldiering', or taking it easy on the job, while at the same time helping them to maintain good piecework pay.

Gilbreth did not time his experiments, being concerned only to eliminate unnecessary physical effort, whereas with Taylor the emphasis was the other way round. Gilbreth never took the view that workers needed tight supervision or control to perform and at first resisted Taylor's theories on the grounds that they did not apply to his own business. The two men finally got to know one another at a meeting in New York's new Engineering Center in 1907. By the time Taylor's *Shop Management* came out in 1910 Gilbreth was a convert, calling it his 'bible' and 'a work of genius'.

Later that year, the term 'scientific management' was adopted by a group of efficiency advocates to cover a number of theories. Taylor had already taken the phrase as his own but others now subscribed to it at a meeting in a New York apartment. The apartment's owner was Henry Gantt (qv), who had worked for Taylor and was to prove influential with his own time-based work-schedule system known as the Gantt Chart. The others present included Gilbreth and Louis Brandeis, a lawyer who had played a key role in promoting scientific management at public hearings on cost-saving in the railroad industry.

The new movement gathered pace rapidly. In 1911, Taylor's *The Principles of Scientific Management* were published over three issues of the *American Magazine*, and the Gilbreths published their own theories as *Motion Study*. The foreword by Louis Brandeis stated: 'Under Scientific Management, men are led, not driven. Instead of working unwillingly for their employer, they work in cooperation with the management.' Idealistically, Brandeis added that this would secure workers 'a very large share of the industrial profits arising from improved industry'.

In the same year, the first conference on scientific management was held at the Tuck School, Dartmouth College, and the Gilbreths brought out a question-and-answer 'primer of scientific management', designed to demystify the new terminology for industrialists and businessmen. Some time after this, relations between Taylor and Gilbreth soured when Taylor publicly asserted that 'motion study' was in effect the same as his own time study. The feud persisted beyond Taylor's early death in 1915, with a Gilbreth paper carrying the subtitle 'An Indictment of Stop-Watch Time Study'. Eventually, the Taylor Society acknowledged that the Gilbreth studies in 'micromotion' had many benefits to offer in the transference of skills, and World War I gave a boost to the whole scientific-management movement. Both Taylor's and Gilbreth's systems were adopted after the war in Japan and, by 1930, motion study was officially recognized by the US engineering profession as a separate discipline from time study.

Until ill-health forced him out, Gilbreth served briefly in the US army during the war, devising systems for rapid gun assembly and helping disabled soldiers recover working functions. Working on appliances for handicapped people was something both Gilbreths did: later in her life, Lillian designed the ideal kitchen layout for heart sufferers and worked on appliance design with General Electric.

As with his early patented inventions, Frank Gilbreth wanted to spread motion study around the world and, in 1921, he was gratified that Britain's King George V and Queen Mary visited his exhibit at the *Daily Mail* Efficiency Exhibition in London. In 1924, he was on his way to board a liner for the world's first international management congress in Prague when he collapsed and died of a heart attack while telephoning home.

Lillian, despite having to raise and manage 11 children between the ages of four and 18 (one had died), immediately shouldered the work of the partnership and took his place at the Prague Congress. In 1926, although the all-male American Society of Mechanical Engineers had once barred her from lecturing there, she was elected its first woman member. By the 1930s, she had turned to consulting and academic work, leaving the teaching of Frank's methods to others. She served on one of President Roosevelt's New Deal commissions for reviving employment opportunities and worked throughout World War II on fatigue elimination in war production.

Lillian Gilbreth continued to head the family consultancy, Gilbreth, Inc., until she was 91. She remains one of the 20th century's most remarkable and multi-talented women, breaking down gender prejudice in an almost universally male profession.

KEY WRITINGS

Gilbreth, F. B. and L. M. (1911) *Motion Study*.
Gilbreth, F. B. and L. M. (1916, 1973) *Fatigue Study*.
A recent biography is (2004) *Making Time: Lillian Moller Gilbreth*, Jane Lancaster, Boston: Northeastern University Press.

18

GARY HAMEL

(b. 1955)

Core competencies and strategic intent

Fastest-rising star of the international guru circuit since 1994, when he published (with University of Michigan professor C. K. Prahalad) the much-acclaimed book *Competing for the Future*, which redefined and reignited interest in the uses of strategy. Essentially it shifted strategic thinking from positioning a company within its industry to changing the rules of that industry and creating new markets. As a result of the book and the lecture-circuit fame that followed, core competencies, strategic intent and industry foresight are just a few of Hamel's trademark concepts that have passed into the language of management.

Hamel started his career as a hospital administrator and switched tracks in 1978 to take a PhD in international business at the University of Michigan, where he met Indian-born Prahalad, then a newly hired associate professor of strategy and now professor of business administration and professor of corporate strategy and international business at Michigan's graduate school of business administration.

The pair quickly sparked ideas off each other and discovered a common belief, as Hamel wrote in the preface to their book, that 'the ultimate test of business-school research is its managerial significance.' They have published seven influential articles in *Harvard Business Review* as well as their ground-breaking book, which advised companies to 'shine their headlights' on potential markets and customers ten years ahead, and to identify their core competencies that would enable them to refocus and reinvent their business for the future.

After ten years teaching strategy at London Business School, Hamel returned in 1993 to base himself in California's Silicon Valley, which he describes as 'a very good vantage point to see the future coming'. Here he heads a consultancy called Strategos Inc. in Menlo Park, just outside San Francisco, which generates annual revenues of around $20m out of advising companies on the Hamel brand of strategy as revolution.

'The capacity for strategic innovation,' he says, 'will be the next competitive edge for companies around the world.' Innovation, he declared in 2000, would be as important to the success of 21st-century companies as the quality movement was in the latter half of the 20th century. Silicon Valley's capacity to generate and incubate innovative ideas became a major inspiration for Hamel's seminars and the main theme of his book *Leading the Revolution*, published before the collapse of so many companies which had created bold new business models based on the Internet.

He is still a visiting professor of strategic and international management at LBS but with his easy, entertaining style of presentation he now rivals Tom Peters as a sought-after conference and seminar speaker, and was reported by the *Financial Times* in 1997 to earn as much as $150,000 for two days' work. He spends much of the year on the road, typically delivering a major speech every week. For his 1998 book, *Alliance Advantage: The Art of Creating Value Through Partnering*, he joined forces with the heavyweight French management thinker Yves Doz, a professor at INSEAD, France's international business school.

Business strategy and strategic planning are riding high on the management agenda again after years of being sidelined in favour of shorter-term measures for operational efficiency such as re-engineering and downsizing, designed to counter the pressures of global competition and economic recession. Today's strategic approach is, however, very different from the systemic matrix planning popularized in the 1980s by Boston Consulting Group with the future of business classified as cash cows, dogs, stars and question marks.

Foremost among the new strategists is Gary Hamel, whose co-authored bestseller *Competing for the Future* sounded a necessary warning bell in the mid-1990s against the reflexive cost-cutting that was damaging companies' long-term growth prospects in the name of next quarter's results.

The book, which in classic fashion developed out of a landmark article in *Harvard Business Review* (July/August 1994), carried two powerful messages: first, that the sustainable health of a business could not be achieved by simply applying an accountant's rule to costs and second, that managers needed to look much farther into the future of the business than they had been accustomed to do. Customers and markets could not be relied upon to stay the same year on year, providing incremental profits: managers should ask themselves what the business would look like in the medium- to long-term future and who their customers would be.

Hamel and Prahalad urged managers to ask themselves two sets of questions about their business, under the headings 'Today' and 'In the Future':

- Which customers do you serve today/will you serve in the future?
- Through what channels do you reach customers today/will you reach customers in the future?
- Who are your competitors today/who will be your competitors in the future?
- What is the basis for your competitive advantage today/what will be the basis for your competitive advantage in the future?
- Where do your margins come from today/where will your margins come from in the future?
- What skills or capabilities make you unique today/what skills or capabilities will make you unique in the future?

'If senior executives don't have reasonably detailed answers to the "future" questions, and if the answers they have are not significantly different from the "today" answers, there is little chance that their companies will remain market leaders,' warned Hamel and Prahalad.

The strength of their arguments against short-term solutions such as downsizing and in favour of seeking new growth strategy became evident in the years immediately following publication of their book. Leading business figures such as Howard Davies, deputy governor of the Bank of England and former chief executive of the Confederation of British Industry (CBI), began quoting the two gurus' devastating phrase 'corporate anorexia' about companies that had slimmed down so drastically that they had no resources to respond when growth opportunities returned.

A senior manager at ICI responsible for Asia Pacific liaison went on record in 1996 as saying that his company had gone so far in cutting corporate functions that it could no longer give promising managers career moves across boundaries and equip them to develop new markets as fully as in the past (Kennedy, Carol: 'The Incredible Shrinking Company', *Director*, April 1996). At the pit of its cost-cutting, ICI had just two executive board directors responsible for splitting global operations between them – one for the eastern hemisphere and one for the west. More recently, the mighty Boeing Corporation was knocked off balance by a surge in its order-book that it no longer had the resources to meet, thanks to downsizing: its share price plunged as a result.

Hamel has since delved deeper into the process of making strategy, which he stresses is distinct from planning. 'Strategy is revolution, everything else is tactics,' he argues. In Hamel's three key concepts, companies should build their *core competencies* to create *strategic intent* for their future business by practising *industry foresight*.

He divides companies into three categories:

- **The rule makers,** i.e. those which built their industries, such as IBM, Coca-Cola and Merrill Lynch
- **The rule takers,** i.e. those which followed in the rule makers' wake but never quite caught up, such as McDonnell Douglas (trailing Boeing) and Avis, chasing Hertz

- **The rule breakers,** which are rewriting industry rules to their own bold agenda. Prime examples are Dell Computer, the Body Shop, Southwest Airlines, Swatch, the Virgin Group and Direct Line, First Direct, and all the other telephone-based financial services.

The key to being a successful rule breaker is a willingness to redefine products and services by following certain guidelines. 'Any company intent on creating industry revolution has four tasks,' writes Hamel in *Harvard Business Review* ('Strategy as Revolution', July/August 1996). 'First, the company must identify the unshakeable beliefs that cut across the industry – the industry's conventions. Second, the company must search for discontinuities in technology, lifestyles, working habits or geopolitics that might create opportunities to rewrite the industry's rules. Third, the company must achieve a deep understanding of its core competencies. Fourth, the company must use all this knowledge to identify the revolutionary ideas, the unconventional strategic options, that could be put to work in its competitive domain.'

Elsewhere in the article, Hamel describes nine 'routes to industry revolution', including:

- 'Radically improving the value equation' (for example, the Swedish IKEA furniture stores, or the US company Fidelity Investments, which lowered the entry level to foreign equity funds to allow customers of modest means a slice of the action)
- 'Striving for individuality' (Levi Strauss now offer 'personal pair' outlets with computer-measured jeans)
- 'Increasing accessibility' (for example, direct telephone banking)

Other management theorists, notably W. Chan Kim and Renée Mauborgne (qv), two professors of strategic management at INSEAD, are working along similar lines of lateral or creative thinking to break through accepted rules in an industry and thereby enhance or enlarge their customer base. Kim and Mauborgne call their theory 'value innovation' because it creates an entirely new dimension of value for the customer and thereby cuts out the competition.

Hamel also argues strongly that strategy should involve creativity at all levels of the organization, not just in the executive offices. 'One thing is certain,' he says. 'If you don't let the revolutionaries challenge you from within, they will eventually challenge you from without in the marketplace . . . When was the last time a Generation-X employee in your company exchanged ideas with the executive committee?'

Hamel summed up his core thinking to the *Financial Times* in April 1997: 'The test for any company today is whether they can tell me the five fundamental ways they are going to change their industry in the next ten years. If they can't, someone else will.'

Hamel later expanded this into his favourite concept of 'bringing Silicon Valley inside' – finding techniques to import the best Valley firms' flair for innovative thinking into existing old-economy or 'legacy' corporations. One of his frequently cited exemplar companies, Enron, went down to the world's biggest bankruptcy in early 2002 amid accounting scandals and a top-level suicide. But Hamel continued to maintain that Enron's boundary-less business model was valid in bringing its competencies of trading and arbitrage to bear on a wide range of market opportunities: it was the implementation and controls that failed.

In 2000, Hamel published *Leading the Revolution*, the fruit of his researches into Silicon Valley practices, on which he based many seminars, identifying 'innovation genes' common to successful Valley companies. The book outlined ten 'design rules for innovation' including internal open markets for talent, ideas and capital, promoting 'unreasonable expectations' of what the business could achieve and defining potential markets in an 'elastic' way – something Enron was to take to extremes in the energy business. In a subsequent edition of *Leading the Revolution*, glowing references to the disgraced company were removed.

KEY WRITINGS

Hamel, G. and Prahalad, C. K. (1994) 'Competing for the Future', Cambridge, Mass.: *Harvard Business Review* (July/Aug), reprint no. 94403.

Hamel, G. and Prahalad, C. K. (1994) *Competing for the Future*, Boston: Harvard Business School Press.

Hamel, G. (1996) 'Strategy as Revolution', Cambridge, Mass.: *Harvard Business Review* (July/Aug), reprint no. 96405.

Hamel, G. (1999) 'Bringing Silicon Valley Inside', Cambridge, Mass.: *Harvard Business Review* (Sept/Oct).

Hamel, G. (2000) *Leading the Revolution*, Boston: Harvard Business School Press.

19

MICHAEL HAMMER

(b. 1948)

The radical redesign of business processes

Mathematician and former professor of computer science at Massachusetts Institute of Technology (MIT) who caused a management revolution in the early 1990s with the 'big idea' of re-engineering – identifying the key work processes in every aspect of a company's operations, following them across departments, stripping them down to their components and maximizing their efficiency. Hammer liked to declare he was 'reversing the Industrial Revolution', which – as Adam Smith described the workings of a pin factory – broke down processes into dozens of individual tasks.

Enthusiastically embraced by companies on both sides of the Atlantic desperate to counter the effects of recession, re-engineering has proved only patchily successful (surveys in the mid-1990s suggested that around 70 per cent of re-engineering efforts failed for one reason or another) and was often used as a cloak for 'downsizing' with cost-cutting redundancies. Yet in 1995 US companies spent more on re-engineering consultancy than the whole country spent on importing coffee.

Hammer became a lecture-circuit celebrity on the back of his 1990 *Harvard Business Review* article, 'Reengineering Work: Don't Automate, Obliterate', which was followed up in 1993 by a hugely bestselling book, *Reengineering the*

Corporation, written with James Champy, a founder of the consultancy CSC Index.

The book sold more than two million copies worldwide and within a year of its publication 69 per cent of US companies surveyed by CSC Index, and 75 per cent of European companies, had undertaken re-engineering projects. Another survey by Price Waterhouse found that 78 per cent of Fortune 500 companies and 68 per cent of UK companies had adopted the technique. Soon re-engineering had moved out of manufacturing into service industries such as banking and into the public sector.

The book defined re-engineering as 'the fundamental rethinking and radical redesign of business processes to achieve dramatic improvements in critical measures of performance such as cost, quality, service and speed'. Its concept of rethinking was to take a blank sheet of paper and design the company as from scratch rather than innovate from existing practices or, in Hammer's colourful phrase, 'pave over the cow paths'. It seemed the answer to every organizational inefficiency.

In practice, however, there were many problems. Although some stunning productivity gains could be cited, and cycle times were often dramatically slashed, re-engineering became too mechanistic in implementation and simply ignored the human dimension. Hammer's early seminars, characterized by an aggressive dynamism and a barking delivery, were notable for a lack of attention to people issues. The charts looked impressive, but what of the people whose jobs were re-engineered out, and the traumatic impact on those who survived?

In 1995 Champy recognized this missing dimension with a book of his own, *Reengineering Management*, which addressed the issues of managing such radical change along with the challenge of inspiring, motivating and rewarding people to cooperate actively with it. Champy has since left CSC Index for Perot Systems, an offshoot of the EDS computer services giant founded by Ross Perot.

Hammer set up his own consultancy in Boston and has been lauded by *Time* magazine as one of America's most influential individuals. He has written two more books expanding and refining re-engineering (a term he and Champy claim to have trademarked in its non-hyphenated spelling). In *Beyond Reengineering* (1996), he took a larger, more humanistic view of the 'process-centred organization', emphasizing the entrepreneurial character of the customer-focused business, the individual ownership of processes and the need for team-work and for employees to feel fulfilled by more than their pay-cheque.

In a new edition of *Reengineering the Corporation*, published in 2001, Hammer maintained his faith in the theory's essential value, claiming that failures were due to many companies having misunderstood or misapplied its principles. BPR is still cited in surveys as one of the most widely used management practices.

Although Hammer is careful to say he discovered rather than invented re-engineering, he is a good example of the one-big-idea guru who built his fame the classic way; from academic backwater research to *Harvard Business Review* article to bestselling book to lucrative consultancy and lecture work. Whatever happens to the reputation of re-engineering as a management theory, Hammer's work will undoubtedly continue to have an influence on the way companies are organized in the 21st century.

Re-engineering was an idea waiting to be reborn, in many ways harking back to the work-study theories of F. W. Taylor's 'scientific management' at the turn of the century. It germinated in study groups at Massachusetts Institute of Technology in the early 1980s where technology-minded academics brainstormed on how computers would shape 'the corporation of the 1990s', and in similar work at the technology-based consultancy CSC Index, also located in Cambridge, Massachusetts. Hammer was a mathematician who had become a professor of computer science at MIT, and James Champy, his eventual collaborator, was the founder of CSC Index, where the term re-engineering was coined.

Like scientific management, re-engineering was a reassuringly hard-nosed term, unlike 'transformation' and some other buzz-words into which consultancies around the world would later absorb its principles. Its core concept centred on the process flows that cut across the departmental functions of a business, from factory floor to invoicing, but its streamlining of those processes by eliminating the number of wasteful tasks or 'hand-offs' was not far removed from Taylor's belief in a 'one best way' to perform every industrial function.

Re-engineering is often known as business process re-engineering, or BPR, though Hammer and Champy eschewed this label, claiming it was too narrow in application and that true re-engineering involved a total rethink of management strategy as well as operational processes. The idea hit its moment as companies in the US and Europe were struggling with the severe recession of the early 1990s and were forced to search for new ways to make their operations more efficient and cost-effective.

Unfortunately, many attempts to implement it went off at half-cock or concentrated on cutting jobs, leading to the concept becoming damningly associated with downsizing and 'corporate anorexia'. This was a term coined by Gary Hamel (qv) and C. K. Prahalad (qv) in *Competing for the Future* to describe companies that had cut beyond the fat into the muscle and were too emaciated to seize growth opportunities. Charles Handy (qv) was quoted in *Fortune* in October 1994 as saying: 'The trouble with reengineering when it is done badly – which it mostly is – is that it leaves people shattered, even the people left behind.'

Champy would later claim that only one in ten companies got re-engineering right. Only one in ten chief financial officers of US corporations in a May 1995 magazine survey (quoted in *The Witch Doctors* by John Micklethwait and Adrian Wooldridge) cited quality and service improvement as a reason for re-engineering rather than cost-cutting – perhaps a significant coincidence.

Certainly re-engineering can claim some spectacular successes – Ford Motor's accounting, Hallmark Cards and Federal Express are three well-known examples, and there are less high-profile examples in Britain such as Pilkington Optronics, the former periscope-maker Barr and Stroud. Rolls-Royce Motor Cars was saved from near-bankruptcy in 1991 by application of re-engineering principles as part of a 'transformation' aided by

Gemini Consulting. In all cases, the initiative was driven by dynamic leadership and in many, notably Rolls-Royce and British Telecom, it was part of a profound culture change.

Hammer always insisted that leadership was crucial to the success of the technique, saying: 'Re-engineering only succeeds when driven from the top levels of an organization.' What has been less recognized until recently is the importance of leadership at many levels, of owning the change processes and of energizing the whole organizational culture through communication and participation.

From being regarded as a change machine in its own right, re-engineering is now more wisely seen as part of an holistic approach, with a recognition that the technique works better for some areas of the business than others, and with more attention paid to human motivation and to the intellectual capital held in the heads of individual employees. The most successful change managers now encourage employees to feel involved and committed in the goals of change; to think of themselves as mini-entrepreneurs with a key role in the ultimate aim of delighting the customer.

In many companies, such as the Munich-based Siemens Nixdorf Informationssyteme (SNI), key workers are effectively responsible for re-engineering their own processes, and their ideas are exchanged and shared on the corporate intranet. To be fair to Hammer's original book, the case studies in *Reengineering the Corporation* did emphasize the added value to both company and individual when employees enjoyed more decision-making over their process work, as with the clerks in Ford's accounts payable department and the credit-checkers at IBM. But the style of Hammer's public speaking and writing has changed dramatically from a seminar he gave in Boston in 1993 when he declaimed with relish that re-engineering was 'not only about cutting the fat from an organization but grinding it up and frying it out'. In the final chapter of *Beyond Reengineering*, he even admits that the process-centred organization could turn into a nightmare.

'It may foster a brutal form of social Darwinism and a perverse modern Calvinism . . . It may also become confusing and disorienting to work and live in a process-centred world . . . Will we face spiritual poverty even as we enjoy material plenty? Will never-ending organizational improvement inevitably produce a culture of tension and stress? Will it destroy our very humanity?' Questions that might have come from Charles Handy himself, the guru who is now backing away from business to study human fulfilment in work and life.

But Hammer goes on to argue that the process-centred world is here and will not go away. 'The question we must confront is not whether to accept it but what we make of it.' And in words that he could never have envisaged in 1994, he claims it can give workers a sense of control and influence which will enhance their lives – even enable them to see their work as a 'service to humanity'.

'In the process-centred world dignity is restored to work, the dignity that was lost to workers who only performed repetitive tasks.'

In 2001 he and Champy published an unapologetic new edition of *Reengineering the Corporation*, updated with several new case studies designed to prove the theory's validity. He also wrote a more wide-ranging but still heavily process-based book on management priorities called *The Agenda*.

KEY WRITINGS

Hammer, M. (1990) 'Reengineering Work: Don't Automate, Obliterate', Cambridge, Mass.: *Harvard Review* (July/Aug).
Hammer, M. and Champy, J. (1993, 1995) *Reengineering the Corporation*, New York: HarperCollins; London: Nicholas Brealey.
Hammer, M. and Stanton, S. A. (1995) *The Reengineering Revolution*, New York and London: HarperCollins.
Champy, J. (1995) *Reengineering Management*, London: HarperCollins.
Hammer, M. (1996, 1997) *Beyond Reengineering*, New York: HarperBusiness; London: HarperCollins Business.
Hammer, M. and Champy, J. (2001) *Reengineering the Corporation*, new edition, London: Nicholas Brealey.
Hammer, M. (2001) *The Agenda*, London: Random House Business Books.

20

CHARLES HANDY

(b. 1932)

The future of work and organizations

Britain's only world-class business guru and philosopher, noted for his studies of organizations and his far-reaching ideas on the future of work and business structures. Since the publication in 1997 of *The Hungry Spirit*, his most philosophical work yet, Handy has declared his intention to draw back from management topics and to concentrate on wider issues of life, society and individual fulfilment.

Handy was born in Kildare into what he calls 'the Parnellian tradition', the son of a southern Irish Protestant clergyman, and says this background is an important key to his development: 'it gave me a slightly irreverent streak and a tendency to ask "Why?"'

After graduating from Oriel College, Oxford, with a first in Greats, Handy worked for Shell International in Malaysia and as an economist in the City of London and then spent a formative two years at MIT's Sloan School of Management. Here he 'sat at the feet' of Warren Bennis (qv), an authority on organization theory but now principally associated with leadership, who remains a good friend and is probably his strongest influence ('Bennis is my godfather'); Ed Schein (qv), the 'career anchor' guru who became identified with the study of corporate culture; and Chris Argyris (qv), the organizational psychologist.

Douglas McGregor, of Theory X and Y fame, had recently died, but his ideas still powerfully influenced a group of disciples at MIT.

Handy has said that his experiences working with the Sloan School gurus 'transformed my life'. It was the end of his fledgling career as a businessman; he returned to London to launch and direct the Sloan Management Programme at the newly established London Business School.

From 1977 to 1981 he was Warden of St George's House in Windsor Castle, a private conference and study centre concerned with issues of ethics and values in society. It was here that he carried out the research for *The Future of Work* (1984), and the appointment marked something of a watershed in his life. Handy went to St George's instead of joining the Church itself, and it enabled him to extend his teaching and thinking beyond business executives and management issues.

Handy's first book, *Understanding Organizations* (1976), has become a bible in some quarters and has been revised several times to take account of the vast changes in business cultures that have taken place since the mid-1970s.

His second book, *Gods of Management* (1978), which explored corporate culture in a highly original manner, is his personal favourite: he feels it is his most creative. 'It was before its time,' he says. 'It's still the best way of getting a quick fix on organizations and to find clues on how they need to change.'

It develops an apparently whimsical concept (first sketched out in *Understanding Organizations*) – that all organizations can be classified according to the characteristics of four ancient Greek gods: Zeus (power, patriarchy, the club culture); Apollo (order, reason and bureaucracy, the role culture); Athena (expert, wisdom, meritocracy, the task culture); and Dionysus (individualism, professional rather than corporate, the existential culture). It is one of the earliest, though underrated, works on company culture.

In the 1980s, Handy turned away from full-time academic work, combining writing and broadcasting with teaching, and thus practising his own blueprint for 'portfolio' living as developed in *The Future of Work*. This stimulating volume threw off scores of ideas around the proposition that lifetime careers are becoming a thing of the past and that those fortunate individuals who are knowledge or brain workers rather than manual workers will in future be able to design a range of jobs for themselves to suit the way they want to spend their time.

The idea had already been touched upon in *Gods of Management* (each of Handy's books in a sense foreshadows the next), and is further elaborated in *The Age of Unreason* (1989, paperback 1990), which Handy regards as his most popular book, vividly encapsulating his principal theories on the implications of change in work and society. It was the first of his books to be published in the United States, and so impressed Robert Horton, then chairman and chief executive of British Petroleum, that he invited Handy to advise the company as a consultant.

Handy's joint study with John Constable of the state of management education, entitled *The Making of Managers* (1988), crystallized a widespread unease about the UK's persistent amateurism and accentuated the need to professionalize management. It led to formation of the Management Charter Initiative, in which several eminent management and professional bodies participated, though the concept of the 'chartered manager' has since become bogged down in arguments over qualifications. Handy's commitment to developing the right calibre of management is directly connected to his belief that managers in the future will no longer be able to rely on the experience of their predecessors to help them make decisions.

'Leaders of tomorrow's businesses will have to be more resourceful and imaginative to enable their businesses to survive,' as an article in *Director* summed it up in September 1989.

Since the early 1990s, Handy has progressively moved more into non-managerial fields of study, and concerned himself with ethics, values and corporate issues beyond the bottom line. Having broadcast regularly for four years in the BBC's radio 'God-slot', *Thought for the Day*, he published an anthology of these philosophical reflections under the title of *Waiting for the Mountain to Move* (1991).

The diversity of Handy's interests and activities is evident from his work for the Royal Society for the Encouragement of the Arts, Manufactures and Commerce, more commonly known as the Royal Society of Arts. He was chairman of the RSA 1988–1989 and subsequently vice-chairman, and played a leading role in the RSA's research project into business organizations of the future, 'Tomorrow's Company'.

Handy's last purely management book, *Inside Organizations*, was tied in with a BBC television series in 1991. It offers 21 managerial concepts for application to business problems, and is aimed at first-time managers in all types of organizations. It is supremely accessible in its language, using metaphors and anecdotes rather than technical jargon.

His two later books, *The Empty Raincoat* (1994) and *The Hungry Spirit* (1997), reflect his growing concern with the individual's struggle to find personal fulfilment in today's shifting world of uncertain work and short-term careers. He is now reluctant to be described as a 'guru' in its business sense, although happy to think of himself passing on wisdom and ideas to individuals in search of them.

While giving up most of his business consultancy and lecture work, he has continued to produce books that combine prescient social observation and philosophy with relevance to a business readership. *The New Alchemists* (1999), a collaboration with his photographer wife Elizabeth, studies the common characteristics of individuals who have created, like the alchemists of old, something out of nothing, whether an entrepreneurial business or a pro-bono social organization. In 2001, *The Elephant and the Flea* explored Handy's continuing fascination with the interdependence of big corporations (the elephants) with the entrepreneurs (the

fleas) who stimulate them. Handy's books today rarely break new ground as they did with *The Future of Work* and *The Age of Unreason*, but they continue to command a wide and devoted readership beyond the world of the business executive.

Charles Handy openly aspires to be numbered among those who 'change the way the world behaves' and who 'affect the way in which managers think'. In this generation his own list of gurus who have achieved such a status would include Drucker, Deming, Bennis, Porter, Peters, Pascale and Mintzberg.

Like Peter Drucker, Handy's eclectic range of interests and wide-angle view of economic and social change make him hard to categorize as a management guru. Drucker has written more on the techniques of management and has nearly 30 years' start on Handy, but both share a curiosity about the directions of society and a gift for extrapolating future trends. (Drucker's *The Age of Discontinuity* did for the 1970s and 1980s what Handy's *The Age of Unreason* may do for the early 21st century – foreshadow cataclysms of change in industry and economics.)

Certain Handy concepts have remained constant throughout his writing – the increasing shift from lifetime employment in a single company to 'portfolio' work, less secure but more fulfilling; the evolution of new organizational forms such as the 'shamrock' company (a core of essential staff flanked by contract specialists and part-time helpers) and the 'Triple I' (information, intelligence, ideas), in which managers will be required to rise to the challenge of managing knowledge workers, individuals with far different aspirations from the hierarchy-conscious personnel of the past.

Increasingly, he is concerned with how companies manage their goals beyond the pursuit of profit, and whether they can develop into communities of human endeavour rather than properties to be bought and sold in the marketplace. He fears, however, that the Western model of company-as-property will prevail over the Eastern model of company-as-community.

For the student of management, business and the organizations that sustain them, Handy's *Understanding Organizations* provides a valuable synthesis of ideas propounded by himself and others. Here you will find explained the major theories of motivation and why we work – the satisfaction theory of Herzberg, the incentive theory of Morse and Weiss, the intrinsic theory of McGregor and Likert (the response of the individual to a worthwhile job).

The book also examines leadership and the culture of organizations, how people behave within them and the power games they play. Handy concludes with a preliminary sketch for his vision of the future organization, which has occupied much of his thinking since, including the changes wrought by communications (fewer people needing to travel physically to their place of work) and leaner organizations paying fees to contract workers rather than salaries and overheads to staff.

Handy says he writes books to clarify his ideas and advises readers of *Understanding Organizations* to 'burn this book after reading it and to write their own – it's the only way to really own the concepts'. It is not, he emphasizes, a book purely for students of business, but concerns organizations of all kinds. He has written separately on schools as organizations and on voluntary organizations.

'Organizations are changing,' he told an interviewer in *Director* magazine in September 1989. 'The days have gone when you went into the kitchens and worked your way up. Soon there won't be promotion prospects after 30. People have got to be prepared to run their own operations – to be competent in all aspects of management.' As the monolithic 'palace' structures of corporations give way, he says memorably, 'we are being thrust into a world of tents.'

In *The Age of Unreason* (his name for the coming era of wrenching change), Handy warns that in the business organization, as in other areas of life, 'the status quo will no longer be the best way forward.' To counter the challenge, he recommends a process he calls 'upside-down thinking', a process not unrelated to Edward de Bono's (qv) 'lateral thinking'. The book shows how the technique can be applied to solving problems of change and, though written for a popular readership, offers stimulating new perspectives to managers and students of management.

The Empty Raincoat (1994), published in the US as *The Age of Paradox*, further developed many of the ideas in *The Age of Unreason*, revealing the hollowness at the heart of economic growth and its impact on human aspirations. The dilemma of greater corporate wealth and fewer jobs that it explored was summed up in the equation offered by the chairman of a large pharmaceutical company: half as many people paid twice as well and producing three times as much equals productivity and profit. The book ranged widely over changing business and society and was a massive bestseller.

Handy followed it up in 1997 with *The Hungry Spirit*, which focused more on the individual at sea in a bewildering world of change. One or two leading business reviewers criticised its idealistic, philosophical tone and the repetition of many earlier ideas, but Handy was looking for, and achieved, a wider, younger readership than is generally associated with management books.

His reputation as a management thinker remains securely based, however, and his first major work, *Understanding Organizations*, is still much in demand as a classic text.

Latterly, Handy's interest has been stirred more by innovative entrepreneurs than by corporate leaders (*The New Alchemists*, 1999) and by social enterprises, in which a new generation of successful self-made business people put back some of their wealth or expertise where it is needed in society (*The New Philanthropists*, 2006). In 2006 he also published a much-praised memoir distilling enduring lessons from his own brand of work–life balance.

KEY WRITINGS

Handy, C. (1976, 1991, 1998) *Understanding Organizations*, London: Penguin Books.

Handy, C. (1978, 1991) *Gods of Management*, London: Souvenir Press; Business Books.

Handy, C. (1984, 1986) *The Future of Work*, Oxford: Basil Blackwell.

Handy, C. and Constable, J. (1988) *The Making of Managers*, London: Longman.

Handy, C. (1989, 1990) *The Age of Unreason*, London: Business Books; Arrow.

Handy, C. (1990) *Inside Organizations: 21 Ideas for Managers*, London: BBC Books.

Handy, C. (1994) *The Empty Raincoat: Making Sense of the Future*, London: Hutchinson; Boston: Harvard Business School Press (as *The Age of Paradox*).

Handy, C. (1997) *The Hungry Spirit: Beyond Capitalism – A Quest for Purpose in the Modern World*, London: Hutchinson; New York: Broadway.

Handy, C. and Handy, E. (1999) *The New Alchemists*, London: Random House.

Handy, C. (2001) *The Elephant and the Flea*, London: Random House.

Handy, C. (2006) *Myself and Other More Important Matters*, London: Heinemann.

Handy, C. and Handy, E. (2006) *The New Philanthropists*, London: Heinemann.

21

FREDERICK HERZBERG

(1923–2000)

Motivation and job enrichment

US clinical psychologist and professor of management at the University of Utah from 1972 until a few years before his death in January 2000. Known as 'the father of job enrichment', his work on human motivation remains a major influence on management thinking with its separation of the elements of a job into those serving animal or economic needs ('hygiene' or 'maintenance' factors) and those meeting deeper aspirations ('motivation' factors). Herzberg gives these a timeless context with biblical analogies and believes that individual needs and expectations 'are shaped by the religious/philosophical system in which one lives'.

More urgently, he relates job satisfaction or dissatisfaction to mental health, and has described his work as originating in his World War II experiences as a US army volunteer posted to Dachau concentration camp after liberation. Here, he 'realized that a society goes insane when the sane are driven insane'. After the war, he worked for the US Public Health Service on research projects, particularly concerning mental illness. Reading all that had been published on industrial psychology up to that time, he identified a void in conceptual thinking that he set out to fill with his behavioural theories.

Herzberg, who coined the concept of 'job enrichment' to add motivational factors (he once said the theory had 'given employment to a hell of a lot of consultants'), was also one of the few management thinkers and writers to have worked at the sharp end of industry as a consultant; in his case, with the telecommunications giant AT&T. He distilled his thinking about motivation in a 1968 *Harvard Business Review* article – 'One More Time: How Do You Motivate Employees?' – which is said to be that journal's biggest-selling article, with well over a million reprinted copies sold.

It was Herzberg's 1959 book *The Motivation to Work*, written in collaboration with two research colleagues, B. Mausner and B. B. Snyderman, that established him as an original thinker about the mainsprings of human activity in the workplace. The type of investigation it used has been followed by at least 16 other studies, some in Communist countries, making the original research, in Herzberg's words, 'one of the most replicated studies in the field of job attitudes'.

The Motivation to Work was based on intensive questioning of 200 Pittsburgh engineers and accountants, asking them to analyse times when they felt exceptionally good and exceptionally bad about their work. The book was the first to discover that satisfaction and dissatisfaction with one's employment arose from quite different factors and were not simply opposing reactions to the same factors.

The factors that led to feelings of satisfaction, Herzberg found, were 'motivation' ones such as achievement, recognition, satisfaction in the nature of the work itself, responsibility, progress and personal growth (of which the last three were the most important). Dissatisfaction nearly always related to 'hygiene' factors such as company policy, working conditions, salary, status and job security.

'Man has two sets of needs,' explained Herzberg in a later book, *Work and the Nature of Man*; 'his need as an animal to avoid pain and his need as a human to grow psychologically.'

Herzberg illustrates his theory by biblical example. 'Motivation' is represented by Abraham, made in the image of God and capable of great achievements in self-development; 'hygiene' by Adam, who was faced after the expulsion from Eden with the need to meet bodily requirements – food, warmth, safety, security, avoidance of pain. Both are part of the human condition at work, argues Herzberg, and a lack in one cannot be compensated by fulfilment in the other. 'Animal-Adam' seeks avoidance of pain from the environment or job; 'Human-Abraham' seeks growth and self-realization from tasks. The individual becomes unhappy without the first factor, but it brings only temporary relief, like an analgesic, and the effects soon wear off without deeper satisfactions.

Herzberg's solution was to evolve an 'industrial engineering' philosophy which would design the 'Abraham' factor into jobs. This technique he called 'job enrichment'.

Where it has been done – for example, by enhancing a worker's accountability or by giving him or her additional authority – the changes have brought substantial benefits.

As jobs become 'enriched', the need for much mundane job supervision disappears, and hitherto unsatisfying supervisory tasks can themselves be enriched by enlarging their responsibilities on a more managerial level.

Herzberg's motivation theories have been reflected in many recent corporate developments such as 'flexitime' and the 'cafeteria' system of choice within a company's benefits system. Nearly 30 years after its publication, *Work and the Nature of Man* was listed by the International Press as one of the ten most important books impacting management theory and practice in the 20th century.

KEY WRITINGS

Herzberg, F., Mausner, B. and Snyderman, B. B.(1959) *The Motivation to Work*, New York: Wiley.
Herzberg, F. (1966) *Work and the Nature of Man*, World Publishing.
Herzberg, F. (1968) 'One More Time: How Do You Motivate Employees?' Cambridge, Mass.: *Harvard Business Review*.
Herzberg, F. (1976) *Managerial Choice: To be Efficient and to be Human*, Dow Jones, Irwin.

22

GEERT HOFSTEDE

(b. 1928)

The causes of cultural diversity

Dutch engineer and psychologist noted for his seminal work on the influences shaping national cultures. In Hofstede's definition, culture is 'the collective programming of the mind which distinguishes members of one group or category of people from another'. These patterns of thinking may be passed on from one generation to another, or by a leader to followers, or as part of shared experience. They then become 'crystallized in the institutions and tangible products of a society, which reinforce the mental programmes in their turn'.

From this, Hofstede evolved his four 'dimensions' governing national cultural diversity – uncertainty avoidance, power distance, masculinity-femininity and individualism-collectivism. A fifth, Confucian dynamism, emerged later while studying Asian economic performance.

Hofstede spent his older childhood and teenage years under the Nazi occupation of the Netherlands, afterwards training as a mechanical engineer and taking a master's in engineering at the Delft Institute of Technology. He then switched to studying psychology, and gained his doctorate from the University of Groningen in 1967. He is one of those rare gurus (F. W. Taylor was the first) who has worked on the factory floor, as foreman and plant manager, before becoming chief psychologist on the international staff of IBM. This became the source of his research on cultural variabilities within organizations for his key book, *Culture's Consequences* (1980).

Hofstede left IBM to take up an academic career as a professor at international management schools including IMD (Lausanne), INSEAD (Fontainebleau) and the European Institute for Advanced Studies in Management (Brussels). In 1980 he co-founded the Institute for Research on Intercultural Cooperation (IRIC) at Tilburg University and in 1985 became professor of anthropology and international management at Maastricht University, teaching there until 1993. In 2001 he rewrote *Culture's Consequences* to incorporate all subsequent research in the field over 20 years, a task that involved consulting some 3,000 separate works.

This revised second edition is primarily aimed at the academic market. In it his theories are applied to new fields including consumer behaviour, political behaviour and linguistics as a reflection of culture. He also explores the relationship between superiors and subordinates and the 'correlation between power distance and corruption'.

He now works with his eldest son, Gert Jan Hofstede, assistant professor of information technology at Wageningen University in the Netherlands. Together with Paul Pedersen of Syracuse University, the Hofstedes recently co-authored a new corporate training manual, *Exploring Culture* (2002), designed to create awareness of the five dimensions and to train groups to deal with different cultures.

Quite why the Dutch seem to have cornered the market in cross-cultural management studies is not clear, but the field has always been led by Geert Hofstede and his younger successor Fons Trompenaars (qv). Perhaps it has something to do with the Netherlands having been a cultural crucible itself over the centuries, as well as being at the geographic mercy of invading armies.

Where Trompenaars' work concentrates on how national differences can be reconciled and integrated in a management context, Hofstede uncovers the deep psychological currents that help to shape those different national cultures. The work of both men is distinguished by vast databases of research drawn from scores of countries. Hofstede's seminal *Culture's Consequences* (1980) was based on around 100,000 survey results in IBM's companies in 72 countries, looking at the differences caused by national macro-cultures impacting on IBM's already strong corporate culture.

Later, while teaching at IMD in Lausanne, he pursued his researches further into national cultures and perceived the same differences as between IBM managers of different nationalities. The four principal dimensions he identifies as governing these cultures are:

- Uncertainty avoidance: this refers to how comfortable or how threatened people feel about ambiguity and the unknown. The former means a low uncertainty-avoidance culture, the latter a high one, often marked by a preference for formal rules.
- Power distance: defined as 'the extent to which the less powerful members of institutions and organizations accept that power is distributed unequally'. People in high power-distance cultures are more comfortable with larger differentials than people in low power cultures.
- Masculinity-femininity: masculine cultures tend to have very marked expectations of gender roles in society while feminine cultures show a greater fluidity. In feminine cultures such as the Nordic countries and the Netherlands, he has said, 'soft' management skills are practised just as much by men as by women.
- Individualism-collectivism: the extent to which a society favours individual over collective action and effort. The more affluent a country becomes, he finds, the more it moves towards individualism. The US has a notably individualist culture, in contrast to Latin-American countries.

Hofstede examines the impact of the major religions on individualism versus group orientation, finding that Protestants score more strongly on the former and Catholics more on the latter. He has also studied and written a paper on 'Confucian dynamism' to explain the rapid development of many Asian 'tiger' economies, looking at the effects of Confucian teachings and ethics on thrift, perseverance, a sense of shame and a belief in hierarchy. He now classes this as a fifth dimension governing culture among peoples.

He believes strongly that knowledge of other languages is essential for understanding the cultures they belong to, and has criticized American researchers in the field for failing in this. As a consultant to the European Commission in Brussels (among many other governmental and commercial organizations), he has observed how older Eurocrats resist the concept of cultural diversity because they see it as a threat to the integration of the European Union. Cultural diversity certainly complicates decision-making, he said in a 2001 online interview with Management First, and the EU will survive to the extent that it manages to deal with that challenge.

'To that extent I believe that it [the EU] is a wonderful laboratory for the rest of the world; a group of countries that are more or less at an equal level of development but with very different histories and a great variety of concepts of good and evil. If these countries succeed in resolving their differences peacefully and in moving together towards the solution of common problems, this will set a ground-breaking precedent.'

KEY WRITINGS

Hofstede, G. (1980) *Culture's Consequences: international differences in work-related values*, Newbury Park, CA: Sage.

Hofstede, G. and Bond, M. H. (1988) 'Confucius and Economic Growth: new trends in culture's consequences', *Organizational Dynamics*, 16 (4).

Hofstede, G. (1991) *Cultures and Organizations: software of the mind*, London: McGraw-Hill.

Hofstede, G. (2001) *Culture's Consequences*, 2nd edition, Newbury Park, CA: Sage Publications.

Hofstede, G., Hofstede, G. J., Pedersen, P. (2002) *Exploring Culture*, London: Nicholas Brealey Publishing.

23

JOHN HUMBLE

(b. 1925)

Management by Objectives as a practical methodology

British management consultant who took Peter Drucker's (qv) concept of Management by Objectives and developed it as a practical tool for managers.

Humble, a Cambridge graduate, is a former director of the UK's first management consultancy, Urwick Orr, whose founder, Lyndall Urwick, introduced the principles of scientific management to Britain in the 1920s. While reviving Urwick Orr's personnel-training side, Humble launched the firm's own brand of MBO, initially called Improving Management Results.

Humble was in the forefront of management development in the UK for many years. In 1967, he joined the Central Training Council of the Department of Employment and later served on the management education committee of the National Economic Development Council. He also headed consulting teams in many sectors of industry from engineering to retail distribution.

His 1965 book, *A Dynamic Approach to Management by Objectives*, was the first on the subject by a British writer. In *Management Objectives in Action* (1970), he recorded the successful application of the practice to organizations in both the public and private sectors, including the Ministry of Defence, Rolls-Royce, Smiths Industries and Imperial Tobacco. MBO consultancy became so popular that it generated a third of Urwick Orr's revenues and Humble made a series of six acclaimed films for management in the late 1960s and early 1970s that were shown in all major British cities.

On subsequent visits to Urwick Orr's international clients, Humble was told by a Russian that his books had been unofficially copied in the Soviet Union as 'Training Manuals for Senior Engineers'. In 1966, he received the British Institute of Management's Burnham Medal 'in recognition of his original work in the area of management objectives'.

The theory of Management by Objectives (MBO) was conceived by Peter Drucker in the 1950s to define the tasks required of the visionary manager, the manager who can see the goals of the business beyond his functional role. Drucker identified eight areas in a business that were suitable for performance objectives: market standing, innovation, productivity, physical and financial resources, profitability, manager performance and development, worker performance and attitude, and public responsibility. Managers also needed, he said, to devise a measuring system for their objectives and a realistic timescale for their achievement.

Every manager, from the chairman to the chief clerk, needs 'clearly spelled-out objectives', said Drucker. These objectives should set out what each manager's unit is expected to achieve, with the emphasis on teamwork: other units cooperate towards the manager's goals, while his unit in turn helps others to achieve theirs. 'These objectives should always derive from the goals of the business enterprise', and managers needed to be able to measure their performance against these goals, said Drucker.

Drucker described MBO as 'a philosophy of management' in which all the functions and activities of the business should be integrated into a whole and implemented through the agreement and feedback of individual managers. John Humble was the first to introduce it to the UK and to develop the philosophy into a practical methodology. He spent three months in the US on a Ford Foundation grant studying best practice in American companies.

Humble defined MBO as 'the attempt to clarify the goals of management objectivity so that the responsibility for achieving the goals was reasonably distributed round the management team, and to check standards of performance against which management effectiveness can be measured'.

The idea of breaking down corporate aims into a series of personal objectives throughout the management team sounds simple but runs the risk of the objectives being too ambitious or too modest to work. Many companies subsequently suffered from too rigid a faith in planning and forecasting and the temptation to pitch their objectives too high without, in the words of a Beecham Group executive, 'legislating for failure'. The reverse danger, of setting objectives too low, tended to be overlooked in Humble's elegant circular structure that moved from strategic planning to tactical planning to unit planning to individual managers' results and back to review, control and strategic planning.

Humble intended to encourage managers throughout the organization to play 'a creative part' in establishing the standards of performance they would be expected to meet; a sort of continuous self-appraisal mechanism working for the corporate good, and at the same time enhancing personal satisfaction. But, as management writer Robert Heller has pointed out, 'the executive soon catches on to the notion that, if he is being held to a plan or objective, the plan had better be one he can meet.'

MBO in its original form has few adherents today, though elements have been adopted by most successful businesses and feature in the widely used Balanced Business Scorecard (see Kaplan and Norton entry).

Humble later switched the focus of his work to studying the impact and integration of information technology on business strategy and, in the 1970s, concentrated on the often controversial role of the multinational corporation and its responsibilities to the communities in which it operates, particularly in the Third World.

KEY WRITINGS

Humble, J. W. (1971) *Management by Objectives*, Maidenhead: McGraw-Hill.

24

ELLIOTT JAQUES

(1917–2003)

Psychological factors in group behaviour and the 'midlife crisis'

Canadian psychologist and doctor of medicine who became a founder member of the Tavistock Institute of Human Relations in London, an organization that did much pioneering work after World War II on the sociology of industry and management. A graduate of both the University of Toronto and Johns Hopkins Medical School, Jaques served as a major in the Royal Canadian Army Medical Corps between 1941 and 1945.

Jaques' principal fame rests on his work in studying the psychological and social factors behind group behaviour, first carried out at the Glacier Metal Company in London in the early 1950s. He also developed a theory of measuring the value and responsibility of work by 'the time-span of discretion' that elapses before decisions are monitored.

In 1945, he coined the term 'midlife crisis' in a study of creative geniuses published in the *International Journal of Psychoanalysis*. He found that many composers and artists changed direction around the age of 35 and concluded that people then began to see their lives as the time left to them instead of the time since birth, with all the questions that implied about things done and undone.

From the mid-1960s to the mid-1980s, Jaques was

associated with Brunel University in Uxbridge, Middlesex, as head of the School of Social Science (1965–1970) and director of the university's Institute of Organization and Social Studies (1970–1985). He was a government adviser to the Board of Trade on overseas marketing and on reorganizing the National Health Service. Jaques retired from Brunel in 1983 and from 1989 was visiting research professor of management sciences at George Washington University, Washington, DC.

Elliott Jaques' studies in worker behaviour at the Glacier Metal Company, carried out between 1948 and 1965, were at least a decade ahead of their time and remain the most extensive of their kind to be carried out on the factory floor. The 'working-through' process he pioneered, using an investigator interacting with a group on its problems, uncovered, most importantly, the need that workpeople feel to have their role and status defined in a way that they and their colleagues can accept. Confusion of roles or unclear boundaries of responsibility lead to frustration and insecurity, and to a tendency in management to avoid authority and accountability.

Jaques' work on wage problems at Glacier Metal led to him formulating a theory of the value of different types of work, based on 'the time-span of discretion' – the length of time that elapses before the actions or decisions of an individual worker are monitored by superiors. The lowest-paid workers tend to have their actions monitored at frequent intervals, whereas high-level decisions may take years to be evaluated. This resulted in a book called *The Measurement of Responsibility* in 1956, five years after his ground-breaking Glacier investigations were published as *The Changing Culture of a Factory*. (Jaques also collaborated with the managing director of Glacier Metal, Wilfred Brown, on the *Glacier Project Papers* in 1965.)

Jaques later developed a theory of bureaucracy in which progress up an organization, with increasing levels of responsibility, was divided into seven main strata defined by differing time-spans of discretion. These ranged from days or weeks to many years, and represented levels at which pay differentials were felt to be fair. Over some 30 years, Jaques refined and deepened the concept into eight strata dealing with levels of capability governed by the time-spans that elapse between a person's ability to handle the cognitive complexity of different tasks (level one being routine, supervised work, while level eight might be the CEO of a corporation such as General Electric or General Motors). The time-span differentials between level one and level eight could range from a day to more than 20 years, and pay at level eight could be 96 times that of level one and still be regarded as a fair differential.

In this model, the fit between time-span and stratum determines how comfortable someone feels in his or her position in a hierarchy, which, controversially in today's thinking, Jaques claimed to be the ideal business organization for differing human capabilities. He dismissed most contemporary management ideas, from self-managing teams to empowerment to organizational learning, as unsupportable.

In *A General Theory of Bureaucracy* (1976), Jaques also examined the different perceptions of a worker when asked to describe his boss. He may see his 'real' boss – the one from whom he feels he has a chance of getting a decision about himself – as someone quite different from the person next in line up the hierarchy.

Jaques quoted from military staff examples to illustrate that real decisions are never made in the way they are supposed to be made in the hierarchy charts. 'They would all be killed while trying to sort out who was giving orders to whom.' He concluded from studying bureaucratic organizations in 20 countries 'that it is never possible to tell from an organization chart just who is manager of whom: in effect, it is a wise manager (or subordinate) who knows his own subordinate (or manager).'*

Jaques' methods of assessing potential capabilities and his openly contemptuous attitude to many modern theories of flat management structure led to him being attacked as 'mechanistic', 'Taylorist' and even 'fascist', but he believed that the key to a successful hierarchy is trust. If the people within it trust its fairness, he maintained, that is its justification. (For current

---

* E. Jaques, *A General Theory of Bureaucracy* (Heinemann, 1976), quoted in *Organization Theory*, ed. D. S. Pugh (Penguin, 1990).

work in a similar area, see the entry on W. Chan Kim and Renée Mauborgne.)

His books were latterly published within his family under the imprint of his wife, human resources consultant Kathryn Cason, who said on his death in 2003: 'It took 25 years for Elliott's work on midlife crisis to be accepted; we don't want to have to wait that long for recognition of his other work.'

KEY WRITINGS

Jaques, E. (1951) *The Changing Culture of a Factory*, London: Tavistock.

Jaques, E. (1956) *The Measurement of Responsibility*, London: Tavistock.

Brown, W. and Jaques, E. (1965) *Glacier Project Papers*, London: Heinemann.

Jaques, E. (1961, 1967) *Equitable Payment*, London: Heinemann.

Jaques, E. (1976) *A General Theory of Bureaucracy*, London: Heinemann.

Jaques, E. (1982) *Free Enterprise, Fair Employment*, London: Heinemann.

Jaques, E. and Clement, S. D. (1991) *Executive Leadership: A practical guide to managing complexity*, Arlington, Va: Cason Hall; Cambridge, Mass.: Blackwell Business.

Jaques, E. (1994) *Human Capability: A study of individual potential and its application*, Falls Church, Va: Cason Hall.

Jaques, E. (1998) *Requisite Organization: A total system for effective managerial organization and managerial leadership for the 21st century*, Arlington, Va: Cason Hall.

Jaques, E. (2002) *The Life and Behavior of Living Organisms*, Arlington, Va: Cason Hall.

Jaques, E. (2002) *Social Power and the CEO*, Arlington, Va: Cason Hall.

Note: Jaques' books and material on his system known as 'Requisite Organization' can be obtained through the Requisite Organization International Institute, Inc., Gloucester, Massachusetts, USA.

25

JOSEPH M. JURAN

(b. 1904)

Company-wide quality cannot be delegated

US electrical engineer, born in Romania, who worked contemporaneously with W. Edwards Deming (qv) on pioneering the quality management revolution that began in postwar Japan. Ironically, no industrialist in the US was interested in the theories of Deming and Juran – the production mentality ruled at the time – until Japanese manufacturing, practising the quality philosophy, began driving American products to the wall.

By coincidence, both Deming and Juran had become interested in the techniques of ensuring manufacturing quality based on statistical control while working in the 1920s at Western Electric, the manufacturing division of Bell Telephone. Juran joined Western in 1924, three years before the famous Elton Mayo (qv) experiments began at Western's Hawthorne plant in Chicago, which revolutionized thinking about motivation and the human element in industry. Here he worked with the brilliant statistician Walter A. Shewhart, who developed a method for controlling quality in manufacturing.

Juran joined the manufacturing side of AT&T in the 1920s, becoming a corporate industrial engineer and later a quality consultant. He articulated precise steps for achieving consistent quality, and was the first to define the Pareto Principle, named for the Italian economist

Vilfredo Pareto (1848–1923), who discovered that most of the wealth in a nation is concentrated in the hands of a few people while the majority are relatively poor. Juran refined this to the now-familiar 80–20 division whereby, for example, 20 per cent of a company's products generate 80 per cent of its revenue, or 80 per cent of sales come from 20 per cent of the sales force.

Juran established his reputation in 1951 with his *Quality Control Handbook*, the first manual of its kind. The Japanese, who had already absorbed Deming's lessons to the extent of instituting a Deming Prize that year, invited Juran to Tokyo in 1953 to give a series of lectures. In the early 1980s, his contribution to Japanese quality achievements was recognized with the award of the Order of the Sacred Treasure, second class, an honour also conferred on Deming.

Juran justifiably claims some of the credit for turning round Japan's poor postwar reputation for quality. In the decades since, his 'Management of Quality' courses have been attended by more than 20,000 managers in over 30 countries. As a consultant, his clients include Texas Instruments, Du Pont, Monsanto, Xerox, Motorola and the US Internal Revenue Service.

Juran's work with Motorola, Texas Instruments and other early converts to the quality discipline led to the development of 'Six Sigma', the zero–defect measurement system that was given its name by Motorola and has become the gold standard of total quality management.

The Juran Institute in Southbury, Connecticut, is now the main channel and repository of his thinking. It provides consultancy, training programmes and professional services based on his work to companies around the world.

Juran's principal contribution to quality management thinking is his methodology for determining the avoidable and unavoidable costs of quality, thus enabling companies to measure the cost of their quality programmes.

Juran devised a structured concept known as CWQM – Company-Wide Quality Management. He believes it essential for senior managers to involve themselves in the process, to define the goals, assign responsibilities and measure progress. Quality, Juran teaches, cannot be delegated.

Like other management thinkers, notably Peter Drucker (qv), Charles Handy (qv) and Rosabeth Moss Kanter (qv), Juran has developed a vision of the future corporation, in which he sees quality targets being incorporated in business plans as routinely as targets for sales, profits, return on capital and earnings per share. Like Moss Kanter, Juran sees greater 'empowerment' of the workforce as a key – in this case to achieving quality through self-organization and self-supervision. For Juran, quality has always been indissolubly linked with human relations and teamwork.

Joseph M. Juran and W. Edwards Deming are so closely linked – by age, experience and their part in the Japanese economic miracle – that it is sometimes hard to differentiate their contributions to the enduring quality movement. Juran set out to develop Company-Wide Quality Management into a full-blown corporate philosophy, and criticized the Deming approach for being more at home with statistics than with management.

Juran's approach is heavily oriented towards the human side of achieving quality, and he praised the Japanese use of quality circles for their effect on human relations in the workplace, while acknowledging that QCs have accounted for less than 10 per cent of Japan's improvement in quality.

The Juran methodology was clearly laid out in *Juran on Planning for Quality* (1988), which set out to demonstrate how quality planning affects different levels of company activity. It outlined the Juran 'quality trilogy' – quality planning, quality management and quality improvement – by which managers learn how to implement strategic quality planning across the company. Key elements include: identifying customers and their needs; creating measurements of quality; planning processes capable of meeting quality goals under operating conditions; producing continuous improvements in market share and premium prices, and in reducing the error rate. The book emphasized the universal application of quality commitment throughout an organization – to all products, both goods and services; to all corporate levels from CEO down; to all corporate functions from general management to product development; and to all industries, in both the manufacturing and service sectors.

A key principle of the Six Sigma system, one of Juran's great legacies, is getting all employees to aspire to rising skill levels named in Japanese martial-arts style – black belt, green belt and so on. In a 94th-birthday interview, Juran observed that a major problem in scaling up the total quality movement across all sectors was the 'cultural resistance' encountered from companies that mistakenly believed their business was 'different' and did not need a system originally developed for manufacturing.

Juran continued in public life into his late nineties and at the age of 92 began work on a five-volume autobiography. A recommended introduction to his work is *Juran: A Lifetime of Influence*, by John Butman (John Wiley, New York, 1997).

KEY WRITINGS

Juran, J. M. (1951) *Quality Control Handbook*, New York: McGraw-Hill.
Juran, J. M. (1988) *Juran on Planning for Quality*, New York: Free Press; London: Collier Macmillan.
Juran, J. M. (1989) *Juran on Leadership for Quality: An Executive Handbook*, New York: Free Press.
Juran, J. M. (1992) *Juran on Quality by Design*, New York: Free Press.

26

ROSABETH MOSS KANTER

(b. 1943)

*The 'post-entrepreneurial' corporation: empowering
individuals as a force for change*

US sociologist, professor of business administration at
Harvard and former editor of the *Harvard Business Review*,
who has established herself as a leading authority on
managing change, developing the 'post-entrepreneurial'
corporation and 'empowering' human potential in
organizations. She is now one of the most sought-after
consultants in the US (clients include IBM, CBS, Procter
& Gamble, Honeywell, Digital, Apple, Xerox and General
Electric) and a celebrated TV performer on both sides
of the Atlantic. A BBC television documentary described
her as 'a fearless critic of management tradition'.

Born in Cleveland, Ohio, Moss Kanter graduated from
the elite female academy Bryn Mawr and took her PhD
at the University of Michigan, later joining the faculty
of Brandeis University as associate professor of sociology before moving to Harvard in 1973. Between 1977
and 1986 she taught at Yale and MIT before returning
to Harvard as professor of business administration. In
1988 she worked as a key economic adviser to Michael
Dukakis in his campaign for the presidency against
George Bush.

Kanter's award-winning first book, *Men and Women
of the Corporation* (1977), analysed the bureaucratic
factors that locked people into pre-determined roles

in a code-named industrial corporation, and how this prevented the business from fully tapping the talent within it.

The Change Masters (1983) compared the characteristics of such change-resisters with those of innovative corporations which stimulated entrepreneurship within themselves and became market leaders. Combining as it did the academic discipline of Kanter's background in organizational sociology with her hands-on experience as a consultant in industry, the book was hailed as 'the thinking manager's *In Search of Excellence*'.

When Giants Learn to Dance (1989) in effect completed a trilogy on the deep changes facing corporate America. Kanter examined a broad range of corporations, large and small, working from the inside on consulting projects, and found that very different organizations were converging towards similar solutions to the problems of competing in the new global 'corporate Olympics'.

The new model corporation Kanter outlines is 'post-entrepreneurial' – lean and athletic with fewer management levels, able to 'do more with less', to anticipate change and open itself up to opportunities such as strategic alliances with other companies. A focal point of the corporate Olympic runner is to achieve synergies, where the whole is worth more than the sum of its parts; Kanter's inside studies of merger and acquisition strategy and culture change are particularly fascinating.

The last third of the book studies the impact of the post-entrepreneurial organization on the people who work in it. The implications for careers (from climbing the corporate ladder to developing portable 'employability'), for pay (as determinants switch from position to performance, from status to contribution) and for the psychological wellbeing of individuals are all explored with stimulating intellectual zeal. The trilogy thus in a sense comes full circle, focusing on the key task of managing the creative potential of the men and women of the corporation as corporate reality changes about them.

The book achieved both intellectual and popular status

within a short time: Tom Peters has described it as 'the benchmark against which management books of the 1990s are measured'.

Rosabeth Moss Kanter has pursued a logical progression from studying how traditional, bureaucratic organizations stultify individual talents to identifying how the 'post-entrepreneurial' corporation is releasing and 'empowering' those talents in flatter, less hierarchical structures.

Men and Women of the Corporation, which won a US award in 1977 for the best book on social issues, discovered that the highest value placed on managers was 'predictability'. Women, whether in the traditional roles of secretaries or company wives (with all their potential for influence in the corporation) were regarded as both unpredictable and incomprehensible.

Kanter's research for this book led her to conclude that there was crucial need for change in the average industrial corporation in order to improve the quality of working life, to create equal employment opportunities for men, women and minority groups, and to enable employees to make better use of their talents to the benefit of the corporation. To achieve this, she perceived that the following changes in organizational structure would be required:

1. Management should be opened up to promotion from a wider range of candidates, including women and hitherto powerless individuals like clerical workers. Changes in certain areas, such as systems of appraisal and career development, would be needed to achieve this. Intermediate jobs would need to be created to bridge these jobs with management.
2. Empowering strategies would be necessary, leading to a flatter hierarchy, decentralized authority and autonomous work groups.

Building on her discoveries about resistance to change, Kanter's second book studied in depth leading companies that could be defined as 'change masters', illuminating the factors that encourage innovation as a way of life, and the problems that the search for innovation brings in its wake. Kanter's principal discovery was that firms prone to innovate have an 'integrative' approach to problems and a willingness to challenge established practices; to judge a course of action by a vision of the future rather than by the accepted ways of the past. Firms unlikely to innovate were typically 'segmentalist' in approach, compartmented by department and unable to see problems whole.

Throughout *The Change Masters*, Kanter argued that the key to a corporate renaissance was 'participation management' or empowerment – making possible the mechanisms by which individuals could contribute their ideas. It is only in integrative companies that individuals can improve their leverage, thus contributing to their own and the corporate success.

When Giants Learn to Dance (1989) extends this philosophy to the future shape and character of the globally competitive corporation, which she describes as 'post-entrepreneurial . . . applying entrepreneurial principles to the giant corporation' in order to make it flexible and responsive to change while maintaining a disciplined efficiency – combining 'the power of an elephant with the agility of a dancer'. In the aftermath of the 'excellence' era, she suggests, companies are facing some problems not addressed by Peters and Waterman, such as 'Who has the power to start or block innovations?' and 'Who gets the financial returns?'

Kanter's detailed and knowledgeable case studies suggest that companies as different as, for example, Eastman Kodak and Apple Computers are increasingly converging towards similar solutions when faced with the challenge of competing in the global 'corporate Olympics'. Her practical experience as a consultant comes through in such examples of the new strategy as 'the corporation as switchboard', where comparatively small head offices manage a network of other organizations, or contract out former company services as market-oriented businesses. (A crucial by-product of the latter, essential to Kanter's argument, is that staff are no longer considered as 'overhead' but as potential sources of value.)

Much of the book is devoted to the study of achieving synergy and all the components required for it, including the flatter

135

management structure which enables greater cooperation across divisions and departments.

Another key idea is encapsulated in the acronym PAL – '*pool* resources with others, *ally* to exploit an opportunity or *link* systems in a partnership'. Companies can become better PALs with suppliers, venture partners, service contractors, customers and unions. In purchasing, for example, they shed the adversarial character of earlier practice, when the prevailing wisdom was to minimize price by maintaining a large vendor base and insisting on short-term contracts. The growth of joint ventures as a means of access to foreign markets has contributed strongly to the new ethos.

Kanter's keen perception of the individual human dimension within organizations leads her to identify the dangers in becoming more 'mean' than 'lean' and to stress, on a personal level, the importance of shared values in the corporation.

The impact of post-entrepreneurialism on individual careers, with rewards linked more to contribution than to position or status, and with a more flexible structure bringing an end to the lifetime career ladder, is fully explored. Management, for its part, becomes even more complex and demanding when it switches from the mentality of boss to that of partner.

Empowering the individual within the company, which this implies, has been a Kanter preoccupation for years. In 1979, her *Harvard Business Review* article 'Power Failures in Management Circuits' (July/August 1979) identified those organizational factors affecting individuals which create power or powerlessness to influence events and people, e.g. discretion, recognition, relevance to central problems, sponsors, peer networks and subordinates.

'The powerless live in a different world . . . they may turn instead to the ultimate weapon of those who lack productive power – oppressive power . . .' This she identified as a prime cause of dissatisfaction with frontline supervisors, a category especially subject to the feeling of powerlessness. Staff professionals and isolated top executives are other susceptible categories, leading in Kanter's view to conservatism and resistance to change in those areas. Women managers experience particular failures of power, she found, because organizations are geared to employing them in routine, low-profile jobs.

Kanter's key message here is: 'By empowering others, a leader does not decrease his power; instead, he may increase it – especially if the whole organization performs better.'

Her seven essential skills for managers of the future, set out in *When Giants Learn to Dance*, are:

• Learn to operate without the hierarchy 'crutch'
• Know how to compete in a way that enhances, not undercuts, cooperation
• Operate to the highest ethical standards
• Possess a dose of humility
• Develop a process focus on how things are done
• Be multifaceted and ambidextrous, work across functions to find synergies
• Be able to gain satisfaction from results and be willing to stake your own rewards on them

Kanter's post-entrepreneurial model corporation is a three-part mix: the values and goals emanating from top management; the channels, forums, programmes and relationships designed in the middle to support those goals and values; and the project ideas bubbling up from below – 'ideas for new ventures or technological innovations, or better ways to serve customers'.

Like other leading gurus – a term she shuns, preferring to be defined as a thought leader – Kanter has turned her attention to globalization and in *World Class* (1995) she examines how the global economy, with its vast expansion of customer choice, is transforming companies of all sizes and the communities in which they operate. It is the best book yet on globalization and what it means in practice to the future of businesses. In a fascinating microcosm, she presents a variation on Michael Porter's 'cluster' theory of industrial success, showing how the city of Boston reinvented itself from a decaying centre of manufacturing to a hive of world-class technology and knowledge businesses, feeding off and reinforcing the city's fabled centres of educational excellence such as Harvard University and Massachusetts Institute of Technology with its leading-edge Media Lab.

She has since published a study of the new economy with the somewhat over-contrived title *E-volve!* and is developing

Internet versions of her methods for managing change in organizations more effectively.

Many of Kanter's most influential writings, including the 'Power Circuits' article from *Harvard Business Review* in 1979, were collected in 1997 in *Rosabeth Moss Kanter on the Frontiers of Management* (Harvard Business School Press).

Her books deserve careful and thoughtful reading: their many-faceted ideas resist easy categorization and will play a shaping role in management theory for years to come.

KEY WRITINGS

Kanter, R. M. (1977) *Men and Women of the Corporation*, New York: Basic Books.

Kanter, R. M. (1983, 1984) *The Change Masters: Corporate Entrepreneurs at Work*, New York: Simon and Schuster; London: Allen & Unwin.

Kanter, R. M. (1989) *When Giants Learn to Dance*, New York and London: Simon and Schuster; (1998) London: International Thomson Business Press.

Kanter, R. M. (1979) 'Power Failures in Management Circuits', Cambridge, Mass.: *Harvard Business Review*; reprinted in *Organization Theory* (1990), ed. D. S. Pugh, London: Penguin Books.

Kanter, R. M. (1992) *The Challenge of Organizational Change*, New York: Simon and Schuster.

Kanter, R. M. (1995) *World Class: Thriving Locally in the Global Economy*, New York: Simon and Schuster.

Kanter, R. M. (1997) *Rosabeth Moss Kanter on the Frontiers of Management*, Boston: Harvard Business School Press.

Kanter, R. M. (2000) *E-volve! Succeeding in the Digital Culture of Tomorrow*, Boston: Harvard Business School Press.

27

ROBERT S. KAPLAN AND DAVID P. NORTON

(b. 1940) (b. 1941)

The balanced scorecard system of performance measurement

The partnership that invented the balanced scorecard, a new kind of performance-measurement tool that allows businesses to measure their non-financial as well as financial results, covering such 'soft' but essential areas as customer satisfaction, quality and product-cycle times and effectiveness of new product development. It has proved the most sustainable big idea of the 1990s, practised by major companies around the world and controlled as a brand by a collaborative franchise set up by its founding partners.

Robert Kaplan is Marvin Bower Professor of Leadership Development at Harvard Business School and has also held a chair of accounting there. He has been on the Harvard faculty of the Graduate School of Industrial Administration at Carnegie-Mellon University, serving as dean from 1977 to 1983.

A graduate in electrical engineering from Massachusetts Institute of Technology, with a doctorate in operations research from Cornell University, Kaplan has received a number of awards for outstanding contributions to the accountancy profession. His research, teaching and consulting work all focus on new cost and performance measurement systems, primarily activity-based costing and the balanced scorecard. He has authored or co-authored more than 100 academic papers and nine books.

David Norton is president and CEO of Renaissance Solutions, Inc., an international consultancy firm specializing in performance measurement and organizational renewal. Before Renaissance, he co-founded Nolan Norton and Company, where he spent 17 years as president before the firm's acquisition by Peat Marwick. He is a Harvard DBA (doctor of business administration) and, like his colleague Kaplan, earned his first degree in electrical engineering.

The balanced scorecard concept had its genesis when the two men worked together in 1990 on a one-year multi-company study called 'Measuring Performance in the Organization of the Future'. The study was carried out by Norton's old company, which had been renamed the Nolan Norton Institute and was the research arm of the accountancy and consulting giant KPMG. Norton was the study leader and Kaplan an academic consultant. Also participating were representatives of a dozen companies from manufacturing and service industries, both heavy-duty and high-tech. All had come to believe that financial performance measurements were no longer enough to enable a company to remain competitive and enhance its economic value.

As David Norton observed in a 2005 interview for this book, 'the idea came at the right time, the right place. The old production economy was giving way to the new service-and-solutions economy and corporate values were shifting to intangibles. Our idea gave executives a tool to deal with the intangibility of the world. It was all about managing change, and it responded to a need.'

The partners were influenced by their systems-driven academic backgrounds – all systems are processes and flows – and by the statistical quality movement that had captured US industry in the 1980s. Harvard Business School was also a forcing bed for action out of ideas: there was, says Norton, an attitude of 'we like your concept but what are you going to do tomorrow?'

As Kaplan and Norton explain in the preface to their

book *The Balanced Scorecard: Translating Strategy into Action* (1996), a number of innovative case studies on performance measurement were reviewed early in the project, among them a new type of corporate scorecard from Analog Devices that contained, in addition to traditional financial measures, others on customer delivery times, quality and cycle times of manufacturing processes and effectiveness of new product development. Analog also had a system for measuring continuous improvement processes.

Group discussions of the scorecard expanded it into four main quadrants: financial, customer, innovation and internal/learning development. The name balanced scorecard was chosen to reflect the balance between long- and short-term objectives, financial and non-financial, lagging and leading indicators, and external and internal performance. Several companies participating in the research team tried it out in pilot schemes and reported back on its working. By the end of 1991, Kaplan and Norton were ready to summarize the group's findings in a *Harvard Business Review* article ('The Balanced Scorecard: Measures That Drive Performance', Jan/Feb 1992). It soon became one of the most requested *HBR* reprints, and a new management tool was born.

When Norton became CEO in 1993 of the newly formed Renaissance Solutions, the scorecard was introduced as a vehicle for helping companies translate and implement strategy. An alliance between Renaissance and the much bigger Gemini Consulting brought it into use in major corporate transformations, and further refined the concept to tie measures together in strategic linkages. This meant that it was possible to tell how current investment or other decisions in one area would impact on another and eventually affect the bottom line.

The first four companies to adopt it in the US – Mobil Oil, Cygna Insurance, Chemical Bank and Brown and Root – all showed dramatic performance improvements by 1998 through tying strategy to their management processes.

The balanced scorecard is now widely used in US

commerce and industry – oil giant Mobil regards it as an irreplaceable agenda for discussion of business strategies, strengths, weaknesses and performance – and its adherents in Europe include some of the UK's major corporations, among them NatWest Bank, British Petroleum, Rolls-Royce Aerospace Group and the UK Ministry of Defence.

The Balanced Scorecard Collaborative (BSCol) was formed in 1998 as a vehicle to preserve the integrity of the idea, Kaplan and Norton having learned from the way in which re-engineering had sacrificed so much credibility by loss of identification with its inventors, Mike Hammer (qv) and James Champy. An idea is like a brand, says Norton, the public face of the partnership. 'You have to be careful that the brand doesn't get away from you.'

BSCol is a vehicle to develop and manage the idea as a change-management tool. It certifies software programs developed by practising companies and Kaplan and Norton publish a set of functional standards. It also runs an annual Hall of Fame ceremony honouring companies that have used the scorecard to exceptional effect.

The balanced scorecard has become indispensable in large companies undergoing radical change programmes, because it measures previously hard-to-quantify activities that are increasingly seen as giving a business its competitive edge, such as customer satisfaction and the building of organizational and employee skills. The rapidly growing awareness that companies must continuously improve or fall by the wayside has given the scorecard an enormous advantage over traditional performance measurements. Historically, these were concerned with financial results and the meeting of targets, but at best they could only provide a snapshot of past performance, not a reliable indicator of how a company might be expected to continue to perform in the future.

As Kaplan explained: 'The financial measures of the most

recent period of performance will tell you something about how well that company operated during that period. But there may be processes that they developed during that period for new products or new capabilities that will create long-term value that have yet to show up in the financial statements. And conversely, some organizations may have cut back on some of those investments in capability; in the short run this will make their financial performance look better, but in the process they have mortgaged their future.'

Kaplan and Norton's recognition that companies needed non-financial indicators of future performance as much as financial measures of past performance to survive in a climate of virtually permanent change has brought the balanced scorecard to the forefront of techniques of change management. Being non-prescriptive and endlessly adaptable, the scorecard can be tailored to any combination of indicators required for a specific business. Its ability to project the impact of business decisions on the company's financial future has also moved it from being primarily a measurement system to a core management system. It is still evolving in the field, and Kaplan and Norton describe the book that followed their three *HBR* articles as 'a progress report'.

The basic principles of the balanced scorecard are simple. Essentially, it looks at a business from four perspectives to gain answers to four key questions:

• The customer perspective: how do our customers see us?
• The internal business perspective: which processes and competencies do we need to excel at?
• Innovation and learning perspective: can we continue to improve and excel?
• Financial perspective: how do we look to our shareholders?

Within these four perspectives, the company decides its objectives and progress towards these is then tracked through specific measures and through initiatives for continuous improvement. The first stage of designing a scorecard is always to formulate a vision or mission statement to drive the objectives. At NatWest, for example, it was 'to be first choice in our chosen markets'. The senior executive management team then works together to

143

translate its corporate strategy into specific strategic objectives. In the customer perspective, for example, it must be specific about its targeted customers and the market segments where it hopes to compete. It should also, in Norton's words, 'look at the world through the eyes of the customer'.

The process of designing a scorecard should take about 16 weeks, though Norton admitted in a 1997 interview that he had 'yet to find an executive team with a complete consensus about building a scorecard'. In less than 50 per cent of companies, he added, was there even consensus about why customers dealt with that company.

Today, according to a report by Cranfield School of Management, 75 per cent of companies that have a performance-management system in place use the balanced scorecard and 25 per cent some variation on quality management. But of that 75 per cent, half are still using BSC as a measurement technique rather than the inclusive philosophy intended by Kaplan and Norton.

Outright failures rarely seem to occur, but if the scorecard works less successfully, suggests Norton, it is when it is used as a measurement rather than a change-management tool. 'Companies need to understand that strategic management is a permanent key competency like IT. We've learned that when people don't use the scorecard well it is because they don't believe this. Our Hall of Fame companies see strategic management as a competitive advantage.'

Scorecards can be used at all levels of an organization so that there is alignment between what top management and front-line employees understand is important – the subject of their latest book, *Alignment* (2006). In some organizations, Norton has reported, employees walk about with their personal scorecards and describe how their own objectives relate to the corporate ones. This accessibility to all levels of the organization is crucial to the successful use of the scorecard system, say its originators. 'Frontline employees must understand the financial consequences of their decisions and actions; senior executives must understand the drivers of long-term financial success.' The balanced scorecard is not the only performance-measurement system to use non-financial criteria, as Kaplan and Norton are the first to admit. But what it does better than any other system, they would claim, is to translate 'a business unit's mission and strategy into tangible objectives and measures'.

The latest big idea emerging from the BSC concept is the development of the office of strategic manager (OSM), a system to sustain momentum when corporate leadership changes. Here, as in their adoption of the BSC generally, military organizations around the world were among the first to perceive the value of sustaining policy through change. Most organizations do not have a process or a responsible individual for managing strategy, notes Norton. It is usually a scattered responsibility across functions, rather as (in IT) the CIO role was in 1980.

'On the OSM, Chrysler was one of our inspirations. They started very early. Responsibility was given to the head of corporate planning and he became responsible for shaping strategy as well as leading the design of the scorecard and metrics. The CEO started looking to him to set the agenda and pretty soon what evolved was the office of strategic manager.'

The OSM function, now catching on in companies practising the BSC, starts with a strategy map showing how to link key internal processes with desired outcomes; the subject of Kaplan and Norton's *Strategy Maps: Converting Intangible Assets into Tangible Outcomes* (2004). The visual impact of such a map forces an organization to take positions on issues important to it – for example, to see how employee satisfaction fits with turnover or how the attention paid to employees equates with that paid to shareholders.

The idea continues to grow and evolve, says Norton. 'One of the talents we have is to extrapolate big directions from small pieces of evidence.' The partners derive inspiration from applications that their Hall of Fame companies have discovered. 'The OSM was such an idea at Chrysler. We asked ourselves, why wouldn't this work everywhere?'

KEY WRITINGS

Kaplan, R. S. and Norton, D. P. (1992) 'The Balanced Scorecard: Measures That Drive Performance', Cambridge, Mass.: *Harvard Business Review* (Jan/Feb).

Kaplan, R. S. and Norton, D. P. (1993) 'Putting the Balanced Scorecard to Work', Cambridge, Mass.: *Harvard Business Review* (Sept/Oct).

Kaplan, R. S. and Norton, D. P. (1996) *The Balanced Scorecard: Translating Strategy into Action*, Boston: Harvard Business School Press.

Kaplan, R. S. and Norton, D. P. (2000) *The Strategy-Focused Organization*, Boston: Harvard Business School Press.

Kaplan, R. S. and Norton, D. P. (2004) *Strategy Maps: Converting Intangible Assets into Tangible Outcomes*, Boston: Harvard Business School Press.

Kaplan, R. S. and Norton, D. P. (2006) *Alignment: Using the Balanced Scorecard to Create Corporate Synergies*, Boston: Harvard Business School Press.

28

MANFRED KETS DE VRIES

(b. 1942)

Psychoanalysing the organization

Dutch-born Manfred Kets de Vries holds the Raoul de Vitry d'Avaucourt chair of leadership development at INSEAD, the international business school in France and at its Asian counterpart in Singapore. He is unique among leadership gurus in being both a trained economist and (since 1982) a practising psychoanalyst, a combination that enables him to take both a cognitive and clinical approach to the study of leadership. It is the second strand that particularly illuminates his work, enabling him to uncover the emotional dynamics between leaders and their organizations and how deep-rooted or buried personality traits affect the way individuals lead and manage others.

Director of INSEAD's Global Leadership Centre, Kets de Vries also directs the school's top management seminar, 'The Challenge of Leadership: Developing Your Emotional Intelligence', and its joint master/diploma programme, 'Consulting and Coaching for Change'. A Harvard Business School MBA and DBA, his international academic background includes professorships there and at Canada's McGill University.

Although best known as a leadership thinker, he is also an authority on executive stress, cross-cultural management, entrepreneurship, family business and the dynamics of corporate change. He is a consultant on organizational change and strategic human resource management to a raft of global companies in Europe, North America, Africa and Asia, and has published over 20 books as author, co-author or editor.

An urbane, accessible personality and something of a Renaissance man, he wears his huge learning lightly and entertainingly, as evidenced in the title and style of his best-known (and prize-winning) book, *Life and Death in the Executive Fast Lane* (1995), as well as *The Happiness Equation: A Winning Formula for Happiness and Success* (2002). His CV notes that he was the first fly fisherman in Outer Mongolia, is a member of the New York Explorers' Club and 'in his spare time he can be found in the jungles of central Africa, the Siberian taiga, the Pamir mountains, or within the Arctic Circle'.

Manfred Kets de Vries gains insights into individual leaders and business organizations by using what he calls a clinical paradigm – in other words, as a psychoanalyst would study a patient. A complicating factor in applying this methodology to organizations, he has said, is that the consultant rarely has the time at his disposal for diagnosis and intervention that a psychoanalyst would have in therapy with a patient.

He specializes in analysing the interface between personality, leadership style and organizational dynamics and has identified six distinct organizational types of individual: dramatic, depressive, suspicious, compulsive, detached and 'cyclothymic' (those who suffer from substantial mood swings). Many of history's most charismatic leaders, he points out, have belonged to the latter group: General Patton, Winston Churchill, Teddy Roosevelt and Benito Mussolini were all manic depressives. What would have been the effect on Patton as a battle commander, he speculates, if the drug lithium had been available in the 1940s?

In his book *The Leadership Mystique* (2001) Kets de Vries looks at the way that negative personality traits in the top executive – the 'shadow side' of leadership – can poison a whole organization.

148

Conversely, he has found, certain 'alexithymic' or 'dead fish' organizations can have a stifling effect on the energy, emotions and creativity of their people. Such organizations might be found among banks, insurance companies or government bodies. In the field of career dynamics, one of his special interests, he sees this as a key issue, finding the right 'psycho structure' to match a personality with an organization that will enable it to function at maximum fulfilment.

Consistently successful and creative companies, in Kets de Vries' experience, are also affected by the personality characteristics of their leaders and somehow embody them in their corporate culture. Such companies stay focused on a single business and are close to their customers; develop a strongly shared and positive culture; are sensitive to their environment; push power down through the organization; run a conservative financing strategy; sustain learning, innovation and entrepreneurship; and promote a working environment that attracts and retains talent. Examples such as Merck, 3M, Coca-Cola and Procter & Gamble are successful over decades, not necessarily because they are led by charismatic individuals, but rather by people who spread positive success factors through having a high emotional intelligence: they are able to manage their own feelings and comprehend those of others, to motivate themselves and enter and develop relationships.

As with the negative leaders, how they become what they are can indeed be a matter of 'life and death', both for them and the organizations they lead. Kets de Vries depicts organizations as having two identities; one being the outward and visible identity of structure, set of policies, mission and so on, and the other a submerged mix of psychological currents; who wields the power, how groups interact with each other, what the real corporate culture is like and what de Vries describes as CORTs – core conflictual relationship themes of people wanting to be admired, to assert themselves, to be independent, to oppose or control others and similar emotional drivers.

De Vries has evolved a concept that he calls the 'authentizotic organization', meaning one in which people 'feel authentic, good about themselves; because they really enjoy their work, they can work to their full capacity'. One of the keys to this is size: Sir Richard Branson, whom de Vries has analysed in depth for a book called *The New Global Leaders* (1999), is not alone in believing that when a group of people working in a building gets to be more than 50, they should be split off into smaller cells, amoeba-like, to sustain the sense of belonging to a dynamic group.

This will be a growing challenge for the future, de Vries believes. 'How, for example, can you create a big company which is simultaneously a small company, and how do you build the interfaces and deal with the transfer of knowledge?' he asked rhetorically in an online interview in 2000. 'All these are complex issues and we can add to them the conundrum of how to develop a career in a very flat organization.'

KEY WRITINGS

Kets de Vries, M. F. R. and Zaleznik, Abraham (1975) *Power and the Corporate Mind*, Boston: Houghton-Mifflin; (1985) Chicago: Bonus Books.

Kets de Vries, M. F. R. (1980) *Organizational Paradoxes: Clinical Approaches to Management*, London and New York: Tavistock/Methuen; (1994) London: Routledge.

Kets de Vries, M. F. R. and Miller, Danny (1984, 1990) *The Neurotic Organization: Diagnosing and Changing Counterproductive Styles of Management*, San Francisco: Jossey-Bass.

Kets de Vries, M. F. R. (1995) *Life and Death in the Executive Fast Lane: Essays on Irrational Organizations and Their Leaders*, San Francisco: Jossey-Bass.

Kets de Vries, M. F. R. (1996) *Family Business: Human Dilemmas in the Family Firm*, London: Thomson Publishing.

Kets de Vries, M. F. R. and Florent-Treacy, Elizabeth (1999) *The New Global Leaders*, San Francisco: Jossey-Bass.

Kets de Vries, M. F. R. (2001, 2006) *The Leadership Mystique*, London: Financial Times/Prentice-Hall.

Kets de Vries, M. F. R. (2002) *The Happiness Equation: A Winning Formula for Happiness and Success*, London: Vermilion.

Kets de Vries, M. F. R. (2004) *Lessons in Leadership by Terror: Finding Shaka Zulu in the Attic*, London: Edward Elgar.

Kets de Vries, M. F. R. (2005) *The New Russian Business Leaders*, London: Edward Elgar.
Kets de Vries, M. F. R. (2005) *Global Executive Leadership Inventory*, New York: Pfeiffer Wiley.

29

W. CHAN KIM AND RENÉE MAUBORGNE

(b. 1952)

Value innovation and 'blue ocean' strategy

Often described as two of Europe's brightest business thinkers, this partnership of professors at INSEAD, the international management school at Fontainebleau, France, has carved out a new approach to growth strategy, from beating the competition in a company's existing markets to creating entirely uncontested market space – what they call 'blue oceans'. Working from a rigorous database of 30 industry sectors over 100 years of evidence, their underlying 'value innovation' theory on how successful new industries are born has shifted much conventional strategic thinking. The French business magazine *L'Expansion* has called them 'the No. 1 gurus of the future'.

Korean-born W. Chan Kim holds the Boston Consulting Group Bruce D. Henderson chair of international management at INSEAD and was previously on the faculty of the University of Michigan business school. His American colleague, Renée Mauborgne, is affiliate professor of strategy and management at INSEAD and a distinguished fellow of the Fontainebleau school. She is also a fellow of the World Economic Forum and an adviser to corporations in Europe, the US and Asia-Pacific.

Since 1997, they have published a string of acclaimed

articles in the *Harvard Business Review* on value innovation and 'fair process', a dimension of human psychology they believe has been under-explored in management practice. The process revolves around establishing trust by employees in the way management decisions are made and which, the partnership believes after ten years' research into a range of international companies, can unlock innovation and build higher performance. It goes beyond theories of employee satisfaction accepted since the 1960s into a new dimension of active commitment and creativity needed in the knowledge economy.

Kim and Mauborgne published their first book, *Blue Ocean Strategy*, in 2005. Their *HBR* articles have sold more than 500,000 reprints. They have also co-founded the Value Innovation Institute, an Internet-based forum for linking innovative ideas with business opportunities.

Conventional business competition strategy, say Kim and Mauborgne, is still stuck in a military-style view of a fixed amount of terrain to be captured or shared. This is a zero-sum game because it accepts that the amount of land (or market space) available cannot be enlarged or multiplied. On the contrary, they argue, new and uncontested terrain or market space can be created that makes the existing competition irrelevant. They call this 'blue ocean' to convey the idea of limitless and uncharted space, in contrast to the 'red ocean' in which existing competitors swim and engage in bloody battle and where there is limited room for growth.

As an example of how new market space can be created even within an existing mature industry, Kim and Mauborgne cite Chrysler's innovation of the people carrier, a concept that combined the loading capacity of a van with the comfort of a family station wagon.

Other management gurus have explored the concept of re-inventing markets in line with companies' core competencies, notably the California-based strategist Gary Hamel (qv) with his then co-author C. K. Prahalad (qv) in *Competing for the Future*

(1994) and in Hamel's later work *Leading the Revolution* (2000), which unfortunately led him to praise Enron as an example of inventing a new business model.

The INSEAD academics have been content to keep a lower profile, painstakingly amassing data on the creation of new industries and evolving models for would-be innovators. In their book *Blue Ocean Strategy*, they introduce a practical set of 'value-innovation' tools with which to break out of over-competitive markets into more profitable blue water. Instead of the customary strategic choice between low cost or value differentiation, their value-innovation model is designed to pursue both goals simultaneously.

The value-innovation process identifies five dimensions in which to challenge conventional competitive thinking. These are:

- *Industry assumptions* (value innovators don't set their strategy within accepted parameters but look for ideas that will give customers quantum leaps in value)
- *Strategic focus* (value innovators aren't obsessed with bench-marking against competitors, which yield only incremental market share; they create new markets that others cannot immediately follow)
- *Customers* (value innovators don't seek to segment different markets among customers; they focus on common factors among them)
- *Assets and capabilities* (value innovators don't start from where they are, concentrating exclusively on their core competencies; they assess opportunities as if they were starting anew, as Virgin did in the 1980s by selling its small music stores and opening entertainment megastores)
- *Product and service offerings* (value innovators seek to provide what most customers value most, even if this transcends the normal boundaries of their business)

To assess the sustainability of a proposed innovation, companies should ask themselves three questions, Mauborgne told an interviewer in 2002. Is there a compelling reason to buy the product or service, does it create demand through an attractive price, and can the company make money from its business model? Many dotcom companies failed because they focused only on price.

Amazon succeeded on both price and buyer usefulness, though it took time to make money. To prevent competitors stealing a march, the innovation needs to combine low cost with the highest buyer utility. Given this, the partnership's research has shown the average time-span between launch and imitation is ten years.

One of their early case studies showed how the French hotel chain Accor created a new market for budget travellers with its Formule 1 concept. Thinking about what most customers look for in a budget hotel, Accor concluded the key factor was a good night's sleep at a modest price. The core necessity for this was a well-insulated room and comfortable bed: guests would trade non-essentials for this.

Through its own questioning of industry assumptions, Accor discovered that it could strip out less-valued services in budget hotels and increase the quality of the core offering to a level far above its price. Managers asked four key questions:

1. Which factors that our industry takes for granted could be eliminated? (Answer: restaurants, bars)
2. Which factors could be reduced well below industry standard? (Answer: 24-hour reception service – check-in and check-out procedures can be done automatically in non-peak periods – and non-essential bedroom fittings such as desks and fitted closets)
3. Which factors should be raised well above industry standards? (Answer: bed quality and soundproofing)
4. Which new factors should be created that the industry has never before offered? (Answer: delivery at one-star prices of better than two-star quality on the features most valued by customers)

The Formule 1 concept not only captured the lion's share of French budget-hotel customers but expanded the market, bringing in truck drivers at one end and business travellers at the other. By going beyond the competition, Accor effectively changed the market.

More recently, Kim and Mauborgne have cited the Canadian Cirque du Soleil as a prime value innovator. This clever idea created a whole new 'blue ocean' in the old and fading market

155

for traditional circuses with their clowns and trained animal acts, themselves now less accepted by the public. Cirque du Soleil combines drama, spectacle, colour and music in a way that is neither old-style circus nor theatre but draws on both to create a new kind of family entertainment.

'Innovation need not be random,' Kim insists. 'It can be repeatable in organizations, but there has to be a climate of trust within the company that generates a genuine and voluntary cooperation.' This is the theory underlying Kim and Mauborgne's other important area of work on 'fair process', a dimension of human psychology that they believe has been under-explored in conventional management practice. People in an organization, their argument runs, release their best creative abilities only when they completely trust the processes by which corporate decisions are made and executed. This has to involve active consultation and explanation by the decision-makers: employees may not agree with the decisions, but they are enabled to understand that the decisions were fairly reached.

Kim and Mauborgne developed their theory from the work of two social scientists in the 1970s. John W. Thibault and Laurens Walker sought to understand what psychological factors lead people to trust a legal system and discovered that they care as much about the fairness of the process itself as about the actual outcome. Researching in industry over a decade, the INSEAD professors became convinced that a direct link existed between such processes and the attitudes and behaviour of people in the organizations.

'Fair process,' says Kim, 'will be a powerful management tool as industry moves out of the production economy into the knowledge economy.' As land, labour and capital rapidly become commodities, what really count are ideas. And since no one can supervise ideas, or dictate where they go, the attitudes and goodwill of the people who generate them become of central importance to the organization employing them.

Fair process, the pair wrote in *Harvard Business Review* (July/August 1997) 'profoundly influences attitudes and behaviours critical to high performance. It builds trust and unlocks ideas. With it, managers can achieve even the most painful and difficult goals while gaining the voluntary cooperation of the employees affected.'

Kim and Mauborgne identify three planks to fair process which they call the 'three Es':

- *Engagement* – participation and open debate between managers and employees
- *Explanation* – employees have an intellectual understanding of how and why decisions were reached
- *Expectation clarity* – clearly setting out what targets are expected and who will be responsible for what

The concept is not the same as consensus. It differs significantly from the Japanese management tradition of seeking harmony through participation: the key to fair process is that an idea is accepted by the majority through understanding, not necessarily agreement. When successful culture change is achieved in an organization, Kim and Mauborgne believe, fair process is always a part of it.

The INSEAD professors believe that although the motivational theories of employee satisfaction propagated by Frederick Herzberg and others worked successfully in the production economy, they are no longer enough in the knowledge economy: if trust and commitment are lacking, good ideas will not be shared and the company's performance will suffer. Nor is their theory restricted to new industries: their fieldwork in old rust-belt industry such as steel produced the same connection between trust in decision-making, innovation and booming productivity.

KEY WRITINGS

Kim, W. C. and Mauborgne, R. (1997, 2004) 'Value Innovation: The Strategic Logic of High Growth', Boston: *Harvard Business Review* (Jan/Feb 1997 and July/Aug 2004).
Kim, W. C. and Mauborgne, R. (1997) 'Fair Process: Managing in the Knowledge Economy', Boston: *Harvard Business Review* (July/Aug).
Kim, W. C and Mauborgne, R. (2002) 'Charting your company's future', Boston: *Harvard Business Review* (June).

Kim, W. C. and Mauborgne, R. (2003) 'Tipping Point Leadership', Boston: *Harvard Business Review* (April).

Kim, W. C. and Mauborgne, R. (2005) *Blue Ocean Strategy: How to Create Uncontested Market Space and Make the Competition Irrelevant*, Boston: Harvard Business School Publishing.

30

PHILIP KOTLER

(b. 1931)

Marketing as a management science

Chicago-born economist, mathematician and sociologist who became the world's leading authority on marketing as an applied discipline capable of raising awareness not only of products and services but of ideas, places, individuals and organizations. His *Marketing Management*, first published in 1967 and in regular new editions since, is the bible of every business school's marketing course. It defined marketing as a function of management and applied a scientific rigour, with models and statistical analysis, to what had been up till then largely a seat-of-the-pants practice, directed largely at selling. His books have now sold more than 3m copies and are read as marketing gospel in 58 countries.

At a New York seminar in the 1980s, Kotler was approached by a businessman who reproached him for America's trials at the hands of Japanese competitors. 'Deming taught quality to the Japanese and you taught them marketing,' said the man. 'The combination defeated us.' Kotler later examined how Japan had mastered global marketing in *The New Competition* (1985).

Kotler trained as an economist and mathematician, taking a master's in economics at the University of Chicago (where he studied under Milton Friedman) in the early 1950s and a PhD at the Massachusetts Institute of Technology under Paul Samuelson, the Nobel laureate. The opposing theories of the free-marketeer Friedman and the Keynesian Samuelson so frustrated him that he quit economics for a post-doctoral year in sociology and a programme in higher mathematics at Harvard. It was here that he met several professors of marketing and became convinced that marketing deserved a more analytical approach.

In 1962 he joined the faculty of Northwestern University, Illinois, where he is now S. C. Johnson and Son Distinguished Professor of International Marketing at the respected J. L. Kellogg Graduate School of Management. He was offered an assistant professorship in either managerial economics or marketing and chose, he says with typical dry humour, 'to teach the subject that I knew less about, namely marketing'.

Existing marketing textbooks seemed to him short on the kind of research and methodology that were common in other disciplines, so he decided to write his own. After his publishers persuaded him to leave out the more daunting academic models and statistics, *Marketing Management* was an immediate success. Four years later, in 1971, he included the excised material in *Marketing Decision-Making: A Model-Building Approach*, which was incorporated by the University of Chicago in its introductory marketing course.

In 1969 Kotler and a colleague, Sidney Levy, began to broaden out the study of marketing to non-business uses, and he has since published books applying marketing to subjects as diverse as healthcare organizations, educational institutions, celebrities, performing-arts bodies, museums, towns and cities seeking investment and, most recently, entire nations.

Though a distinguished academic, Kotler has the knack of distilling the essence of his work in simple concepts: that marketing is basically a matter of exchange in different contexts; that it is 'the art of creating genuine customer value' and of 'filling needs profitably'.

He has updated his masterwork every three years or so and likes to joke that only the most current edition is correct because marketing moves so fast that 'the answers of yesterday lead to the errors of today.'

His current seminars stress such themes as relationship marketing, speed as a competitive weapon and the role of superior IT systems. In the mid-1980s he took issue with the eminent Theodore Levitt (qv), the first management thinker to treat marketing seriously. Levitt had argued that companies should pursue standardized global products and marketing messages, emulating big brands like Coca-Cola and McDonald's. Kotler argued that this was to ignore crucial differences in culture, tastes, income, distribution and many other factors. His approach was 'think global but also local' – a concept now known as 'glocal'.

Kotler continues to teach, consult and run seminars alongside a prolific writing programme (15 books, many co-authored, and over 100 articles in leading management reviews). In 1985 the American Marketing Association made him the first recipient of its Distinguished Marketing Educator Award. In accepting it, Kotler said: 'Marketing is not the art of finding clever ways to dispose of what you make. Marketing is the art of creating genuine customer value. It is the art of helping your customers become better off. The marketer's watchwords are quality, service and value. Can you imagine what the world would be like if the marketing concept became a universal principle?'

Before the 1960s, marketing was not seen as a serious function of strategic management, more as a grubby commercial business left to the sales department. That changed in 1960 with the publication of an article in *Harvard Business Review* by Theodore Levitt ('Marketing Myopia', July/August 1960) and four years later Philip Kotler began work on the classic textbook that would launch a thousand marketing courses – *Marketing Management: Analysis, Planning, Implementation and Control*, to give its full title, now in its 11th (2005) edition.

Marketing Management broke entirely new ground from the existing lightweight books on the subject. It was divided into six main sections and 26 subsections covering every aspect of planning and managing the marketing function, from the societal, managerial and strategic underpinnings of marketing theory and practice, through analysing consumer and organizational buyers to evaluating and controlling market performance.

As befitted its author's polymathic background in economics, mathematics and sociology, it was grounded in decision theory, organizational behaviour, economic science and social psychology and was quickly adopted by Stanford, Wharton and other leading US business schools. Since then, MBAs around the world have been trained on Kotler's teaching that the customer is paramount and that successful companies don't just sell but build relationships with targeted customers and deliver satisfaction to them.

'Authentic marketing is not the art of selling what you make but knowing what to make,' he wrote in the book's introduction. 'It is the art of identifying and understanding customer needs and creating solutions that deliver satisfaction to the customers, profits to the producers and benefits for the stakeholders. Market leadership is gained by creating customer satisfaction through product innovation, product quality and customer service. If these are absent, no amount of advertising, sales promotion or salesmanship can compensate.'

If the core concept of economics is scarcity, that of politics is power and that of sociology is the group, then the core concept of marketing, Kotler argues, is exchange – the exchange of values between two parties. Marketing thus becomes a social process, composed of human behaviour patterns, not merely a function of adding to business profits. This humanistic view led Kotler to broaden out the study of marketing into non-business activities, including the marketing of individuals, cities and even countries. He believes that it is his work on this, rather than his classic textbook, that ranks among the most important marketing milestones of the 1960s because it enabled him to 'take marketing into new sectors of society and show its potential contributions'.

The idea that marketing had a role in non-profitmaking organizations was controversial when Kotler first aired it in 1969 in an article with Sidney Levy in the *Journal of Marketing*, but within two years it had become accepted by fellow academics. Kotler followed this in 1971 with another controversial breakout from conventional thinking, collaborating with Gerald Zaltman on 'Social Marketing: An Approach to Planned Social Change', which extended the concept into new, political territory. A third contentious publication was 'Demarketing – Yes, Demarketing', in *Harvard Business Review* in 1971, based on Kotler's and Levy's observations that some firms actively discourage some customers and encourage others, and advancing the idea that companies and indeed society can use marketing theory in reverse to dampen excessive or socially undesirable demand.

Books with various co-authors poured out on marketing in non-business contexts: *Marketing for Non-Profit Organizations* (1975, 5th edition 1996); *Strategic Marketing for Educational Institutions* (1985, 1995); *Marketing for Healthcare Organizations* (1987); *High Visibility* (1987, 1997), on celebrity marketing; and a raft of others on cultural organizations, hospitality, tourism, the performing arts. In 1993 Kotler published *Marketing Places: Attracting Investment, Industry and Tourism to Cities, States and Nations*, and in 1997 *The Marketing of Nations: A Strategic Approach to Building National Wealth*. In 1986 he advanced the concept of 'megamarketing', using political skills and understanding of public opinion to break into blocked or protected markets.

Kotler has identified a number of different levels at which marketing operates, from the lowest level of selling up through targeting specific groups and needs to anticipating needs and finally shaping demand by extending and creating new lifestyles through innovation, such as Sony achieved with the Walkman.

All his work has the common theme that organizations compete for customers and cannot succeed by trying to satisfy all segments; they must select and focus on well-defined target groups whose needs they understand. Marketing, he argues, must match the organization's supply capabilities to appropriate market opportunities.

Throughout his career Kotler has been driven by a love of problem-solving and working out concepts to completion. In a paper circulated privately to one of his classes, he was quoted as saying: 'I operate on the assumption that "progress" is possible, even in the face of much contradictory evidence. I prefer to believe that human beings can improve their condition by applying collective intelligence to solving shared problems.'

Kotler's work is made handily accessible in *Kotler on Marketing* (1999), which covers his thinking under four headings – strategic marketing, tactical marketing, administrative marketing and transformational marketing.

KEY WRITINGS

Kotler, P. (1967, 1997, 2000, 2005) *Marketing Management: Analysis, Planning, Implementation and Control*, Englewood Cliffs, N.J.: Prentice-Hall.

Kotler, P. and Levy, S. J. (1969) 'Broadening the Concept of Marketing', *Journal of Marketing* (January).

Kotler, P. and Zaltman, G. (1971) 'Social Marketing: An Approach to Planned Social Change', *Journal of Marketing* (July).

Kotler, P. and Levy, S. J. (1971) 'Demarketing – Yes, Demarketing', Cambridge, Mass.: *Harvard Business Review* (Nov/Dec).

Kotler, P. and Lilien, G. (1971, 1983) *Marketing Decision-Making: A Model-Building Approach*, New York: Holt Rinehart and Winston; (1992, 1996) revised as *Marketing Models*, Englewood Cliffs, N.J.: Prentice-Hall.

Kotler, P. (1980, 1996, 2005) *Principles of Marketing*, Englewood Cliffs, N.J.: Prentice-Hall; London: FT/Prentice-Hall.

Kotler, P. (1986) 'Megamarketing', *Harvard Business Review* (March/April).

Kotler, P. (1987, 1997) *Marketing – An Introduction*, Englewood Cliffs, N.J.: Prentice-Hall.

Kotler, P. and Roberto, E. (1989) *Social Marketing: Strategies for Changing Social Behaviour*, New York: Free Press.

Kotler, P. (1999, 2001) *Kotler on Marketing: how to create, win and dominate markets*, New York: Free Press.

Kotler, P. (2003) *Marketing Insights from A to Z*, Chichester: John Wiley and Sons.

31

JOHN P. KOTTER

(b. 1947)

Leadership and organizational change

Harvard professor whose work since the early 1980s has focused on managerial qualities and behaviour and is now predominantly associated with the leadership of organizations. Like Warren Bennis (qv), the elder statesman among leadership gurus, he has made detailed studies of what differentiates leaders from managers, with a substantial body of casework that began with his first, much-praised 1982 book, *The General Managers*.

Where the two differ is that Bennis, 22 years Kotter's senior, has studied individuals across a variety of occupations in attempting to identify common principles of leadership, while Kotter sets his research firmly in a corporate framework and argues that leadership is a 'process' that sets off hundreds or thousands of 'leadership acts' within the organization.

Kotter's 1990 book, *A Force for Change: How Leadership Differs from Management*, demonstrates this process in action in businesses such as NCR, American Express and SAS. The message of *A Force for Change*, one that Bennis has also expressed, is that thousands of companies are over-managed and under-led because too few executives, while managerially competent, have a clear understanding of what leadership is. Both Kotter and Bennis believe that while leadership qualities may be inherent in some, they can also be imbibed and taught. Kotter's international bestseller *Leading Change* (1996) presented an eight-step leadership process for implementing successful corporate transformation.

Since 1990, Kotter has held the Konosuke Matsushita chair of leadership at Harvard Business School, endowed by the Japanese entrepreneur who founded the giant electrical engineering firm. In 1997 he published a study of Matsushita, one of the most charismatic business leaders Japan has produced, under the title *Matsushita Leadership: Lessons from the 20th Century's Most Remarkable Entrepreneur*, which provided a rare insight into the arcane world of Japanese business philosophy. Kotter's half-dozen other books on leadership are highly regarded, along with *Corporate Culture and Performance* (1992), in which, with co-author James L. Heskett, he analysed the factors common to successful change programmes in large companies – most of them, unsurprisingly, linked to strong and committed leadership.

A graduate (in electrical engineering) of Massachusetts Institute of Technology, recipient of a master's degree in management from the Sloan School of Management and a Harvard doctorate in organizational behaviour, Kotter was one of the youngest individuals to be given a full professorship at Harvard Business School in 1980, at the age of 33.

Kotter is a prolific and award-winning contributor to *Harvard Business Review* and is probably the world's most sought-after speaker on leadership and organizational change.

'Leadership produces change. That is its primary function.' That was the key statement in Kotter's influential book *A Force for Change* (1990), which defined the differences between leadership and management and the relationship between the two, based on rigorous casework within large US corporations. Since his first major book, *The General Managers* (1982), which analysed the capabilities and working methods of 15 general managers in a variety of companies, Kotter has always founded his research firmly on observation within organizations.

The General Managers, like Henry Mintzberg's *The Nature of Managerial Work*, exploded some long-held beliefs, principally the myth of the 'generalist' professional manager who could step into any business and run it. Instead, he discovered that the most effective GMs executed their work through a knowledge of the business and networks of other people in the organization, built up over a long period. He also illuminated the daunting complexity of the general manager's job and the dual competencies needed for handling both job responsibilities and developing relationships – skills in the latter role being particularly noticeable in the highest performers. Although nearly 20 years out of date in its research (executive mobility is much higher in the late 1990s), *The General Managers* remains a seminal work in its field.

In *A Force for Change*, Kotter applied a similar methodology of observation and identified the principal tasks of leadership as:

- Establishing direction, developing a vision and strategies for the future of the business
- Aligning people – getting others to 'understand, accept and line up in the chosen direction'
- Motivating and inspiring people by appealing to very basic but often untapped human needs, values and emotions

Management roles, on the other hand, were defined as:

- Planning and budgeting, setting short- to medium-term targets
- Establishing steps to reach them and allocating resources
- Organizing and staffing, establishing an organizational structure to accomplish the plan, staffing the jobs; communicating the plan, delegating responsibility and establishing systems to monitor implementation
- Controlling and problem-solving, monitoring results, identifying problems and organizing to solve them

Both are 'complete action systems', because leadership as well as management involves implementation. Organizations need both strong management and strong leadership to succeed;

strong management and weak leadership can produce stifling bureaucracy, whereas strong leadership without strong management can turn messianic and cult-like.

Direction-setting should not be confused with long-range planning, says Kotter. 'Planning is a managerial process that is not the same as, nor ever a substitute for, the direction-setting aspect of leadership, a process that produces vision and strategies, not plans . . .'

Planning works as a complementary activity to direction-setting: 'a competent planning process serves as a useful reality check on direction-setting activities . . . Likewise, a competent direction-setting process provides a focus in which planning can then realistically be carried out; it clarifies what planning must be done and what planning is irrelevant.'

Similarly, Kotter argues, alignment is very different from the managerial process of organizing – it is 'a complicated communications challenge . . . Organizations that are both well led and well managed understand all this.'

The third task of leadership, motivation, is also very different from the incentives that managers employ in getting targets met. Management processes are about control and monitoring whereas leadership processes 'accomplish their energizing effect, not by pushing people in the right direction . . . but by satisfying very basic human needs: for achievement, belonging, recognition, self-esteem, a sense of control over one's life and living up to one's ideals'.

Having examined these tasks in action in a number of closely observed companies, Kotter moves on to determine the inherent attributes commonly found in leaders. Such individuals, he concludes, always seem to have:

- Above-average energy levels
- An inner drive often associated with high personal standards, a certain dissatisfaction with the status quo and a tendency to push for continuous improvement
- Above-average intellectual skills, e.g. in absorbing and processing large quantities of diverse information
- Mental or emotional health
- Integrity

Early broadening experience also helps: Kotter's research suggests that leaders in big jobs have almost always had an earlier opportunity to grow beyond the narrow base of most managerial careers.

A further message of the book is that effective leadership today is rarely the result of one person but of hundreds of individuals at middle levels in the organization. As early as 1984, Procter & Gamble's paper products division was pursuing a policy of group management in which the new divisional head invited his eleven direct reports to form a divisional 'board' and set strategy and direction. The result in 1986, after resources were diverted to a new product development, was the stunning rise of the Pampers brand of disposable nappies, from 40 per cent to 58 per cent of the market.

In *The Leadership Factor* (1987) Kotter had presented extensive evidence that the typical business organization did a poor job of finding people with leadership potential and developing it. Asserting that leadership is 'no longer the domain of the CEO or a few top managers, but is increasingly needed in nearly all managerial jobs', he examined 15 US firms with high reputations for leadership development to identify the practices they followed, concluding among other things that a common factor was 'moderately strong corporate cultures'.

From here, after *A Force for Change*, it was a natural progression to *Corporate Culture and Performance* (1992), in which Kotter and co-author James L. Heskett demonstrated, again through a detailed study of successful turned-around companies, that cultures which encourage leadership up and down the hierarchy help organizations to adapt to change and thereby prosper. 'The single most visible factor that distinguishes major cultural changes that succeed from those that fail is competent leadership at the top . . . Unlike even the very best management process, leadership has as its primary function the production of change.'

Most companies, argued Kotter and Heskett, lack adaptive cultures, and 'only with leadership does one get the boldness, the vision and the energy needed to create large and difficult changes . . .' Their ten case studies, including British Airways, General Electric, ICI and Nissan, all had a history of major cultural change – and subsequent enhanced performance – after an individual with a past track record of leadership was appointed at the top.

Leading Change (1996) pursued this theme by examining 100 cases of large-scale change, the book's title deliberately challenging the more common concept of 'managing change'. It identified eight best–practice stages in the process, all of them 'a leadership activity', in which managers and executives:

- Help push up a sense of urgency
- Organize a guiding change coalition
- Create an appropriate change vision
- Communicate that vision to everyone
- Empower people to act on that vision
- Create short-term wins to build credibility
- Use that momentum to take on bigger change problems
- Institutionalize new approaches in the organizational culture

Kotter intends to develop his leadership studies further in future, believing that it is still growing in importance as a subject, and is one about which we still know relatively little.

KEY WRITINGS

Kotter, J. P. (1982) 'What Effective General Managers Really Do', Cambridge, Mass.: *Harvard Business Review* (Nov/Dec).

Kotter, J. P. (1982) *The General Managers*, New York: Free Press.

Kotter, J. P. (1987) *The Leadership Factor*, New York: Free Press.

Kotter, J. P. (1990) 'What Leaders Really Do', Cambridge, Mass.: *Harvard Business Review* (May/June), reprint no. 09309.

Kotter, J. P. (1990) *A Force for Change*, New York: Free Press.

Kotter, J. P. and Heskett, J. L. (1992) *Corporate Culture and Performance*, New York: Free Press.

Kotter, J. P. 'Leading Change: Why Transformation Efforts Fail', Cambridge, Mass.: *Harvard Business Review* (March/April), reprint no. 95204.

Kotter, J. P. (1996) *Leading Change*, Boston: Harvard Business School Press.

Kotter, J. P. (1997) *Matshusita Leadership*, Boston: Harvard Business School Press.

Kotter, J. P. (2002) *The Heart of Change*, Boston: Harvard Business School Press.

32

THEODORE LEVITT

(b. 1925)

Understanding the true role of marketing

The first management theorist to emphasize the importance of marketing, German-born Levitt is emeritus professor of business administration at Harvard Business School, where he has been an academic luminary for over 40 years. He is unusual in having established his reputation as a guru on the basis of a single article – 'Marketing Myopia', published in the *Harvard Business Review* in the summer of 1960. It has since sold more than 500,000 reprinted copies.

In this extraordinarily influential article, Levitt argued powerfully that 'an industry is a customer-satisfying process, not a goods-producing process'. He suggested, for example, that railway managers helped to cause problems in their industry by viewing their business as railways, a technical product, rather than transport, a customer business. This was the approach reversed by Lord King and Sir Colin Marshall at British Airways, and which led to a dramatic turnaround in the airline's performance and in the perception of it by its customers. Before Levitt, it has been said, marketing was a poor relation in the world of senior management.

Levitt can claim to have had more articles published in the *Harvard Business Review* than any other guru. He edited the journal from 1986 to 1990, when he was succeeded by Rosabeth Moss Kanter. Of his five books on marketing, he regards *The Marketing Imagination* (1983) as his most important. He believes the secret of success in marketing is constantly to 'ask questions to develop your sensitivity and sensibility . . . Perceptiveness requires cognitive effort and personal involvement. You bring something to what you see.'

Like other gurus, notably Kenichi Ohmae (qv), Levitt has recently diversified into the subject of the global market-place and 'global branding'. Selling the same product worldwide, whether baked beans or cameras, is a subject of divided opinions among gurus; Ohmae, for example, taking the view that acting as an 'insider' in the territory you are selling in is more important than selling a standard product from a central point, whereas Levitt inclines to the latter view.

Levitt's view of his own influence is modest. 'What I've achieved, I think, is to make myself effective in some way, kept myself intellectually curious, alive and productive, and made myself interesting to myself' (*Makers of Management*, Clutterbuck and Crainer).

Theodore Levitt's ground-breaking article 'Marketing Myopia' started by pointing out that every industry was once a growth industry. After growth continues for a while, managers tend to believe it will always do so. Seeing no competition for their product, they pin their faith on improvements in productivity and cost reduction. The result is stagnation or decline.

Levitt proceeds to demonstrate that only 'a thoroughly customer-oriented management' can keep a growth industry growing 'even after the obvious opportunities have been exhausted'.

Detroit's automobile industry provided a key case study for Levitt's thesis. Ruled by the production ('Fordist') philosophy, it went on giving the customer what it believed the customer should have. 'Detroit never really researched the customer's wants,' wrote Levitt. 'It only researched the kinds of things which it had already decided to offer him.'

It was not until Japanese and European manufacturers won huge sales with compact cars that Detroit woke up to the reality of a shift in its traditional customer base.

Other long-successful industries, Levitt suggested, could be overtaken by the same nemesis unless they reversed the habits of an organizational lifetime and realized that 'an industry begins with the customer and his needs, not with a patent, a raw material or a selling skill.'

Selling, Levitt insisted, was not the same as marketing. 'Selling concerns itself with the tricks and techniques of getting people to exchange their cash for your product. It is not concerned with the values that the exchange is all about. And it does not, as marketing invariably does, view the entire business process as consisting of a tightly integrated effort to discover, create, arouse and satisfy customer needs.'

The difference between marketing and selling, Levitt continued, was 'more than semantic. Selling focuses on the needs of the seller, marketing on the needs of the buyer. Selling is preoccupied with the seller's need to convert his product into cash; marketing with the idea of satisfying the needs of the customer by means of the product and the whole cluster of things associated with creating, delivering and finally consuming it.'

In a truly marketing-oriented firm, says Levitt, what is offered for sale is much more than the basic product or service – how it is made available to the customer, for example, under what conditions and terms of trade. 'Most important, what it offers for sale is determined not by the seller but by the buyer . . . the product becomes a consequence of the marketing effort, not vice versa.'

Taking a deliberately bizarre example of an industry that could have prevented its demise by understanding the wants of its customers, Levitt cites the makers of buggy whips in the early days of the automobile. 'No amount of product improvement could stave off its death sentence. But had the industry defined itself as being in the transportation business rather than the buggy-whip business, it might have survived. It would have done what survival always entails, that is, changing. Even if it had only defined its business as providing a stimulant or catalyst to an energy source, it might have survived by becoming a manufacturer of, say, fanbelts or air cleaners.'

In *The Marketing Imagination*, Levitt argued that competitive success rested on realizing five factors:

1. The purpose of a business is to create and keep customers.
2. To do this, goods and services must be produced and delivered that people want and value, at prices and conditions that are more attractive than those of competitors.
3. To continue, enough profits must be made to keep investors.
4. To achieve this, all companies must clarify their purposes, strategies and plans, and clearly communicate them to the workforce. The larger the enterprise, the greater the need for a clearly written and reviewed set of goals.
5. All enterprises must have a system of rewards, audits and controls to ensure the proper pursuit of those goals.

The organization, Levitt constantly preaches, must think of itself less in terms of producing goods or services and more in terms of buying customers. To achieve this, the chief executive's leadership is all-important.

Today marketing is no longer, as Levitt called it in 1960, a 'stepchild'. Getting and staying close to the customer was enshrined by Tom Peters and Robert Waterman's *In Search of Excellence* as a prime component of the top-performing company. But that was in 1982. More than 20 years earlier, the idea was sufficiently novel for Levitt's *Harvard Business Review* article to start an earthquake in management thinking.

KEY WRITINGS

Levitt, T. (1960) 'Marketing Myopia', Cambridge, Mass.: *Harvard Business Review*.

Levitt, T. (1962) *Innovation in Marketing*, New York: McGraw-Hill.

Levitt, T. (1969) *The Marketing Mode*, New York: McGraw-Hill.

Levitt, T. (1983) *The Marketing Imagination*, New York: Free Press.

Levitt, T. (1990) *Thinking About Management*, New York: Free Press.

33

RENSIS LIKERT

(1903–1981)

How leadership styles link with business performance

US social psychologist and researcher who founded in 1949 a pioneering establishment for research into human behaviour in organizations, the Institute for Social Research at the University of Michigan. His work had a lasting effect on organizational theory and the study of leadership. He is best known for his *New Patterns of Management* (1961), in which, based on extensive questioning of employees in industrial firms, he argued that the management of organizations could be categorized along a line graduating from System 1, exploitative and authoritarian, to System 4, participative and based on overlapping work groups. He also invented the concept of 'linking plans' – individuals capable of linking each work group to the organization.

A lasting by-product of his studies within organizations was the invention of the Likert Scale for attitude measurement. The scale, a common feature of most attitude surveys today, ranges from favourable ('strongly agree') to unfavourable ('strongly disagree') with a neutral midpoint for each statement. The scale's values range from one to five or seven, the midpoint reflecting an undecided position. Statistical analysis then determines the relative significance of each statement.

Like Douglas McGregor (qv), Likert rejected traditional

assumptions about human behaviour under management and proposed new methods based on a better understanding of people's motivation and potential.

Likert gained a PhD from Columbia University in 1932, and his work there was later published as 'A Technique for the Measurement of Attitudes'. He then became director of research at a life-insurance office in Hartford, Connecticut, where he began to study management practices. In 1939 he moved to the Department of Agriculture in Washington as director of programme surveys.

From 1949 to 1969 he ran the Institute for Social Research and on retirement formed his own consulting firm. His books are underpinned with numerous original research studies, the last of them being written with his wife and co-researcher, Jane Gibson Likert.

Rensis Likert believed that participative management was the best kind, and the most likely to produce results. Some of his contemporary management thinkers criticized him for flatly assuming that group discussion was the only way to good decision-making and thereby abandoning or ignoring the search for better techniques of problem-solving or decision-making.

Kepner and Tregoe in *The Rational Manager* (1965) commented that managers would find this both difficult and 'far removed from the practical reality they must contend with every day'.

Likert's primary objective at the Institute for Social Research was to identify different styles of leadership and correlate them with business performance. His research method was based on detailed questionnaires to employees of US companies, asking them a series of questions about their supervisors. He then drew up a profile of each supervisor or manager in the light of how he was viewed by the people who worked under him. From these profiles Likert established his System 1 to 4 progressive chart of management styles:

1. Exploitative authoritarian: management by fear and coercion, where communication is top-down, decision-making

is done at the top with no shared processes, and superiors and subordinates are psychologically far apart.

2. Benevolent authoritarian: management by carrot rather than stick, but subordinates are still basically subservient; such information as flows upwards is mainly what the boss is thought to want to hear, and policy decisions are taken at the top, with only minor ones delegated to a lower level.

3. Consultative: management uses both carrot and stick and does try to talk to employees; communication flows both ways but is still somewhat limited upwards; important decisions are still taken top-down.

4. Participative: management provides economic rewards and is concerned to get employees involved in groups capable of making decisions; it sets challenging goals and works closely with employees to encourage high performance. Communication flows easily in both directions and sideways to peers; superiors and subordinates are psychologically close. Decision-making is done through participative processes: work groups are integrated into the formal structure of the organization by creating a series of overlapping groups with each linked to the rest of the organization by a 'linking pin' – preferably a team leader or departmental manager, who will be a member of both group and management.

Likert's research suggested that departments which were low in efficiency tended to be in the charge of 'job-centred' supervisors; that is, Taylorist managers who keep their subordinates busily engaged in a 'specified work cycle in a prescribed way and at a satisfactory rate as determined by time standards'.

Supervisors with the best record of performance tended to be 'employee-centred', to regard their chief task as dealing with people rather than work and who focused on building effective work groups that in turn were set high achievement goals. Such supervisors exercised general rather than detailed supervision of their subordinates and were more concerned with overall targets than with methods. They also allowed the maximum participation in decision-making.

In *New Ways of Managing Conflict*, Likert and his wife profile the System 4 Total Model Organization (System 4T), which adds certain characteristics to System 4, such as high levels of perform-ance goals, transmitted by leader to subordinates; a high level of skill and knowledge on the part of the leader; and the leader's capacity to provide planning, resources, equipment and help for subordinates. System 4T is the optimum Likert structure in terms of linkages and group working relationships, and he conceives it as the best means of dealing with conflict in an organization.

Likert argues that the nearer an organization approaches to System 4T, the more its productivity and profitability will improve and conflict be reduced. Beyond this, he also suggests a System 5 for the future, in which all authority on a hierarchy basis will disappear, such authority as individuals retain deriving only from their 'linking pin' roles and the overlapping of groups.

The basic principle behind the work of both Likert and McGregor is that effective modern organizations must see them-selves as interacting groups of people with supporting relation-ships to each other. The ideal goal is to achieve an organization in which the organization's objectives become of personal signifi-cance to everyone working in it. In pursuit of this, management must be a relative process, always adapting itself to the individual human beings who are led by it.

KEY WRITINGS

Likert, R. (1961) *New Patterns of Management*, New York: McGraw-Hill.

Likert, R. (1967) *The Human Organization: Its Management and Value*, New York: McGraw-Hill.

Likert, R. and Likert, J. G. (1976) *New Ways of Managing Conflict*, New York: McGraw-Hill.

34

DOUGLAS McGREGOR

(1906–1964)

Theory X and Theory Y: authoritarian vs participative management

US social psychologist specializing in human behaviour within organizations, and famous for his formulation of 'Theory X' (authoritarian management) and 'Theory Y' (participative management), first propounded in his 1960 book *The Human Side of Enterprise*. He was, says a recent book reassessing his importance in management thinking (*Douglas McGregor Revisited*), the first to apply the findings of behavioural science to the world of business: 'McGregor challenged managers to think of human organizations more as a biologist than a mechanic.'

For some years president of Antioch College, McGregor was professor of management at the Massachusetts Institute of Technology from 1954 until his death in 1964.

McGregor shared many of his ideas on human wants with Abraham Maslow (qv) and Rensis Likert (qv). Maslow experimented with Theory Y in a California electronics plant and concluded that it did not wholly work in practice. Further work on motivating human achievement which revealed Theory Y as insufficiently flexible was done after McGregor's death by David C. McClelland of Harvard.

However, in 1994 Robert H. Waterman Jr revealed in *Frontiers of Excellence* that in 1956 McGregor was invited by an executive of Procter & Gamble, David Swanson, who had been a student of McGregor's at MIT, to design a detergent plant in Augusta, Georgia, on Theory Y principles. Swanson had served with the US army in Korea and returned to civilian life convinced that military command-and-control structures were totally unsuitable for a business organization, which should be drawing out responsibility and potential in the individual.

The Augusta plant, designed for a non-hierarchical organization working in self-managed teams, was an immediate success. By the mid-1960s it was 30 per cent more productive than any other P&G plant. The company spread the principle through other plants and kept the story secret for 40 years, regarding it as a competitive advantage.

Since the mid-1990s, self-managed teams have become an accepted part of organizational change and empowerment. McGregor's legacy as a teacher and thinker influenced a whole generation of management theorists, including Charles Handy (qv) and Warren Bennis (qv). It has made him one of the most powerful, if under-recognized, gurus of the 20th century.

Douglas McGregor believed that the way an organization was run stemmed from the beliefs of its managers. 'Behind every managerial decision or action are assumptions about human nature and human behaviour,' he wrote in *The Human Side of Enterprise*, probably the most widely read and quoted of all the books on motivation in industry published since World War II.

The research behind Theory X and Theory Y was not original but, as McGregor acknowledged, it was synthesized and formulated from the ideas of others (including, as Peter Drucker has observed, those Drucker himself had presented in three early books: *Concept of the Corporation, The New Society* and *The Practice of Management*).

McGregor had already suggested the term Theory X to define a set of assumptions that had ruled management thinking since the writings of Henri Fayol. Theory X assumes that most people are lazy, dislike work and need a mixture of carrot and stick to perform; that they are basically immature, need direction and are incapable of taking responsibility. Theory Y assumes the opposite; that people actually have a psychological need to work and want achievement and responsibility – that they are adult, in fact. On this reading, Periclean Athens was a Theory Y society, Sparta a Theory X society.

McGregor believed that Theory X owed its origins to the banishment of Adam and Eve from Eden into a world where they were forced to work to survive. 'The stress that management places on productivity, on the concept of "a fair day's work", on the evils of featherbedding and restriction of output, on rewards for performance – while it has a logic in terms of the objectives of enterprise – reflects an underlying belief that management must counteract an inherent human tendency to avoid work.'

Like Maslow with his hierarchy of needs, McGregor identified a series of human wants in ascending order, from the most basic physiological urges through a desire for safety and security (and security in the workplace) to the 'social needs' such as belonging, acceptance by one's peers and the giving and receiving of affection. Above those again came the 'egoistic needs' – those that relate to an individual's self-esteem, his need for self-respect, self-confidence, autonomy, achievement, competence and knowledge; and to reputation, status, recognition and the respect of one's peers. Ultimately in McGregor's pyramid came the needs for self-fulfilment, for realizing one's individual potential and for continuing in self-development.

'Man is a wanting animal – as soon as one of his needs is satisfied, another appears in its place,' wrote McGregor in *The Human Side of Enterprise.* 'This process is unending. It continues from birth to death. Man continuously puts forth effort . . . to satisfy his needs.'

Since most modern managements by McGregor's time were providing relatively well for both physiological and safety needs, the motivational emphasis had shifted to social, egoistic and self-fulfilment needs. 'Unless there are opportunities at work to satisfy these higher-level needs, people will be deprived; and their behaviour will reflect this deprivation,' wrote McGregor.

If management continued to focus its attention on physiological needs, therefore, providing rewards was unlikely to be effective, and the only alternative under this philosophy would be reliance on the threat of punishment. Thus part of Theory X validates itself, 'but only because we have mistaken effects for causes'.

McGregor continues: 'The philosophy of management by direction and control – regardless of whether it is hard or soft – is inadequate to motivate because the human needs on which this approach relies are relatively unimportant motivators of behaviour in our society today. Direction and control are of limited value in motivating people whose important needs are social and egoistic . . . So long as the assumptions of Theory X continue to influence managerial strategy, we will fail to discover, let alone utilize, the potentialities of the average human being.'

Theory Y, the management approach designed to tap these potentialities, was based on McGregor's observations of the way management thinking had moved a considerable way from the traditional 'hard' approach and the 'soft' reaction that followed the Depression years. He formulated six basic assumptions for Theory Y:

1. 'The expenditure of physical and mental effort on work is as natural as play or rest. The average human being does not inherently dislike work. Depending upon controllable conditions, work may be a source of satisfaction (and will be voluntarily performed) or a source of punishment (and will be avoided if possible).

2. 'External control and the threat of punishment are not the only means for bringing about effort towards organizational objectives. Man will exercise self-direction and self-control in the service of objectives to which he is committed.

3. 'Commitment to objectives is a function of the rewards associated with their achievement. The most significant of such rewards, e.g. the satisfaction of ego and self-actualization needs, can be direct products of effort directed towards organizational objectives.

4. 'The average human being learns, under proper conditions, not only to accept but to seek responsibility.

5. 'The capacity to exercise a relatively high degree of imagination, ingenuity and creativity in the solution of

organizational problems is widely, not narrowly, distributed in the population.

6. 'Under the conditions of modern industrial life, the intellectual potentialities of the average human being are only
   partially utilized.'

Such assumptions, McGregor pointed out, had a deep implica-
tion for management. Where Theory X offered management an
easy scapegoat for failure – the innate nature and limitations of
its human resources – Theory Y placed all problems 'squarely in
the lap of management'. If employees were lazy or unwilling to
show initiative or responsibility, if they were indifferent or intran-
sigent, the fault lay in management methods. In other words,
McGregor was redefining the old military adage 'There are no
bad troops, only bad officers.'

McGregor admitted that Theory Y was not perfect and remained
to be tested in a variety of organizations. Abraham Maslow (qv)
found it to be wanting in a well-meaning experiment run on its
principles in a California electronics factory. Maslow believed it
placed too much of a burden on individuals who actually wanted
guidance, direction and some form of authority.

Peter Drucker has commented: 'It has now become clear that
Theory X and Theory Y are not, as McGregor maintained, theories about human nature . . . Ordinary, everyday experience teaches
us that the same people react quite differently to different circumstances. They may be lazy and resist work to the point of sabo-
taging it in one situation. They may be motivated to achievement
in another one. It is clearly not human nature nor personality
structure that is at issue.'

Drucker also referred to the work of David C. McClelland
of Harvard, especially his book *Motivating Economic Achievement*
(Free Press, 1969), who concluded that the desire to achieve is
conditioned largely by culture and experience, both of which
can be changed.

McGregor never claimed that Theory Y denied all need for
authority, only that it denied that authority was appropriate for
all purposes, including the goal of 'obtaining commitment to
objectives'.

'Theory Y assumes that people will exercise self-direction and
self-control in the achievement of organizational objectives to the

degree that they are committed to those objectives . . . Managerial policies and practices materially affect this degree of commitment.'

Put simply, McGregor believed that human beings were capable of far greater potential than the industrial management of his time could understand. Theory X denied even the existence of that potential; Theory Y challenged management 'to innovate, to discover new ways of organizing and directing human effort, even though we recognize that the perfect organization, like the perfect vacuum, is practically out of reach'.

History, starting with the Procter & Gamble plant in Augusta, Georgia, continues to vindicate the essential rightness and power of his thinking.

(All quotations from McGregor are from *The Human Side of Enterprise*, reproduced in *Organization Theory*, ed. D. S. Pugh (Penguin, 1990).)

KEY WRITINGS

McGregor, D. (1960) *The Human Side of Enterprise*, New York: McGraw-Hill.
McGregor, D. (1966) *Leadership and Motivation*, MIT Press.
McGregor, D. (1967) *The Professional Manager*, New York: McGraw-Hill.
Recommended reading: *Douglas McGregor Revisited*, by Gary Heil, Warren Bennis and Deborah C. Stephens, New York: Wiley, 2000.

35

ABRAHAM MASLOW

(1908–1970)

The 'hierarchy of needs' in motivation

New York-born behavioural scientist who has been called the greatest psychologist since Freud. Peter Drucker describes him as 'the father of humanist psychology': what he did, says leadership guru Warren Bennis, was to 'give man ownership over his human potentials'. Maslow invented the term 'hierarchy of needs' to account for the roots of human motivation in the workplace, identifying the physical and psychological essentials for satisfaction. He is still regarded today by many HR practitioners as the most influential thinker in the field of people management.

He trained at the University of Wisconsin and broke an academic career between 1947 and 1949 to work in industry, returning to teaching at Brandeis University, Massachusetts, where he became a professor and head of department. He then spent some further time in industry, studying Douglas McGregor's Theory Y in action at a California electronics factory, where he concluded that McGregor's theory, which he had much admired, did not work in reality because it ignored the need for the structure and certainties provided by the authoritarian Theory X.

Maslow's essential optimism about the good qualities of human nature was part of its time in the climate of

the postwar years, and his ideas were influential on other behavioural scientists such as Chris Argyris (qv), McGregor himself (qv), Rensis Likert (qv) and Frederick Herzberg (qv). He believed that enlightened management based on trust was 'the wave of the future' because the more educated and 'psychologically healthy' employees became, the less businesses would be able to function competitively if run on authoritarian lines. He conceded that this strategy needed time to prove itself, but concluded that human nature had been 'sold short' by authoritarian management.

Maslow's 'hierarchy of needs' postulated that once an individual's basic psychological needs had been satisfied – and these included not only warmth, food and sexual fulfilment, but also a safe, structured environment – the higher needs of love, esteem and fulfilment of personal potential would be released. His greatest insight was to realize that none of these wants is absolute; as soon as one is satisfied, the fact of its satisfaction ceases to be important.

The five-layer pyramid that Maslow used to illustrate his principle started with a broad base of bodily needs – such as food, oxygen, water, vitamins, activity, sleep, sex and avoiding pain – and progressed upwards through the need for safety and security, the need for love/belonging, the need for self-esteem and esteem by one's peers and, at the apex, the need for the self to grow and feel fulfilled. Maslow characterized the first four as 'deficit needs'; if you don't have enough of any of them, you feel it, but if you do have them, you feel no particular satisfaction and they cease to be motivating. At the fifth level, by contrast, which he called 'self-actualization', the needs become stronger as they are fed and as people strive to fulfil their potential.

In his 1961 book *Toward a Psychology of Being*, Maslow described self-actualizing people as being spontaneous and creative, not restricted by convention, tending to focus on problems outside themselves and having a clear ability to distinguish between the genuine and the phoney. But he reckoned that only about 2 per cent of the world's population were able to reach the 'peak experiences' of life through full self-actualization.

Peter Drucker challenged some of Maslow's assumptions in his classic work *Management: Tasks, Responsibilities, Practices* (1974), saying that:

> What Maslow did not see is that a want changes in the act of being satisfied. As the economic want becomes satisfied, that is, as people no longer have to subordinate every other human need and human value to getting the next meal, it becomes less and less satisfying to obtain more economic rewards. This does not mean that the economic rewards become less important. On the contrary, while the ability of the economic reward to provide a positive incentive diminishes, its capacity to create dissatisfaction, if disappointed, rapidly increases. In Herzberg's words, economic rewards cease to be 'incentives' and become 'hygiene factors'. If not properly taken care of – that is, if there is dissatisfaction with the economic rewards – they become deterrents.
>
> This we now know to be true of every one of Maslow's wants. As a want approaches satiety, its capacity to reward, and with it its power as an incentive, diminishes fast. But its capacity to deter, to create dissatisfaction, and to act as a disincentive, rapidly increases.

Drucker pointed out that once a need was satisfied, ever-greater incentives were needed to maintain the same level of satisfaction, and that in the economic sphere, the danger was that additional rewards would become progressively viewed as rights or entitlements.

Maslow was a profound influence on Douglas McGregor's development of 'Theory X and Theory Y' behaviour, and his experience in the California electronics industry proved valuable in applying practical research to McGregor's Theory Y proposition that most people want to work, achieve and take responsibility; in short, that they are naturally mature, responsible beings as opposed to the Theory X view of them as basically immature and in need of direction.

Maslow's discovery – in a company which believed wholeheartedly in Theory Y – was that even an organization composed of strong and mature individuals needs the security of some structure and some direction. He criticized McGregor, his mentor, for 'inhumanity' to the weak, the vulnerable and the immature, who could not take the burden of individual responsibility. Nevertheless, he remained a convinced advocate of the underlying soundness of Theory Y and his solution was that Theory X could and should be replaced by an improved version of Theory Y. This would be more demanding in many ways than the authoritarian prescription, because it required more of individuals.

By extension, as Drucker points out, this argument applies with even more force to flexible, free-form organizations, because these place a greater load on their members than do the traditional, control-and-command structures.

Maslow's work remains a key point of reference in the field of human resources. He was 40 years ahead of his time in anticipating the needs of the digital economy, in which human potential is now recognized to be the primary competitive advantage. In 1998 an early work of his, *Eupsychian Management* (the Greek word means ideal or enlightened), was reissued as *Maslow on Management*, with additional commentary by two other writers. In the main text, Maslow envisages ways of achieving the kind of self-managed society that he believed would develop among people who are highly committed to and identified with their work. It remains a goal worth striving to attain.

KEY WRITINGS

Maslow, A. H. (1961) *Toward a Psychology of Being*, Princeton, NJ: D. van Nostrand Co.; 3rd edition (1998) published by John Wiley, New York.
Maslow, A. H. (1970, 1987) *Motivation and Personality*, New York: Harper and Row.
Maslow, A. H. with Deborah C. Stephens and Gary Heil (1998) *Maslow on Management*, New York: Wiley.
Stephens, Deborah, ed. (2000) *The Maslow Business Reader*, New York: Wiley.

36

ELTON W. MAYO

(1880–1949)

Human relations in industry and respect for individuals

Australian-born Mayo is regarded as the founder of industrial sociology, particularly the 'human relations movement', based on his discoveries in the Hawthorne
experiments of 1927–1932 of what really motivates
workers to higher performance, although recent research
suggests that his findings may have been flawed by
ignoring an inconvenient part of the data.

A graduate of Adelaide University and a medical
student in London and Edinburgh, Mayo taught mental
and moral philosophy at the University of Queensland
between 1911 and 1919. In 1923 he emigrated to the
United States, where he worked first on a three-year
research project at a Pennsylvania textile mill, prior to
joining Harvard University as associate professor of industrial research in 1926.

Mayo spent most of his career at Harvard, ending up
as professor of industrial research in the Graduate School
of Business Administration. He was also a consultant on
industrial problems to the postwar British Labour government led by Clement Attlee.

Elton Mayo's most important finding was to identify the roots of work satisfaction as non-economic and to connect them more with the interest taken in a worker's performance than with financial reward. In this, he reversed the emphasis on the incentive of monetary reward which had been the conventional wisdom ever since the writings of F. W. Taylor. Workers rejected 'Taylorism', Mayo explained, because in spite of its aids to efficiency it was basically an imposed system, not one that took account of the employees' own views.

The vital importance of management-worker communication, a key Mayo discovery, laid the foundation for the work of many later management thinkers and writers, including Peters and Waterman (*In Search of Excellence*) and the 1950s school of sociologists headed by Chris Argyris, Frederick Herzberg and Abraham Maslow.

The Hawthorne experiments with which Mayo's name is for ever linked were named after Western Electric's Hawthorne Works in Chicago. They ran from 1927 to 1932 under Mayo's leadership (and a further five years after that), and were conducted by a team of Harvard scientists and between 75 and 100 investigators working with 20,000 Western Electric employees.

The experiments arose from an earlier series of tests by Western Electric which had involved changes in working conditions and produced unexpected results in employee performance. Two teams of workers took part in these tests, in which the lighting conditions for one group only were improved. Production in that group rose dramatically – but so it did in the group for which the lighting remained unchanged.

Mayo took this further, making as many as ten changes in working conditions such as shorter hours, varied rest-breaks and a number of incentives. Mayo's research team spent a great deal of time with the work groups – each consisting of six women – discussing the changes before they were put into effect. Output increased each time a change was made. Yet when the teams were asked to return to their original working conditions, with a 48-hour week, no incentives and no rest-breaks, output rose again – indeed, to the highest ever recorded at Hawthorne. Other significant results included a decline in absenteeism of 80 per cent.

The only explanation, Mayo concluded in one of his later

works, was that the employees had gained enormously in work satisfaction by the feeling that they were teams of individuals, not cogs in a machine, and by the communication between researchers and workers, leading to everyone feeling more valued and responsible for her performance and that of the group as a whole. This sense of cohesiveness and self-esteem was more important to performance than any number of improvements in the working environment.

It has recently been suggested, however, that Mayo deliberately distorted his conclusions by playing down the importance of the pay incentives that the Hawthorne test team had been offered for greater productivity. In their book *Management Innovators* (Oxford University Press, 1998), Daniel A. Wren and Ronald G. Greenwood claim that Mayo ignored the statement of the personnel manager at Hawthorne that 'economic and financial factors are of considerable importance in the test room. The employees are anxious for high earnings.'

This would have been understandable at any time, but particularly in the Depression, which by 1932 was having its most devastating effects. Richard Donkin, in his history of work, *Blood, Sweat and Tears* (Texere, 2001), says Mayo used the Hawthorne experiments to reinforce his own convictions about management-worker relations in the backlash against Taylorism, but given the financial incentives that were on offer he failed to establish a conclusive link between higher productivity and the workers suddenly feeling good about being consulted. 'Hawthorne occupies a tainted pedestal in industrial research,' says Donkin, though it undoubtedly made a case for human relations in the workplace, and the time was ripe for it.

Mythology being what it is in management thinking as in any other sphere of human susceptibility, Mayo's reputation as the godfather of the human relations school of management is unlikely to lose its hallowed status.

Although Mayo did not crystallize his findings until years after the Hawthorne experiments, a contemporary series of interviews in the Chicago works established an equally important discovery: that worker-management conflict may often be due less to the ostensible reasons for a dispute, such as tea-breaks or insufficient light, than to basic emotional attitudes. Workers were ruled by the 'logic of sentiment', thought Mayo, whereas managers were activated by the 'logic of cost and efficiency'. Thus, without understanding and compromise, conflict was inevitable.

The ultimate importance of the Hawthorne experiments was their demonstration, in Mayo's view, that the dour Taylorist philosophy of self-interest was disproved: that workers valued spontaneous cooperation and creative relationships among those with whom they worked, and would perform accordingly. 'The desire to stand well with one's fellows, the so-called human instinct of association, easily outweighs the merely individual interest and the logic of reasoning upon which so many spurious principles of management are based,' wrote Mayo in *The Social Problems of an Industrial Civilization*.

Mayo was not, however, against scientific management, for all that he debunked Taylor's rigid application of it. 'Observation – skill – experiment and logic – these must be regarded as the three stages of advancement,' he observed in the same book. Mayo believed that his findings disproved what he called the 'rabble hypothesis' of society as 'a horde of unorganized individuals', each of whom 'acts in a manner calculated to secure his self-preservation or self-interest'.

Two later sociological writers, D. C. Miller and W. H. Form, developed eight principal conclusions from Mayo's researches in their book *Industrial Sociology*, quoted in J. A. C. Brown's *The Social Psychology of Industry* (1954):

1. Work is a group activity.
2. The social world of the adult is primarily patterned about work activity.
3. The need for recognition, security and sense of belonging is more important in determining a worker's morale and productivity than the physical conditions under which he works.
4. A complaint is not necessarily an objective recital of facts; it is commonly a symptom manifesting disturbance of an individual's status position.
5. The worker is a person whose attitudes and effectiveness are conditioned by social demands from both inside and outside the work plant.
6. Informal groups within the work plant exercise strong social controls over the work habits and attitudes of the individual worker.

192

7. The change from an established to an adaptive society . . . tends continually to disrupt the social organization of a work plant and industry generally.
8. Group collaboration does not occur by accident; it must be planned for and developed. If group collaboration is achieved, the work relations within a work plant may reach a cohesion which resists the disrupting effects of adaptive society.

Another writer on industrial psychology in the 1950s, Gordon Rattray Taylor, estimated from his observations of firms which had put similar principles into practice that by using such methods Britain could expand its national income by 50 per cent within five years without additional capital investment, and that the price of many manufactured goods could be reduced by a third. Needless to say, the experiment has never been carried out on a sufficiently wide scale to prove or disprove his theory.

Mayo's discovery of the importance of the peer group at work led him to conclude that within each formal organization existed many informal ones which could be encouraged to greater productivity by being led to do it themselves, through interest and respect on the part of their managers.

More profoundly, Mayo believed that by creating such an atmosphere of spontaneous cooperation in industry, society at large could help to combat the postwar collapse in traditional values. This, for him, remained one of the most important tasks facing a manager. The whole human relations movement, as engendered by Mayo's work, became concerned with discovering, through scientific research, how to harness the motivation and commitment of individuals to corporate goals.

Even if flawed, Mayo's contribution to management thinking was seminal. It revealed the importance, in hard bottom-line terms, of human emotions, reactions and respect to the business of managing others. It also pioneered the whole concept of proper management-worker communication – again a new idea because of the respect for the individual it required between bosses and workers.

Management, Mayo demonstrated once and for all, could only succeed in leading an organization's employees if the workers, in their informal groups, accepted that leadership without reservation. In his own words, Mayo identified the importance of the Hawthorne findings as specifying, quite clearly, that the relation of working groups to management was one of the fundamental problems of large-scale industry. Organizing teamwork – developing and sustaining cooperation – had to be a major preoccupation of management. Above all, management needed to think less about what 'we' wanted to get across to 'them' than to listen to what 'they' wanted to know and would be receptive to.

'The human relations prescription, though rarely practised, remains the classic formula,' wrote Peter Drucker in 1973. It is still too rarely practised, though every management pays lip service to it.

KEY WRITINGS

Mayo, E. (1933) *The Human Problems of an Industrial Civilization*, London: Macmillan.
Mayo, E. (1949) *The Social Problems of an Industrial Civilization*, London: Routledge and Kegan Paul.

37

HENRY MINTZBERG

(b. 1939)

How strategy is made and how managers use their time

Canadian-born professor of management studies at McGill University, Montreal, and professor of organization (until 1999) at INSEAD, the international business school at Fontainebleau, France. His immensely influential work falls into three main categories: strategy-making; what managers actually do with their time (as opposed to what they think they do) and how their mental processes work (the 'right brain, left brain' theories); and how organizations design themselves to suit their needs.

Mintzberg, originally an engineering graduate of McGill who later studied at the Sloan School of Management, Massachusetts Institute of Technology, is one of the most accessible of management writers, with an easy style and refreshingly iconoclastic approach. He has written over 100 monographs and articles as well as nine books. His reputation is high among those who study the arts of strategic management and planning, about which he wrote a typically provocative history in 1994 entitled *The Rise and Fall of Strategic Planning*.

His teaching work is more international and multicultural than that of any other leading guru. He helped set up a cooperative venture by five business schools in Canada, England, Japan, France and India which aims to create a next-generation programme of management

education for practising managers in the context of their own jobs and the needs of their organizations. Mintzberg's view of conventional MBA courses is that they have minimal value in the real world of business: he likes to observe that 'you can't create a manager in the classroom.'

Mintzberg's reputation was made by *The Nature of Managerial Work*, published in 1973, and the article in *Harvard Business Review* in 1975 which brought it to a wider public ('The Manager's Job: Folklore and Fact'). In researching the book, he spent a week in each of five middle- to large-sized organizations – a consulting firm, a technology company, a hospital, a consumer goods company and a school system – observing how chief executive officers used their time, as well as reporting other studies of managers lower down the line, ranging from factory supervisors to hospital administrators.

Far from confirming any grand all-embracing role, such as Peter Drucker proposed in his analogy of the manager as orchestra conductor, Mintzberg found that a manager's time is constantly being fragmented by interruptions, but that these appeared to produce an adrenalin of their own and to convince the manager that he was achieving a great deal through responding to the pressures of the job over a great many issues, even in summary and incomplete fashion.

'Jumping from topic to topic, he [the manager] thrives on interruptions and, more often than not, disposes of items in ten minutes or less. Though he may have fifty projects going, all are delegated. He juggles them, checking each one periodically before sending it back into orbit.'

The four definitions of managerial work laid down by Henri Fayol in 1916 – planning, organization, coordination and control – have very little bearing on actual daily routine, Mintzberg discovered. Yet, as he explained in the *Harvard Business Review* article condensing the essence of his 1973 book: 'Without a proper answer, how can we teach management? How can we design planning or information systems for managers? How can we improve the practice of management at all?'

Half the activities engaged in by Mintzberg's five CEOs lasted less than nine minutes and only 10 per cent exceeded one hour in duration. 'The chief executives met a steady stream of callers and mail from the moment they arrived in the morning until they left in the evening . . . A diary study of 160 British top and middle managers found that they worked for half an hour or more without interruption about once every two days.

'The traditional literature notwithstanding, the job of managing does not breed reflective planners; the manager responds to stimuli as an individual who is conditioned by his job to prefer live to delayed action.'

The manager also spends as much time dealing with people outside as inside the company, Mintzberg found. 'He shuns written reports, skims periodicals and merely processes his mail.' He prefers to pick up his information verbally, at meetings and on the telephone, and indeed relies heavily on gossip and hearsay, inside and outside the company, to keep him up to date.

Indeed, Mintzberg concluded in a memorable finding, 'the executives I was studying – all very competent by any standard – were fundamentally indistinguishable from their counterparts of 100 years ago (or 1,000 years ago, for that matter). The information they need differs, but they seek it in the same way; by word of mouth. Their decisions concern modern technology, but the procedures they use are still the same as the procedures of the 19th-century manager.

'Managers seem to cherish "soft" information, especially gossip, hearsay and speculation. Why? The reason is its timeliness: today's gossip may be tomorrow's fact. The manager who is not accessible for the telephone call informing him that his biggest customer was seen golfing with his main competitor may read about a dramatic drop in the next quarterly report. But by then it's too late.'

Furthermore, 'managers apparently do not write down much of what they hear. Thus the strategic data-bank of the organization is not in the memory of its computers but in the minds of its managers.'

Out of all this mass of material, which baldly contradicted most conventional wisdom about a manager's activities, Mintzberg identified ten principal managerial roles, grouped into three main areas – interpersonal, informational and decisional.

Interpersonal roles, in his definition, comprise three functions essential to a manager: those of figurehead, leader and liaison. The first two are self-explanatory (the figurehead performs ceremonial roles such as making presentation speeches, meeting visiting dignitaries and lunching important clients; the leader hires, trains and motivates employees) while the third covers a manager's network of relationships within and without the organization, outside his vertical chain of command, and mainly in pursuit of building up a private information system. 'Managers spend as much time with peers and other people outside their units as they do with their own subordinates, and surprisingly little time with their own superiors.'

Informational roles involve those of monitor (keeping tabs on what's going on); disseminator (transmitting essential information to subordinates); and spokesman (the public voice of the unit). 'The manager emerges as the nerve centre of his organizational unit. He may not know everything, but he typically knows more than any member of his staff . . . Many of these contacts are with other managers of equal status, who are themselves nerve centres in their own organization. In this way the manager develops a powerful database of information. The processing of information is a key part of the manager's job . . . In large part, communication is his work.'

Decisional roles, not surprisingly, are described as the most important. Mintzberg divides this category into four – entrepreneur, disturbance handler, resource allocator and negotiator.

As entrepreneur, the manager 'seeks to improve his unit and to adapt it to changing conditions', sometimes juggling as many as 50 different projects at a time, such as initiating a PR campaign, dealing with a poor cash-flow position, reorganizing a weak department or looking after the various stages of an acquisition. As disturbance handler, the manager reacts to events and change beyond his foresight or control: a strike, the bankruptcy of a major customer or the failure of a key supplier.

It is here that Mintzberg parts company most strikingly with Drucker's comparison of the manager's role to that of an orchestral conductor. 'In effect, every manager must spend a good part of his time responding to high-pressure disturbances.'

As resource allocator, the manager must decide how best to deploy the assets of the organization, including its human assets and, most importantly, the manager's own time. As negotiator, he is responsible for all the variety of decisions involved in dealing with other individuals; whether these concern a difficult sales contract, the threat of a strike, staff grievances or attracting a new star player to the team.

All the variables contained within these permutations led Mintzberg to conclude that management is an art rather than a teachable science, and that it requires a continuous process of self-education and assessment. He also pointed out that the roles are part of an integrated whole and cannot easily be separated when, for example, efforts are made to split a managerial job into internal and external roles, though not all managers, he found, give equal attention to all roles. (Sales managers tend to emphasize the interpersonal side, production managers the decisional roles and staff managers the informational roles.)

In summarizing the theme of his findings for the *Harvard Business Review* in 1975, Mintzberg said the pressures of his job 'drive the manager to be superficial in his actions – to overload himself with work, encourage interruption, respond quickly to every stimulus, seek the tangible and avoid the abstract, make decisions in small increments and do everything abruptly . . . The danger in managerial work is that (managers) will respond to every issue equally (and that means abruptly) and that they will never work the tangible bits and pieces of informational input into a comprehensive picture of their work.'

Management schools, he concluded, would only begin 'The serious training of managers when skill training takes a serious place next to cognitive learning . . . Cognitive learning no more makes a manager than it does a swimmer. The latter will drown the first time he jumps into the water if his coach never takes him out of the lecture hall, gets him wet and gives him feedback on his performance.'

Managerial skills such as developing peer relationships, resolving conflicts, handling information and negotiations need to be practised, and the manager should be introspective enough about his work to go on learning on the job.

'No job is more vital to our society than that of the manager,' declared Mintzberg. 'It is the manager who determines whether our institutions serve us well or whether they squander our talents and resources. It is time to strip away the folklore about managerial work, and time to study it realistically so that we can begin the difficult task of making significant improvements in its performance.'

From analysing the components of managerial work, Mintzberg moved on to study the design of organizations in *The Structuring of Organizations* (1979) and *Structures in Fives: Designing Effective Organizations* (1983).

He concluded that most organizational structures fall into five basic categories: simple structure, machine bureaucracy, professional bureaucracy, divisionalized form and adhocracy – a term recently appropriated and redefined by Robert Waterman to describe the ideal conditions for a flexible, innovation–inducing organizational structure. (Waterman, author of *The Renewal Factor* and co-author with Tom Peters of the massively selling *In Search of Excellence*, acknowledges Mintzberg as one of his own most influential gurus.)

Mintzberg's simple-structure organization is just that: a centralized, perhaps autocratic arrangement typical of the entrepreneur-founded company. There will be only a small hierarchy, and control is exercised by a strong chief executive. It is the sort of organization that attracts strong loyalty because of its simplicity, flexibility, informality and 'sense of mission' – but it is desperately vulnerable to the accidents of fate: 'one heart attack can literally wipe out the organization's prime coordinating mechanism.'

The machine bureaucracy, by contrast, gains its strength from what Mintzberg calls its 'technostructure' – its financial controllers, strategic planners, production experts. It is best at mass-production tasks and is characterized by many layers of management and formal procedures. It tends to be slow on its feet when reacting to change, and poor at motivating its employees. A large car-assembly plant would be a typical example.

The professional bureaucracy is built less on hierarchy than on shared expertise – it might be a professional practice of some kind, a school or a hospital. Its administration is governed by standards set by independent professional bodies. It will tend to be more democratic and more highly motivated – among the professionals, if not their support workers – than the machine bureaucracy, but with its lines of authority less clearly set out.

The divisionalized form is reflected in the typical large

multinational or industrial corporation where a small central core controls key guidelines for a number of otherwise autonomous units. Essentially, Mintzberg sees this as an off-shoot of the machine bureaucracy – several machine bureaucracies, in fact, operating under a central staff. It may have started life as a single machine bureaucracy which hived off into divisions as a result of geographic market diversifications.

The adhocracy is most often found in the new technology industries, which need constantly to innovate and respond quickly to changing markets. It is characterized by flexible, cross-border teams collaborating on specific projects as required, and among Mintzberg's five categories of organization 'shows the least reverence for the classical principles of management'.

Mintzberg's adhocracy has two subsections: the operating adhocracy, a creative unit working in the competitive marketplace, such as an advertising agency or software development company, and the administrative adhocracy, which may be research-based, like NASA.

Within Mintzberg's five basic organizational structures are five common elements: the 'strategic apex' of top executives (strongest in the simple structure); the 'technostructure' of key individuals in finance, training, personnel, planning and production (strongest in the machine bureaucracy); the 'operating core' of those at the coalface of the organization (nurses and teachers in a professional bureaucracy, buyers and sales staff in a manufacturing machine bureaucracy); the 'middle line' of managers who link the strategic apex with the operating core (strongest in the divisionalized form); and finally, the 'support staff', who work in areas such as R&D, salaries, public relations and so on. In a manufacturing company their role, though important, is not the fulcrum that it is in the adhocracy, which relies on the quality of its R&D.

'If Simple Structure and Machine Bureaucracy were yesterday's structures, and Professional Bureaucracy and the Divisionalized Form are today's, then Adhocracy is clearly tomorrow's,' writes Mintzberg. But he does not rule out further evolutions of structure as different influences exert their pull, and he has identified one for the future, where ideological influences are involved, which he calls the 'missionary'. Examples include the Israeli kibbutz and the Japanese manufacturing company.

In 1989 Mintzberg distilled 20 years of his thinking into *Mintzberg on Management*, the best introduction to his work, which also includes a chapter on 'crafting strategy' – how this important managerial function works – and the concept that helped shape his understanding of the process, the different part played by the right and left hemispheres of the brain in managerial work.

Briefly, Mintzberg has established a theory that successful chief executives favour the right-hand or intuitive side of their brain more than the left-hand or analytical side. Creative strategy, he argues, requires 'right brain' thinking and there is more than logical planning to the effective management of an organization. 'Effective managers seem to revel in ambiguity, in complex, mysterious systems with relatively little order.'

The split-brain theory of right (intuitive) versus left (logical) thinking originated in the work of neurosurgeon Roger Sperry, a 1981 Nobel laureate, but Mintzberg was the first to introduce the concept to management.

He supports his theory with some general observations of managers at work, while emphasizing that, as a theory, it still remains largely in the realm of speculation.

Nevertheless, he is convinced that 'the important policy-level processes required to manage an organization rely to a considerable extent on the faculties identified with the brain's right hemisphere.'

And in typically iconoclastic style, he adds that if his suggestions turn out to be valid, teachers of management had better 'revise drastically some of their notions about management education. Unfortunately, the revolution in that sphere over the last 15 years – while it has brought so much of value – has virtually consecrated the modern management school to the worship of the left hemisphere . . . There is a need for a new balance in our schools, the balance that the best of human brains can achieve, between the analytic and the intuitive.'

In recent years, Mintzberg has been conducting further research on what managers do, spending time observing them at work in jobs ranging from the chief executives of Britain's National Health Service and the Royal Bank of Canada to the warden of a Canadian mountain park and the conductor of the Winnipeg Symphony Orchestra. Most leading management writers, he comments, tend to emphasize one part of the manager's job – as doer, thinker, leader, controller – to the exclusion of the others. Even in the list of tasks or roles found in classic management literature, 'the integrated work of managing' still gets lost in the process of describing it.

To overcome this, Mintzberg constructed a model of managerial activity 'from the inside out', set out as concentric circles from 'the largely cerebral roles of conceiving and scheduling at the core to the more tangible roles of getting things done', and then laid his fieldwork observations over this model.

'From the outside (or most tangible level) in, managers can manage action *directly*, they can manage *people* to encourage them to take the necessary actions, and they can manage *information* to influence the people in turn to take their necessary actions. In other words, the ultimate objective of managerial work, and of the functioning of any organizational unit, the taking of action, can be managed directly, indirectly through people, or even more indirectly by information through people.

'The manager can thus choose to intervene at any of the three levels, but once done, he or she must work through the remaining ones . . . The level a given manager favours becomes an important determinant of his or her managerial style, especially distinguishing so-called "doers" who prefer direct action, "leaders" who prefer working through people, and "administrators" who prefer to work by information' ('Rounding Out the Manager's Job', *Sloan Management Review*, Fall 1994).

In his initial study of chief executives, Mintzberg found that perhaps 40 per cent of their time was devoted exclusively to communicating, just gaining and sharing information. 'In other words, the job of managing is fundamentally one of processing information, notably by talking and especially by listening.'

Mintzberg's long-held scepticism about management education controversially boiled over in a 2004 book, *Managers Not MBAs*, which argued that conventional MBA programmes, focusing as they do on case-study analysis, leave graduates with an inadequate idea of real management practice and may even have a corrupting effect on it. He went so far as to declare: 'No one should be allowed out of a conventional MBA programme without having a skull and crossbones stamped on his or her forehead over the words: Warning, NOT prepared to manage.'

KEY WRITINGS

Mintzberg, H. (1973, 1980) *The Nature of Managerial Work*, New York: Harper and Row.

Mintzberg, H. (1979) *The Structuring of Organizations*, New Jersey: Prentice-Hall.

Mintzberg, H. (1983) *Structures in Fives: Designing Effective Organizations,* Jersey: Prentice-Hall.

Mintzberg, H. (1989) *Mintzberg on Management*, New York: Free Press; London: Collier Macmillan.

Mintzberg, H. (1994) *The Rise and Fall of Strategic Planning*, New York: Free Press; London: Prentice-Hall.

Mintzberg, H. (1994) 'Rounding Out the Manager's Job', *Sloan Management Review*, Vol. 36, No. 1.

Mintzberg, H. (1996) 'Managing Government, Governing Management', Cambridge, Mass.: *Harvard Business Review* (May/June).

Mintzberg, H. (1996) 'Musings on Management', Cambridge, Mass.: *Harvard Business Review* (July/Aug).

Mintzberg, H. et al. (2004) *Strategy Bites Back*, London: FT/Prentice-Hall.

Mintzberg, H. (2004) *Managers Not MBAs*, London: FT/Prentice-Hall.

38

KENICHI OHMAE

(b. 1943)

Lessons from Japanese global business strategy

Japan's only world–class management guru, Kenichi Ohmae is the former head of McKinsey's Tokyo office and a leading international exponent of global business strategy.

Ohmae, who holds a doctorate in nuclear engineering from MIT, joined McKinsey in 1972. He has published around 30 books and articles on strategy and is renowned for the insights he offers into Japanese strategic thinking and its relationship to Japan's competitive strength in world markets.

In Ohmae's view, Western management thinkers have rarely succeeded in analysing Japanese strategic management styles, focusing instead on tactics like quality circles and company songs. There is a failure, Ohmae considers, to recognize the most fundamental difference between Eastern and Western strategy – that Japanese companies plan for the long term, Western ones for short-term profits.

Ohmae's two most influential books are *The Mind of the Strategist*, first published in 1982, and *Triad Power* (1985), in which he argued that companies which fail to establish themselves inside all three major trading blocs – Europe, the US and the Pacific Rim – become fatally vulnerable to competition from those which do so. The 'three Cs' – commitment, competitiveness and creativity – form his prescription for success in the triad. *The Mind of the Strategist*, subtitled in its first edition *The Art of Japanese Business*, is a highly readable exploration of techniques that can be developed to match the mixture of analysis and intuition which many Japanese business leaders bring to their strategic planning.

Following the publication of *In Search of Excellence* by two of his US McKinsey colleagues, Tom Peters and Robert Waterman, Ohmae embarked on his own study of excellent companies for the Japanese market.

A colleague of Ohmae's at McKinsey summed up his approach as: 'He questions everything. He's always asking "Why?".' His 1990 work, *The Borderless World*, predicted the sweep of globalization and reinforced his gadfly reputation with its bold contentions, among them his view that the trade imbalance between the US and Japan is an 'illusion created by accounting systems that are tragically out of date'.

In 1995 he left McKinsey to enter local politics in Tokyo, and published *The End of the Nation State*, a title that may, in the light of the armed struggles in central and eastern Europe, prove as premature as Francis Fukuyama's *The End of History*.

Ohmae is professor of public policy at UCLA and dean of his own graduate school of management in Japan. He is active in advising Asian governments and Chinese regional administrators as well as multinational corporations around the world. Internationally, his many educational commitments include board membership of the Center for Advanced Studies for Management at the University of Pennsylvania's top-rated Wharton School.

His latest book, *The Next Global Stage* (2005), analyses such borderless 'platforms' for economic progress as the spread of the English language and software programs and examines corporate strategy in a virtual world where customers, competitors and companies themselves are harder to identify.

Of all the scores of books produced by management gurus since World War II, Kenichi Ohmae's *The Mind of the Strategist* has a good claim to be the most practical teaching aid to the development of higher management skills. His objective was to show how outstanding strategists – who in Japan often lack a formal business education – go about developing the ideas that solve problems and create opportunities for their companies. It is less a formula than a set of concepts and approaches which can help anyone to develop this valuable mental agility.

What business strategy is all about, says Ohmae, 'what distinguishes it from all other kinds of business planning, is . . . competitive advantage.' Corporate strategy, he argues, implies an attempt 'to alter a company's strength relative to that of its competitors in the most efficient way'.

Intuition and insight, in Ohmae's view, are more effective keys to successful strategy than rational analysis, though this has its place in the process. 'In what I call the mind of the strategist, insight and a consequent drive for achievement, often amounting to a sense of mission, fuel a thought process which is basically creative and intuitive rather than rational,' he writes.

He defines creative insight as 'the ability to combine, synthesize or reshuffle previously unrelated phenomena in such a way that you get more out of the emergent whole than you have put in'. If creativity cannot be taught, he maintains, it can certainly be consciously cultivated. How it can be cultivated in people with no natural talent for strategy, or in a corporate culture at odds with creative thinking, forms the core of Ohmae's book.

An earlier book, *The Corporate Strategist* (1975) attempted to do it in a specifically Japanese context. *The Mind of the Strategist* is larded with Japanese case studies – how Honda, Toyota or Matsushita, for instance, created new markets or challenged successful competitors – but its application is universal.

The book is organized under three main headings: 'The Art of Strategic Thinking', 'Building Successful Strategies' and 'Modern Strategic Realities'. The first explores the basic mental processes involved – dissecting a problem or situation into its constituent parts; asking the right 'solution-oriented' questions; constructing 'issue diagrams' and 'profit diagrams' to facilitate getting to the right diagnosis.

Ohmae identifies the 'four routes to strategic advantage' – strategy based on a company's key factors for success in its capability to increase market share and profitability; strategy based on exploiting any relative superiority; strategy based on aggressive initiatives, challenging accepted assumptions; and strategy based on 'strategic degrees of freedom' (SDF) – development of innovations such as new markets or products.

All four options are examined in depth with case studies drawn from Japanese industry. As an example of aggressive initiative, he cites Toyota's Taiichi Ohno questioning the need to stockpile large quantities of components for the production line. Ohno's question eventually led to the introduction of 'just-in-time', and a revolution in production systems worldwide.

'If, instead of accepting the first answer, one . . . persists in asking "Why?" four or five times in succession, one will certainly get to the guts of the issue, where fundamental bottlenecks and problems lie.'

Strategic degrees of freedom also require the recognition of changes in the users' (customers') objective function (such as a preference for compact physical size in stereo equipment over performance measured by power output – part of Sony's rise in the market – or the perception by Honda and other car companies that many customers were switching from speed and prestige to convenience, economy and utility).

'Stretching one's mind to find the SDF by which the new objectives can be satisfied is one way to become a pioneer in the new-business game,' Ohmae observes.

Ohmae advises trainee strategists not to worry overmuch about details that seem to threaten their plans. Write down each point of uncertainty, he counsels, and assess its positive or negative outcome. If the overall result won't be affected by a few negative factors, follow the example of Japanese entrepreneurs such as Konosuke Matsushita and Soichiro Honda and persist with execution of the plan.

Responsiveness to changing customer objectives lies at the root of Ohmae's system for constructing a business strategy. His three points of the 'strategic triangle' are the corporation (its strengths, weaknesses and resources), the customer and the competition.

'Customer-based strategies are the basis of all strategy,' asserts Ohmae. He is convinced that a corporation's foremost concern

208

should be the interest of its customers as opposed to that of its shareholders or other parties. 'In the long run the corporation that is genuinely interested in its customers is the one that will be interesting to investors.'

Ohmae's book goes on to analyse competitive advantage by price, volume and cost and their effect on profitability. 'If, for example, you can get a better price because of better design, you may be able to achieve better profit performance than your competitors.'

Having set out strategic mechanisms for single businesses, Ohmae then integrates them into a corporate structure, looking at such techniques as Product Portfolio Management (PPM), a corporate idea for large, diverse businesses, based on the principles of managing an investment portfolio.

In the 'Strategic Realities' section, Ohmae set his planning process against five 'key economic trends' which he believed would have an important impact on business strategies in the 1980s. In 1982, these were:

1. Continuing low growth
2. Market maturity and strategic stalemate
3. Uneven distribution of resources (e.g. Opec oil)
4. Growing international complexities
5. Irreversible inflation

Ohmae listed seven major changes that he thought likely to influence business strategies in the 1990s:

1. A shift from labour-intensive to capital-intensive industries
2. A shift from multinational to 'multi-local' companies
3. A shift in the fixed to variable cost ratio
4. A shift from steel to electronics-based industries
5. A shift in business unit definition
6. A shift from international to local financial management
7. A shift to a coordinated corporate value system

Ohmae's iconoclastic books on global business strategy have made him an international celebrity on the lecture circuit. He says that he is now more interested in 'society, social systems and large corporate activities on a global scale . . . Interdependence is the key to making our world work.'

The Borderless World (1990) had an important message for large companies which remains even more relevant over a decade later. 'Too few managers,' says Ohmae, 'consciously try to set plans and build organizations as if they see all key customers equidistant from the corporate centre . . . The word "overseas" has no place in Honda's vocabulary because it sees itself as equidistant from all key customers.'

In *The Invisible Continent* (2000), Ohmae elaborates on this theme by postulating that to be successful in the new economic environment set by the Internet and other global changes, business organizations needed to be able to operate in four different dimensions: the familiar visible world of local dealings; the borderless, global interconnection of businesses and customers that was developing even before the Internet accelerated it; the dimension of electronic trading and financial transactions; and 'the dimension of high multiples' – the effect that markets and investors had on the new economy, in many cases wildly over-valued, as history was soon to bear out.

Competition in this new world, Ohmae writes, is 'no longer definable in any predictable way', but it will become fairer, he contends, because the consumer will choose the winners and losers 'in a purer way than ever before'.

KEY WRITINGS

Ohmae, K. (1982, 1983) *The Mind of the Strategist*, New York: McGraw-Hill; London: Penguin Business Library.

Ohmae, K. (1985) *Triad Power: The Coming Shape of Global Competition*, New York: Free Press.

Ohmae, K. (1990) *The Borderless World*, New York: HarperBusiness; London: Collins.

Ohmae, K. (1995) *The End of the Nation State*, London: Collins.

Ohmae, K. (2000) *The Invisible Continent*, London: Nicholas Brealey.

Ohmae, K. (2005) *The Next Global Stage*, New Jersey: Wharton School Publishing.

39

RICHARD T. PASCALE

(b. 1938)

Continuous renewal in organizations

Leading business consultant, associate fellow of Oxford University and for 20 years a member of the faculty at Stanford University's Graduate Business School, Pascale's comparative research into US and Japanese companies in the 1970s contributed to his important role in developing, in collaboration with McKinsey, the famous 'Seven-S' framework of guiding management concepts. Tom Peters and Robert H. Waterman Jr, who were later to deploy this tool in their record-selling book *In Search of Excellence*, were two of the McKinsey team involved.

The 'hard-S' factors were strategy, structure and systems; the 'soft-S' factors – at which Japanese companies excelled – were style, shared values or 'superordinate goals', skills and staff. Superordinate goals were the hidden key to the power of the soft S factors, the glue, in Pascale's description, that held the other six parts of the framework together.

Pascale turned his research, with co-author Anthony Athos, into a hugely influential bestseller in 1981, a year ahead of *Excellence*. *The Art of Japanese Management* used the Seven-S framework to illuminate brilliantly the differences in management culture between Japan and the

US, encapsulated in close-up studies of Matsushita Electric and ITT and their respective chief executives' management styles.

In the late 1980s Pascale moved to a new perspective on management priorities in a world where nothing could be safely predicted except chaos and discontinuity. His powerful book *Managing on the Edge* (1990) examined how underlying paradigms or habits of thought in organizations filter and subtly distort a full understanding of change.

A central theme of the book, which was hailed by the *Financial Times* as more intellectually stimulating than *In Search of Excellence*, is that the ultimate, largely ignored task of management is one of creating and breaking paradigms, and that success in organizations breeds failure unless there is a system in place that constantly encourages debate, even contention and conflict, leading to a process of continued renewal.

From his San Francisco base, Pascale has contributed a number of key articles to *Harvard Business Review* in recent years, as well as a BBC television series and video course on corporate transformation. As a visiting scholar at New Mexico's Santa Fe Institute during the 1990s, he became involved in leading-edge work on complex adaptive systems, those ecological phenomena of living organisms found in every natural environment from the cosmos to the garden pond. He went on to use living-systems models in his work as a consultant to such corporations as Shell, BP, Hewlett-Packard and Sears, as well as the US army.

All this study and experience is distilled in *Surfing the Edge of Chaos*, his much-heralded book of 2000, in which he sets out to present a radical new management model based on 'the nature of nature'. He is convinced, he said in an interview that year, that we are now in 'the century of the living sciences' and that living systems are particularly suited to the workings of the digital economy. As a management theory, he believes it will last 'at least 30 years and perhaps 100'.

The Art of Japanese Management hit its moment precisely, as did *In Search of Excellence* a year later. US business leaders were increasingly worried about the growing power of Japanese companies and the competitive edge they were gaining in Western markets. The book that could crack the Japanese secret for them was bound to become a bestseller.

Pascale and Athos identified not only the reasons for Japanese competitive excellence but what enabled organizations in Japan to continue performing to superior standards over time. The answer was the Seven-S model, and how the best Japanese enterprises used the Western managerial 'hard-S' levers to a more productive purpose by allying them with the 'soft-S' levers.

In one of the most gripping narratives to be found in management literature, Pascale and Athos held a mirror up in turn to leading exemplars of the two business cultures – Matsushita Electric, run by its founder Konosuke Matsushita, and ITT, then managed by the formidable hard man of American business, Harold Geneen.

Like Peters and Waterman after them, Pascale and Athos found that many of the best-performing US companies that had sustained their vitality over time were just as efficient as the Japanese at synchronizing hard and soft-S values. 'The best firms link their purposes and ways of realizing them to human values as well as to economic measures like profit and efficiency,' they observed.

Remarking that many observers of the Japanese phenomenon tended to view it through American cultural filters and therefore assumed the soft-S factors to be mere froth, the authors produced a memorable image: 'That "froth" has the power of the Pacific.'

In particular, Pascale and Athos were the first to single out the importance of 'superordinate goals' or shared values in providing an organization with a compelling purpose or vision. This insight laid the foundation of today's concept of vision statements. The book analyses superordinate goals in relationship to the company in six different contexts:

- As an entity
- External markets

- Internal operations
- Employees
- Society and the State
- Culture, including religion

In their study of the two multinationals, Matsushita and ITT, Pascale and Athos drew comparisons in such areas as marketing, financial methods, research, strategic planning policies and – the key factors – in the styles of management practised by Konosuke Matsushita and Harold Geneen.

The authors found the US company generally comparable with the Japanese one as far as hard-S factors were concerned. The crucial difference lay in the soft-S areas: in consequence, they suggested, US companies tended to be wasteful of human resources while the Japanese, as is natural to their culture of interdependence and consensus, have a far more productive and collaborative boss/subordinate relationship.

The originality of the book lay in its holistic approach and cultural perspective on management. This laid the groundwork for much subsequent writing on corporate culture. *The Art of Japanese Management* continues to be essential reading.

Pascale's first major solo book, *Managing on the Edge*, proved just as important to management thinking in its time. Like Peters' *Thriving on Chaos*, it addressed the need for a radical reappraisal of conventional management wisdom, especially in the area of managing change and disruption in the business environment.

Although Pascale had worked with Peters and Waterman prior to *In Search of Excellence*, he came to feel that *Excellence* and other books like it were shallow and had resulted in a number of management fads that failed to address the needs of managers wanting to develop and maintain excellence within their organizations.

Managing on the Edge, subtitled *How the Smartest Companies Use Conflict to Stay Ahead*, took the decline of successful corporations as its point of departure and examined how underlying paradigms or mindsets blind managements to the first weak signals of change. A central premise of the book was that the ultimate, and largely ignored, task of management is one of creating and breaking paradigms. Constructive use of contention,

215

Pascale argued, coupled with persistent self-questioning, is one of the most effective ways of doing this.

Pascale's thesis was that success breeds failure unless there is a system that constantly encourages debate and thus leads to a process of continued organizational renewal. Excellent organizations often persist with perceptions formed in the period of their greatest success and never question these orthodoxies. Their great strengths become the roots of weakness because they resist change and are unable to see environmental change happening around them.

The book identified a process of questioning and renewal that is partly organizational and partly a matter of attitude. In order to be creative and to adapt to changing circumstances, the organization needs to have controlled conflict. The book gave case examples, featuring some of America's leading multinational companies (the transformation of Ford got 60 pages), of how organizations can foster the creative tensions necessary for renewal.

Pascale explained how certain pioneering Western and Japanese companies – he rated Honda one of the best-managed companies in the world – become 'engines of inquiry', mechanisms for continuous learning and renewal. He described the specific mechanisms by which Honda channels the forces of constructive contention in a way that keeps the company 'in a sort of restless, uneasy state, which enables it to get a great deal out of its people and itself as an entity'.

Citicorp was cited as an example of a company that was 'living dangerously' by maintaining a 'Darwinian' culture in which jobs are always at risk and judged by each day's performance. Under Walter Wriston, who changed Citicorp's perception of its business as one of moving information rather than one of moving money, the company harnessed tension to make an aggressive impact in a staid industry. But such a level of tension, creating a lot of personal insecurity, could turn against itself if the balance were lost.

The same failure of success can occur if a company such as Hewlett-Packard takes its mission of vision and values to such lengths that they become a behavioural straitjacket. 'So if there is one prescription,' Pascale has commented, 'it is that there is no prescription. Or that any prescription taken to extremes is going to cause trouble.'

Pascale's work over the 1990s at the Santa Fe Institute, studying the self-organizing behaviour of complex living systems, fed into his consultancy work for Shell, BP, Hewlett-Packard and other major multinationals. Some of these multinationals, as well as the US army, were already experimenting with these concepts in their search for renewal and change. Pascale found that amongst the key principles of complex living systems that were common to self-renewing and change-friendly companies, was acceptance of the necessity to disrupt equilibrium in order to foster innovation, in the same way that fire is essential in forest and savannah to encourage new growth, or hurricanes at sea to regenerate ocean life.

In *Surfing the Edge of Chaos* (2000), the book which puts all his work in this area into a business context with detailed case studies of the major corporations involved, Pascale offers four 'bedrock principles' applicable to the business organization, which is also a living system. Apart from 'equilibrium is the precursor to death', the three others are:

- When threatened or galvanized by opportunity, 'living things move towards the edge of chaos' where change happens.
- When this happens, living systems self-organize to enable new entities to evolve.
- Living systems cannot be directed along a linear path – they need to be disturbed to provoke beneficial change.

Pascale, a thoughtful and scholarly man whose one-a-decade books stand in marked contrast to the frenzied output of some other leading gurus, is convinced that in his work with complex adaptive systems – now penetrating the study of economics as a whole – he has found a management theory that will last perhaps as long as the 21st century. This, he predicts, will be the 'century of the living sciences'.

KEY WRITINGS

Pascale, R. T. and Athos, A. (1981, 1982, 1986) *The Art of Japanese Management*, New York: Simon and Schuster; London: Allen Lane; Penguin Books.

Pascale, R. T. (1990) *Managing on the Edge*, New York: Simon and Schuster; London: Viking.

Pascale, R. T., Goss, T. and Athos, A. (1993) 'The Re-invention Roller Coaster', Cambridge, Mass.: *Harvard Business Review* (Nov/Dec).

Pascale, R. T., Millemann, M. and Gioja, L. (1997) 'Changing the Way We Change', Cambridge, Mass.: *Harvard Business Review* (Nov/Dec).

Pascale, R. T. (2000) *Surfing the Edge of Chaos*, London: Texere.

40

TOM PETERS AND
ROBERT H. WATERMAN JR

(b. 1942) (b. 1936)

The 'excellence' cult and prescriptions for managing chaotic change

Tom Peters and Robert Waterman will for ever be linked because of the phenomenal success of *In Search of Excellence*, although it was the only book the two former McKinsey consultants wrote together. Since its publication in 1982, each has carved out his own distinctive niche in authorship and on the lecture trail, but Peters has gone on to become the world's best-known management guru, bringing showmanship and entertainment to a role that hardly existed before their book appeared.

Excellence is by far the world's bestselling business book. It was slow to take off on both sides of the Atlantic, but its reputation rocketed by word of mouth and suddenly companies were ordering '50, 100, 200 copies to give to their executives', as the British publisher recalls. It reached the million mark in sales in record time, within a year, and has now sold over 10m copies. Despite the fact that two-thirds of its 'excellent' companies have since faded in performance — Peters began his 1987 book *Thriving on Chaos* with the bold words, 'There are no excellent companies' — *In Search of Excellence* still endlessly reprints in paperback and it continues to walk off the airport book-stalls where most business books are sold in the UK.

Its iconic status seems unlikely to be affected by Peters' 'confession' late in 2001 in the US business magazine *Fast Company* that he and Waterman had 'faked the data' and that the book was 'flawed as hell'. Taken out of context, the quotes appeared hugely damaging, but were typically flip comments on the instinctive methods the McKinsey pair had used in picking their 43 exemplars of excellence. They were going for 'soft' people skills (the key to the Seven-S strategy) over the hard systems and numbers-oriented management in vogue in the late 1970s, although at the time they had no provable data that these were linked to excellent results. In the event their eight principles such as 'close to the customer' and 'productivity through people' have stood the test of time and become mainstream management wisdom.

Before joining McKinsey in 1974, Peters worked in the Pentagon for two years, where he became 'fascinated by complex organizations'. He then took a master's degree in civil engineering at Cornell University before serving in Vietnam. Later, he took an MBA at Stanford and worked again in Washington for the Office of Management and Budget. Today, he and Michael Porter can probably claim to be the most sought-after and expensive management lecturers in the world. The Tom Peters Group has built a huge business in videos, cassettes and TV series as well as personal appearances and consultancy work.

Bob Waterman is the complete temperamental opposite of the excitable, hyperactive Peters, whose shirts are rapidly soaked with sweat as he delivers his quickfire, floor-pacing lectures. A tall, laid-back Californian, Waterman says he could, if he chose, do as many lectures as Peters – roughly one every other day – but he observes laconically: 'Why kill myself?' Running his own consultancy in San Mateo, outside San Francisco, for two days a week, giving a couple of dozen lectures a year and acting as a director of several companies, including a multinational power producer, suits him better than Peters' hectic travelling schedule.

The continuing royalties from *Excellence* and his corporate work give him the financial freedom, he says, to do what he wants, and he has started a career counselling business with his wife Judy, along with developing a computerized self-evaluation system to enable people to learn more about their true motivations and skills.

Waterman spent 21 years with McKinsey, initially working on the restructuring and decentralization of large organizations. He worked in Japan and Australia and in 1976 returned to San Francisco, where the partnership with Peters began. Both men left the firm after *Excellence* was published – Peters first, then Waterman in 1986 – and although they considered another co-authorship, McKinsey was not enthusiastic once Peters had left, so Peters wrote the sequel, *A Passion for Excellence*, with Nancy Austin.

Peters' work took a new direction with *Thriving on Chaos* (1987), which inaugurated a genre of books on managing change. He has since led the movement to flatter, nimbler organizational structures and preached the virtue of the virtual company in books such as *Liberation Management* (1992), *The Pursuit of Wow!* (1994) and *The Tom Peters Seminar: Crazy Times Call for Crazy Organizations* (1994). *Circles of Innovation* (1997) was an eccentric publication, laid out in the style of seminar slides with a great deal of Peters' verbal gimmicks such as 'Yikes!' and words inexplicably separated into their component letters by hyphens.

His latest book, *Re-Imagine!* (2003), is even more unconventional, a coffee-table tome designed for short attention spans with bite-sized ideas and bullet points crammed into the page margins. In essence it simply summarizes Peters' familiar arguments for re-inventing businesses and embracing change, even when apparently destructive.

Its most interesting aspect is Peters' re-assessment of the 43 'excellent' companies exemplified in the McKinsey pair's 1982 bestseller. Quoting research from Forbes.com, he demolishes the accepted wisdom that two-thirds of them fell from grace soon after *In Search of Excellence* was published, showing that a $10,000 investment in the Excellence index would have easily outperformed the Dow Jones over 20 years, yielding $140,050 compared with $85,500.

Waterman's more conservative approach produced *The Renewal Factor* in 1987 and *The Frontiers of Excellence* in 1994, which developed some of the ideas from *In Search of Excellence*, chiefly the principle of learning from best practice, but which also focused on the need for managers to ride and manage change and to put people first. Waterman maintains today that the principles laid down in *Excellence* are still valid and that the claim that two-thirds of the companies faltered is based on the decline of stock-market prices, which were at a high when the book came out.

In hindsight, he says, he would have chosen a different group of companies, but some, such as General Electric, 3M, Merck and Intel, continue fully to justify the 'excellent' tag. In any case, he points out, he and Peters observed in the book that 'many of our excellent companies probably will not stay buoyant for ever' – a comment that subsequent critics conveniently overlooked.

Waterman's own favourite management reading includes what he calls the 'heavy-duty' theoretical works of Karl Weick on organizations, Alfred Chandler's *Strategy and Structure*, the work of Chester Barnard, Elton Mayo's Hawthorne experiments ('he showed that just paying attention to things gets more done'), Drucker's *Managing for Results*, Mintzberg on how managers spend their time, and Warren Bennis, especially his earlier works on organizational development ('a little like Drucker but more theoretical').

Another book that influenced him was James Gleick's *Chaos*, a brilliant tour de force on the unpredictable nature of life. 'It's important stuff, an entirely new branch of mathematics. It's as if calculus were reinvented. It has a lot to say about the inherent unforecastability of things, and why things we put a lot of faith in don't work. It has a lot to say about stock markets.'

Waterman believes that F. W. Taylor's work has been 'something of a touchstone' and that we are 'still living in a world created by Taylor: the specialization of work, mechanizing things, dividing work up into functions'. However much they would deny it, he suggests, many – if not most – managers are still Taylorists at heart.

While Peters drives frenetically on round the management circuit, Waterman says in his laid-back way: 'I've said pretty much all I have to say about business management.' He is now developing ideas in a different area, that of the environment and natural resources. But he expresses satisfaction that his participation as a director of companies gives him a welcome practical touchstone for his management theories, 'to see if the stuff really works'.

Peters and Waterman have almost branded the word 'excellence' as a branch of management theory. Their phenomenally successful book has spawned a host of imitators and was the subject of a fascinated study by Japan's Kenichi Ohmae, also a McKinsey man. At the time, though, Waterman says they had no idea it would prove such a watershed.

Its simple idea was the extension of a McKinsey project begun in 1977, to analyse the lessons from 43 of *Fortune*'s top 500 companies that had consistently beaten their competitors over 20 years by six financial yardsticks:

- Compound asset growth
- Compound equity growth
- Ratio of market value to book value
- Return on capital
- Return on equity
- Return on sales

Peters and Waterman developed the famous McKinsey 'Seven-S' formula to analyse an organization: structure, strategy, systems, style of management, skills (corporate strengths), staff and shared values. Applying this framework to their 43 companies, they identified their eight by now well-known characteristics shared by all of them:

- A bias for action: getting on with it
- Close to the customer: learning from the people they serve
- Autonomy and entrepreneurship: fostering innovation and nurturing 'champions'
- Productivity through people: treating the rank and file as a source of quality
- Hands-on, value-driven: management showing its commitment
- Stick to the knitting: stay with the business you know
- Simple form, lean staff: some of the best companies have a minimum of headquarters staff
- Simultaneous loose-tight properties: autonomy in shop-floor activities plus centralized values

All their 43 companies, Peters and Waterman found, were 'brilliant on the basics'. Also, in almost every case, a strong leader had been influential at some stage in forming the culture of excellence.

Five years after the book's publication, two-thirds of those companies had hit trouble in varying degrees, among them Atari, Avon, Wang and DuPont. Only 14 could still be classified as excellent by the original criteria.

Peters and Waterman individually concluded that nothing in today's chaotic business environment stays the same long enough for excellence of the sustained type possible before 1982 to be developed. In *Thriving on Chaos* Peters cited IBM – 'declared dead in 1979, the best of the best in 1982, and dead again in 1986'. People Express, one star of their book, collapsed completely.

Excellence, suggested P&W, required re-defining – excellent firms were now those that believed only in constant improvement and the demands of constant change.

A key concept behind *Thriving on Chaos*, a title that struck a chord with many gurus in the late 1980s, was the need to move from a hierarchical management pyramid to a horizontal, fast, cross-functional, cooperative one.

Peters evolved 45 precepts for managers of every level. They ran as follows:

- Specialize/create niches/differentiate
- Provide top quality
- Become a service addict
- Achieve total customer responsiveness
- Become true internationalists, both small and large firms
- Strive to achieve uniqueness
- Listen to customers, end users, suppliers, retailers
- Make manufacturing the prime marketing tool
- 'Over-invest' in people, frontline sales, service, distribution (make these the company heroes)
- Become customer-obsessed
- Develop an innovation strategy
- Use multifunction teams for all development activities
- Substitute pilots and prototypes for proposals
- Ignore 'Not Invented Here'; practise 'creative swiping'
- Use systematic word of mouth for launching
- Applaud champions
- Symbolize innovativeness
- Support failures by publicly rewarding well-thought-out mistakes
- Measure innovation
- Make innovation a way of life for everyone
- Involve all personnel in virtually everything
- Organize as much as possible around teams
- Listen/celebrate/recognize
- Invest time in recruiting
- Invest in human capital as much as hardware
- Provide bold financial incentives for all
- Guarantee continuous employment for a large slice of the workforce
- Radically reduce layers of management
- Re-conceive middle managers as facilitators instead of guardians
- Reduce and simplify paperwork and bureaucratic procedures
- Challenge conventional management wisdom on a day-to-day basis
- Develop and live an 'enabling and empowering vision'

(effective leadership at all levels is marked by a core philosophy [values] and a vision of how the enterprise or department wishes to make its mark)
- Lead by personal example
- Practise visible management
- Become a compulsive listener
- Ensure that frontline people know they are the heroes
- Examine each act of delegation and increase it radically
- Pursue horizontal management
- Focus on exactly what you have changed recently – what your subordinates have changed
- Create a sense of urgency
- Develop simple systems to encourage participation and understanding
- Simplify control systems (e.g. performance appraisals, setting of objectives, job descriptions)
- Share information with everyone
- Set conservative financial targets
- Demand total integrity in all dealings, both inside and outside the firm

Waterman's prescriptions for renewing vitality and performance in *The Renewal Factor* numbered just eight:

- Informed opportunism: 'the renewing companies treat information as their main strategic advantage, and flexibility as their main strategic weapon.'
- Direction and empowerment: 'the renewing companies treat everyone as a source of creative input . . . Their managers define the boundaries and their people figure out the best way of doing the job within these boundaries.'
- Friendly facts, congenial controls: 'the renewing companies treat facts as friends and financial controls as liberating.'
- A different mirror: ability to step outside the company and look at it from a different perspective.
- Teamwork, trust, politics and power: the first two are common to all renewing companies, the last two never found.
- Causes and commitment: 'commitment results from management's ability to turn grand causes into small actions so everyone can contribute.'

- Attitudes and attention: 'visible management attention, rather than exhortation, gets things done.'
- Stability in motion: renewing companies have a 'habit of habit-breaking'.

Peters was the first major guru to use the Web as a personal marketing tool. His site, www.tompeters.com, is an attention-grabbing announcement board of his current activities, what he's reading and thinking, with interactive links. His recent publishing ventures have been linked to a project called Reinventing Work, small quirky books aimed at developing marketable skills in a world of free agents rather than corporate careers.

Peters and Waterman together were responsible for popularizing the study of management to a mass readership, and initiating a new direction in management thinking. No other authors have come near their feat with *Excellence* in the number of copies sold. They illuminated many issues, such as corporate culture and values, which are just as valid today as in 1982. As the business environment changed and became subject to more shocks and discontinuities, they responded with their individual views of managing change – a concept that few companies understood a decade ago, but which is now central to industrial survival.

KEY WRITINGS

Peters, T. and Waterman, R. H. Jr (1982) *In Search of Excellence*, New York and London: Harper and Row.

Peters, T. and Austin, N. (1985) *A Passion for Excellence*, London: Collins.

Peters, T. (1987, 1988) *Thriving on Chaos*, New York: Alfred A. Knopf; London: Macmillan.

Waterman, R. H. Jr (1987) *The Renewal Factor*, New York: Bantam.

Peters, T. (1992) *Liberation Management*, New York: Alfred A. Knopf; London: Macmillan.

Peters, T. (1994) *The Tom Peters Seminar: Crazy Times Call for Crazy Organizations*, New York: Vintage; London: Macmillan.

Peters, T. (1994) *The Pursuit of Wow!*, New York: Vintage; London: Macmillan.

Waterman, R. H. Jr (1994) *The Frontiers of Excellence*, London: Nicholas Brealey Publishing.

Peters, T. (1997) *Circles of Innovation*, London: Hodder and Stoughton.

Peters, T. (1999) *The Brand You 50, The Projects 50, The Professional Service Firm 50*, New York: Alfred A. Knopf.

Peters, T. (2003) *Re-Imagine!: Business Excellence in a Disruptive Age*, London: Dorling Kindersley.

41

JEFFREY PFEFFER

(b. 1946)

Key success factors in managing people

Professor of organizational behaviour at Stanford Graduate School of Business, where he has taught since 1979, Pfeffer is a leading authority on people-based strategy as the route to competitive advantage. His arguments, like his affable, straight-talking manner, are deceptively simple and common-sense, but as he likes to say: 'common sense is not all that common.' The fact remains that, for all the thousands of companies boasting 'our people are our greatest asset', only a few actively practise that mantra and enjoy the profits that result.

In *The Human Equation* (1998), the book that propelled him into the ranks of significant management thinkers, Pfeffer identified seven practices in the motivation and talent-building of employees that he claimed would boost performance in almost any company by 40 per cent. So why don't more organizations put these practices in place? Pfeffer's wry conclusion: because it takes time, hard work and consistent leadership attention. 'The scarcest resource in most organizations is time and attention – what leader has enough?' he commented in a 1998 interview. 'Too often quarterly financial results crowd out the long-term management of people.'

Pfeffer, whose career has also included professorships at the University of Illinois, UCLA Berkeley and Harvard

Business School, has a 'one-eighth rule' about getting management to accept the people-profits evidence that he produces in his book. Half won't believe the connection; of those who do, half will only try once to put things right instead of realizing the need for a systemic approach; and of the firms that do make a comprehensive effort, probably only half will persist with it long enough to reap real benefits.

The Stanford professor was among the first to stress the critical importance of implementation in corporate strategy that later became the theme of such bestsellers as *Execution: The Discipline of Getting Things Done* (2002), by Larry Bossidy, chairman of AlliedSignal and architect of its merger with Honeywell. Pfeffer went on to create 16 principles for 'getting things done' in his 1999 book *The Knowing-Doing Gap: How Smart Companies Turn Their Knowledge Into Action*. Its chief message was that, for all the tens of billions spent on business education and training, most 'knowledge management' is wasted when it comes to effecting change in organizational practices.

When Jeffrey Pfeffer taught an MBA course at Stanford in 1994 called 'Competitive Advantage Through People', and later took it successfully to executive seminars around the world, he found himself wondering why the principles of profits-through-people were being widely accepted at the very time that more and more companies were laying off staff to cut costs. The newly fashionable re-engineering with its streamlined processes and downsizing seemed to be reviving Frederick W. Taylor's early 20th-century ideas and crediting them with high performance results.

Pfeffer and others, including Gary Hamel (qv) and C. K. Prahalad (qv), concluded that many organizations were storing up significant problems for themselves by choosing a short-term cure for recession that would in future starve them of much-needed expertise. In *The Human Equation*, Pfeffer set out to challenge such errors of conventional wisdom. Organizations do have choices when faced with the need to reduce costs, he argues: some of the most successful US companies in their sectors enjoy high staff commitment and performance because they have a policy of avoiding downsizing wherever possible. Charles Schwab, the discount brokerage house, strives to maintain employment even during market downturns because it does not want to lose the competitive advantage that it believes comes from its investment in staff training.

Pfeffer asks employers to reflect on how they view their people: as costs to be reduced, recalcitrant shirkers who have to be closely controlled, or as intelligent, motivated and trustworthy individuals who are the company's most competitive assets. He is a Theory Y thinker (see Douglas McGregor entry) who argues that people not only work harder when they have some control over their work environment, but also 'work smarter' if they can use knowledge gained from extra training.

His seven people-management practices of successful organizations are:

- Security of employment
- Selective hiring (it is important to recruit people compatible with the organization's culture or security of employment will backfire as a policy: in hiring, basic attitudes are more important than specific skills which can easily be taught)
- Self-managed teams
- Higher than average pay if justified by organizational performance
- Extensive training
- An egalitarian attitude to status in the organization
- Extensive sharing of information

The last principle is nearly always a mark of high-performing companies. Pfeffer cites the case of Whole Foods, which grew in the 1990s from $100m to $1bn in sales: this US company shares so much detailed financial and performance data with its people – many of whom own shares in the company – that the Securities and Exchange Commission regard Whole Foods' employees as insiders when considering share dealings. When the company's CEO was asked why it even shared details of salaries, he said to keep such information secret would imply that the organization trusted some employees and not others – the wrong message if you are trying to harness everyone's energy and commitment.

Building trust is a keystone of Pfeffer's philosophy, and an important part of trust in his view is a no-blame culture. A corporate emphasis on accountability is one of the pieces of conventional wisdom he challenges because it often leads to a destructive blame hunt. Pfeffer often cites the US airline industry as an example. Southwest Airlines defeated the much bigger United's attempt to match its no-frills, low-cost shuttle operations, and there was one big cultural reason. If a plane was late or something else went wrong with the schedule, United wanted to fix the blame somewhere; Southwest just wanted to fix the problem. Staff morale between the two was like chalk and cheese.

Another piece of conventional wisdom challenged by Pfeffer is the belief that 'what gets measured gets managed.' But measuring everything is not the answer: the secret is measuring those practices that are key to a company's success, and each company has to decide this for itself. At the SAS Institute, a highly successful developer of statistical software in the US, the CEO understood that in a knowledge-intensive business, what counts is the quality of its people and how they are hired and retained. So SAS talks more about its numbers of job applicants and staff turnover than about its sales.

Both of these principles of conventionally held good management practice are also put under the critical microscope in Pfeffer's second major book, *The Knowing-Doing Gap*, written with his colleague Robert Sutton, professor of organizational behaviour at the Stanford School of Engineering. They hinder the implementation of strategy because they are accepted at face value without critical examination, and that goes for 14 other flawed practices cited in the book.

Top of the list, Pfeffer and Sutton argue, is the 'cult of knowledge management' whereby business schools and business literature have purveyed an intellectualized view of corporate success where analysis and prescription flourish without any real idea of translating them into action. 'The one thing that business schools don't do is train students to do anything,' says Pfeffer, a view shared by the Canadian Henry Mintzberg (qv), a noted scourge of the practical value of MBA courses. The irony, as Pfeffer notes, is that the top job sought by business–school graduates is management consulting, which often pays twice the salary levels of those actually doing the job rather than talking about it.

'Knowledge is no longer a source of competitive advantage because everyone knows the same things in their area,' says Pfeffer. 'All have the same access, read the same journals. The real difference is taking knowledge and doing something with it.' The latest book by Pfeffer and Sutton, *Hard Facts, Dangerous Half-Truths and Total Nonsense* (2006), attacks commonly held management wisdom from a different angle; that of blindly copying so-called best practice in other companies instead of using 'evidence-based management' to drive their decision-making.

Pfeffer and Sutton are members of a small band speaking out against the massed voices of business education, but the argument their book propounds – learn by doing, even by failing – has always been the dynamic of Silicon Valley, where Stanford has its base. Stanford interacts much more with local industries than its eastern-seaboard peers – Andy Grove, CEO of Intel, teaches a popular course there – and its professors arc thoroughly grounded in the real world of business. Pfeffer himself is on the boards of four technology-related companies but is on record as saying (shortly before the dotcom crash of 2000–2001) that 'Silicon Valley is great in building technology, terrible in building companies. On the whole, these are not organizations built for sustainability . . . Here the long term is lunch-time.'

KEY WRITINGS

Pfeffer, J. (1998) *The Human Equation: Building Profits by Putting People First*, Boston: Harvard Business School Press.
Pfeffer, J. and Sutton, R. I. (1999) *The Knowing-Doing Gap: How Smart Companies Turn Their Knowledge Into Action*, Boston: Harvard

GUIDE TO THE MANAGEMENT GURUS

Business School Press.
Pfeffer, J. (2000) *Hidden Value: How Great Companies Achieve Extraordinary Results With Ordinary People*, Boston: Harvard Business School Press.
Pfeffer, J. and Sutton, R. I. (2006) *Hard Facts, Dangerous Half-Truths and Total Nonsense: Profiting from Evidence-Based Management*, Boston: Harvard Business School Press.

42

MICHAEL PORTER

(b. 1947)

*Strategies for competitive advantage, both national and
international*

Ranked by the management consultancy Accenture as
the world's most prominent business intellectual, the
formidably brilliant Porter is acknowledged as the leading
expert on competition and competitive strategy. He leads
Harvard's Institute for Strategy and Competitiveness, set
up jointly by the university and its business school as a
vehicle for furthering globally his work on competitiveness in nations, regions and cities, and the implications
of competition for corporate strategy.

Porter is one of only 15 Harvard faculty members to
be granted a university professorship, which carries the
prestige of universal scholarship as opposed to achievement in a specific discipline such as business administration. The first of his 17 books, *Competitive Strategy*
(1980), is now in its 53rd edition and is regarded as the
definitive work in its field.

His 'five-forces' model of the factors that drive competition in any industry are viewed by many MBA students
as the key to analysing the effectiveness of every business activity from marketing to product development.
Other hugely influential ideas have been his exposition
of the 'value chain' – how a company performs and costs
its activities relative to its competitors – and his 'cluster'

235

theory of the way in which interdependent industries lead to success in a particular area.

In the summer of 1990, *Business Week* described Porter as 'a business phenomenon in his own right' and one of the highest-paid academics anywhere. He is booked for lectures six months in advance and has sold millions of dollars' worth of video seminars. Porter himself acknowledges that he has become a 'brand' for which buyers are willing to pay.

Porter joined the Harvard faculty at the age of 26 after earning an economics doctorate there. Earlier, at Princeton, he had graduated in aeronautical engineering and reached professional standard at golf. His last major book, *The Competitive Advantage of Nations* (1990), analyses the reasons for ten countries' ability to gain global market share in certain industries. (The UK comes out with a depressingly peripheral list, aside from chemicals and pharmaceuticals: Porter deems it a world leader, for example, in auctioneering and biscuit manufacture. Britain scores only seven world-challenging categories to Switzerland's 16 and Denmark's 11.)

A useful introduction to Porter's work is *Michael Porter on Competition* (1998), a compendium of some of his key texts.

The very words 'competitive strategy' or 'competitive advantage' are enough to identify Michael Porter wherever management gurus gather. Some critics claim that his ideas for analysing markets and industries are based on old economic theories, and Porter himself has acknowledged his debt to Joseph A. Schumpeter, among others, in *The Competitive Advantage of Nations*. What he does brilliantly, however, is to package and simplify analytical models that would otherwise be dauntingly difficult for most working businessmen to understand. His seminars, in particular, are as lively as those of Tom Peters.

On joining the Harvard faculty, Porter was among the first to project corporate strategy in marketplace terms rather than as a theoretical concept linking various functions in an organization.

His basic tool for managers seeking to analyse their own company's competitive position employs five factors or forces that drive competition:

- Existing rivalry between firms
- The threat of new entrants to a market
- The threat of substitute products and services
- The bargaining power of suppliers
- The bargaining power of buyers

He then identifies five generic descriptions of industries: fragmented, emerging, mature, declining and global.

Porter says a firm may possess two kinds of competitive advantage: low cost or differentiation. 'Competitive advantage is a function of either providing comparable buyer value more efficiently than competitors (low cost) or performing activities at comparable cost but in unique ways that create more buyer value than competitors and, hence, command a premium price (differentiation).'

Firms that operate in a number of different countries can locate processes where the best advantage lies – for example, low labour costs, or proximity to vast markets like Japanese firms based in the UK – but at the same time, Porter argues, the most competitive ones come from home bases that are themselves strong and competitive. This sharpens the instinct to succeed and provides valuable cluster support from equally successful linked industries that act as buyers and suppliers.

This theory, developed over several books and numerous articles, reaches its full flowering in *The Competitive Advantage of Nations*, which takes as its key a 'diamond' of factors that makes some nations (and consequently their industries) more competitive than others. The four points of this diamond are:

- *Factor conditions:* the nation's position in factors of production (such as skilled labour or infrastructure) necessary to compete in a particular industry
- *Demand conditions:* the nature of home demand for the industry's product or service and how discriminating it is

GUIDE TO THE MANAGEMENT GURUS

- *Related and supporting industries:* the presence or absence of supplier industries and related industries that are internationally competitive themselves
- *Company strategy, structure and rivalry:* the conditions governing how firms are created, organized and managed, as well as the nature of domestic rivalry. Tough domestic rivalry breeds international success.

Firms gain competitive advantage outside their home markets, Porter argues, when their own countries provide a dynamic competitive environment, characterized by an accumulation of specialized assets and skills and a constant stimulus to upgrade and improve their products and processes. Clusters or mutually supporting industries are important to success; one reason why Britain's performance has declined over the years.

Among Porter's strategic recommendations for the competitive company are:

- Sell to the most sophisticated and demanding buyers: they will set a standard for the organization
- Seek out buyers with the most difficult needs: they become part of a firm's R&D programme
- Establish norms of exceeding the toughest regulatory hurdles or product standards: these provide targets that will force improvement
- Source from the most advanced and international home-based suppliers: those with competitive advantage already will challenge the firm to improve and upgrade
- Treat employees as permanent instead of adopting a demoralizing hire-and-fire approach
- Establish outstanding competitors as motivators

One of Porter's favourite methods of identifying a firm's competitive position is to analyse its 'value chain' – all the activities it performs and how they interact. Examining these components sheds light on the roots of costs and how they behave, and picks out existing and potential sources of differentiation. 'A firm gains competitive advantage by performing these strategically important activities more cheaply or better than its competitors.'

Kathryn Rudie Harrigan, a former student of Porter's – and

now a guru in her own right as well as being professor of strategic management at New York's Columbia University – says the ideas in *Competitive Strategy* are required reading in every US business school and most executive education programmes. 'The framework he popularized forms the cornerstone for the next decade of research concerning strategy formulation . . . The first chapter of the book he edited about global competition* provides what has become the dominant framework for looking at issues in global strategy.'

KEY WRITINGS

Porter, M. E. (1980) *Competitive Strategy: Techniques for Analysing Industries and Competitors*, New York: Free Press.
Porter, M. E. (1985) *Competitive Advantage*, New York: Free Press.
Porter, M. E. (ed.) (1986) *Competition in Global Industries*, Cambridge, Mass.: Harvard Business School Press.
Porter, M. E. (1990) *The Competitive Advantage of Nations*, London: Macmillan.
Porter, M. E. (1998) *Michael Porter on Competition*, Boston: Harvard Business Press.
Porter, M. E. (2001) 'Strategy and the Internet', Cambridge, Mass.: *Harvard Business Review* (March).

* *Competition in Global Industries*, ed. M. E. Porter (Harvard Business School Press, 1986).

43

C. K. PRAHALAD

(b. 1941)

Finding rich markets by serving the world's poor

Now acknowledged as a leading guru in his own right after years in the shadow of Gary Hamel (qv), his high-profile collaborator on *Competing for the Future* (1994), Prahalad has always had a following among cognoscenti who understood his intellectual contribution to that best-seller. Since the book came out with its ground-breaking ways of reinventing businesses, he has regularly featured among the world's top ten management thinkers. His latest big idea, backed up by rigorous research and a powerful moral conviction, is that the 4–5bn people at the bottom of the world's earnings pyramid could form huge new markets for multinational corporations, to the benefit of both.

A charismatic professor at the University of Michigan, where he holds two chairs, in business administration and corporate strategy and international business, Prahalad has also been a visiting professor at INSEAD, the international business school in France, and held senior appointments at the Indian Institute of Management, Ahmedabad. Always known as 'CK', Prahalad is in fact his first name, the initials standing for Coimbatore, his Indian home town, and Krishnarao, the first name of his father, a Madras judge and noted Sanskrit scholar.

240

The young Prahalad was studying for a PhD in physics at Harvard when he accepted a job – just for a year – at the nearby Union Carbide battery plant. His innovative thinking produced many efficiency reforms and he stayed for four years, having learned much about 'the extraordinary wisdom of ordinary people'.

After taking his PhD, Prahalad returned to teach at the Indian Institute of Management, but his global thinking was ahead of Indian business culture in the 1970s and he returned with his young wife to the US with just $18 in funds. He was teaching at the University of Michigan in 1981 when he met Gary Hamel, a PhD student there.

They began sparking ideas off each other in a partnership that would last more than ten years despite – or perhaps because of – being complete opposites, in much the same way as the exuberant Tom Peters (qv) and the laid-back Bob Waterman (qv) of *In Search of Excellence* fame. A profile of Prahalad in the US journal *Fast Company* once likened the relationship with Hamel to that of 'Felix and Oscar on crack', a reference to the characters in Neil Simon's play *The Odd Couple*.

Their ideas broke surface with a mighty splash in 1990 with an acclaimed article in *Harvard Business Review*, 'The Core Competence of the Corporation'. Core competences – what a company does that gives it competitive advantage – became part of management language when the article turned into *Competing for the Future*, one of the most successful business books in publishing history (see Gary Hamel entry).

'Industry foresight' was another of the book's phrases that entered the business lexicon: the authors offered a model for shining a company's headlights into the future and assessing how it could create new profit growth from its skills core; how incumbent managers, as Prahalad put it, could 'imagine the future and influence the evolution of industries'.

The pair published several more admired articles in *HBR* and other journals before embarking on separate books. In 2004, Prahalad published *The Future of*

Competition: *Co-Creating Unique Value with Customers*, co-authored with a marketing academic, Venkat Ramaswamy. This explored the concept of co-opting customers through the Internet to engage in providing more value for themselves – as, for example, Amazon does through getting book-buyers to share opinions, and eBay does by creating a virtual auction room for anything and everything. To some extent, core competences then become less important than how proficient companies are at providing customers with the experiences they seek.

Since 1997, however, Prahalad had been nursing a truly big idea and proselytizing it to the multinational companies among which he moved as a strategy consultant. This idea was creating wealth at the 'bottom of the pyramid' (BOP), that vast unserved market of the world's poorest who live on less than $2 a day but are still potential consumers for the right products at the right price. A simple example is the shampoo market in village India, served by perceptive multinationals with branded products sold in single sachets.

Such markets have to be built instead of entered, argues Prahalad, and this requires a dramatic change in corporate price-performance expectations along with technical innovation and the vision to re-engineer products or services. But over seven years he assembled case-study proof that it could be done and the result, *The Fortune at the Bottom of the Pyramid* (2004), is one of the most original and morally impressive business books of its time.

Less than two years after *Competing for the Future* became a wildfire bestseller, propelling both its authors into fame and wealth as star gurus of corporate strategy, Prahalad spent the Christmas holiday of 1995 nagged by a seemingly unanswerable question: why, with all the world's technological and managerial expertise, did so many billions of people remain locked in poverty around the globe?

Finding a solution to the plight of those at the bottom of the economic pyramid became an obsession, and it was clear to Prahalad that it needed 'a clean sheet of paper' approach. While many international organizations were trying to encourage local entrepreneurship, it wasn't enough. It needed the mobilization of big multinational firms with their investment capacity, linked to local knowledge. This would produce a two-way benefit, bringing consumer quality to the poor and opening up a whole unserved market for multinationals. 'The most untapped opportunity in the world is 5bn people who have been below the radar screen for all large companies,' he explains.

Some companies in India already understood this. Both Hindustan Lever, the Indian subsidiary of Unilever, and Procter & Gamble had a flourishing business in shampoo sold in single sachets that were affordable even in the poorest households. Such market-tailored products can also lift the 'poverty penalty' that burdens millions of Indians, forced by their lack of financial credibility to pay up to 25 times what wealthy customers would be charged. Prahalad relates how those living in Dharavi, a shantytown outside Mumbai, pay 600–1,000 per cent interest to moneylenders: a bank entering this market could make a good profit at 25 per cent, even accepting – as Prahalad does not – that BOP customers are a higher risk.

After the success of his book with Hamel, Prahalad – to whom 'the entrepreneurial drive is the ultimate in self-expression' – co-founded a technology firm called Praja, whose business was knowledge-sharing and data analysis, and became galvanized by the power of the Internet to mobilize economic activity. In 1997, he linked up with a fellow academic from the University of Michigan Business School, Stuart Hart, to produce a paper called 'The Strategies for the Bottom of the Pyramid'. Not a single journal, Prahalad said later, would publish it.

Once circulated on the Web, however, it began to stimulate interest and action in companies as heavyweight as Hewlett-Packard, Monsanto and DuPont. Then two co-authored articles by Prahalad were published in *Strategy+Business* and *Harvard Business Review* in January and September 2002, respectively, and corporate America began to pay serious attention to the BOP market. Globally, Prahalad values this market at $13tn.

He is still only at the beginning of his proselytizing mission, in which he says things like 'convert the pyramid into your diamond' and eloquently puts the case for the power of business to create prosperity and a more stable world. *The Fortune at the Bottom of the Pyramid* (2004) presents a dozen well-researched case studies in businesses as diverse as cement, banking, mobiles and healthcare. The mountain of detail, sometimes overwhelming, is there to prove to sceptics that the model works for companies willing and imaginative enough to rethink and re-cost their market offerings for this huge collective pool of untapped buying power. Bill Gates called the book 'a blueprint for how to fight poverty with profitability'.

Cemex, for example, is already known as one of the world's most innovative companies in a mundane, mature industry. Founded in 1987 in Mexico, it is now the world's third largest cement-manufacturing company: by 2002, sales had reached $6.54bn with margins of 44 per cent. Its products, especially ready-mixed cement, go to customers whose delivery requirements may change at short notice, making for tricky distribution problems. Cemex solved this by employing satellite navigation to liaise its trucks with each other and the customers, thus offering a unique competitive advantage in delivery.

In 2001, Cemex devised an entirely new channel for selling its products and simultaneously improving housing in poor areas. The scheme is known as 'Patrimonio Hoy' – meaning wealth or legacy today – and it taps into the desire of people in Spanish cultures to leave a solid asset to their children, such as a house. Cemex creates small savings groups, usually women, with the incentive of access to credit and eventually the ability to add a kitchen or bathroom to their homes. After three years the scheme had mustered 36,000 customers with access to $10m credit, and although the profit benefits are still working through, the firm has ambitious expansion plans and has gained enormous kudos in terms of corporate social responsibility.

The Cemex scheme follows Prahalad's 'three-A' principles for creating consumer capacity among the poor: affordability, access (distribution must be rethought for local conditions) and availability, because BOP decisions to buy are based on cash in hand.

A few steps up the BOP ladder, the same principles have accounted for two big breakthrough successes in the Indian healthcare and hotel sectors. An eye hospital in south India can now perform cataract operations for $25 a time, making a profit even though 60 per cent of its patients are non-paying. Its visionary founder was inspired by the principle behind the McDonald's fast-food chain, of step-by-step process flow and standardized quality. The hospital treats only cataracts and all non-surgical patient care is carried out at minimal cost by young technicians – high-school graduates who are intensively trained to perform one skill to a consistent standard.

In another breakthrough, the Taj group, famous for its luxury hotels, has innovated a 'smart basics' concept, in which comfortable, modern, well-equipped rooms are provided for $20 a night, opening up a vast new market for Indian travellers on a tight budget. The target is for 500–1,000 such hotels with up to 225 rooms each.

Prahalad is out to persuade large companies that their interests ultimately converge with those of the world's poor, and he hopes the business schools 'will make this part of what business is about, not just part of CSR [corporate social responsibility]'. His book explodes a number of myths. BOP customers, he argues, do not necessarily represent a higher risk than top-of-the-pyramid customers. They are just as brand conscious as richer consumers and they are getting increasingly connected to information networks through Internet cafés and chat rooms.

Above all, as he said in an interview in London in 2004, 'some of the greatest companies in the world – Marks and Spencer, Sainsbury's, Woolworth, Singer, Sears, Wal-Mart – were created on the custom of ordinary people. We tend to forget our own history.

'All that we need is 20 companies to lead the way – others will follow. It will make value for shareholders but also create social collateral in the poorest countries where people can live with dignity and choice.'

KEY WRITINGS

Hamel, G. and Prahalad, C. K. (1990) 'The Core Competence of the Corporation', Boston, Mass.: *Harvard Business Review* (May/June).

Hamel, G. and Prahalad, C. K. (1994) *Competing for the Future*, Boston, Mass.: Harvard Business School Press.

Hamel, G. and Prahalad, C. K. (1996) 'Competing in the New Economy: Managing Out of Bounds, *Strategic Management Journal* (March).

Prahalad, C. K. and Ramaswamy, V. (2004) *The Future of Competition: Co-Creating Unique Value with Customers*, Boston, Mass.: Harvard Business School Press.

Prahalad, C. K. (2004) *The Fortune at the Bottom of the Pyramid: Eradicating Poverty Through Profit,* New Jersey: Wharton Business School Publishing.

44

REG REVANS

(1907–2003)

Managers educating each other through 'action learning'

Underrated British (Southampton-born) inventor of 'action learning', in which working teams of managers educate each other amid the real risk, confusion and opportunity of the workplace itself. The idea has become an accepted part of management education and is considered by many to be one of the key management ideas of the last 50 years, though only the Japanese have fully acknowledged the importance of Revans' early work – as a foundation stone of their quality-circle philosophy. In British industry, Sir Arnold (later Lord) Weinstock of the General Electric Company was one of the first to perceive its value and he became an important advocate.

Revans trained first as a physicist at the famous Cavendish Laboratories in Cambridge in the 1920s, studying under Ernest Rutherford, the father of nuclear physics, and working with Albert Einstein. The Cavendish shaped Revans' analytical powers of the mind and taught him, he has said, to 'keep away from experts with prefabricated answers'. He wrote his first paper on action learning in 1937 while working as an education officer for the county of Essex. After World War II, when he became the first director of education and training at the National Coal Board, he developed his theories more fully while studying how miners and colliery managers worked out and solved problems on the job.

Revans was known to feel bitter about his position as a guru without honour in his own country. Management consultant Bob Garratt, who worked with Revans in industry, says his theories form 'one of the few bodies of management work which are highly scientifically and mathematically based, beautifully researched'. Garratt suspects it was this that 'frightened people off', especially in the late 1960s and early 1970s when British management education came heavily under the whole influence of US west-coast psychotherapy and the whole humanist, sociological approach to industry. But the theory still 'works wonderfully', says Garratt.

Revans' ideas have played an important role in management training in continental Europe. A programme in Belgium based on Revans' theories was described as being partly responsible for Belgium's 102 per cent increase in industrial productivity between 1971 and 1981. (For comparison, Japan's figure is 85 per cent and Britain's 28 per cent.)

In the 1970s Revans became president of the European Association of Management Training Centres, and an EC report later paid tribute to his work ('Education in the European Community', 1978). There is now a Revans Centre for Action Learning and Research at the University of Salford, near Manchester.

Revans said of his book *Action Learning* (1980) that he bought most of the copies as scrap. It did not sell, yet it was the culmination of some 40 years' working and thinking by Revans, who wrote his first paper on training in 1937, when he was responsible for technical and professional education on Essex County Council.

Over the next 20 years he developed the radical theory that managers learned better from each other in working management situations than they ever could in a classroom. The message was driven home for him while working in a training and development capacity in the coal-mining industry, where he observed how miners had to 'carry the educational can' in working with young newcomers to the pits. They had to combine the teaching of technical knowledge with sensitivity to the fears and insecurity of youngsters working underground for the first time.

Revans identified these abilities as essential to the manager of any large enterprise. In doing so, as one appreciation of his work puts it, he 'became a forerunner of the whole socio-technical school of management which was to blossom in the 1960s'.

From his observations in the pits, Revans concluded that miners and managers should also learn from and with each other, and he proposed the formation of a staff college through which people in the industry with common problems could be brought together to exchange ideas for practical solutions. This was the core of action learning, which Revans later took into National Health Service hospitals.

Revans also studied the effect of the size of a business on the morale of people working for it, and concluded well ahead of E. F. Schumacher (a colleague of his on the Coal Board) that 'small is beautiful.'

'What does make Revans unique,' wrote Ronald Lessem of City University Business School, 'is the way he has linked together industrial relations (artisan and scribe), human relations (self and others), technological change (education and industry) and the whole question of scale (centre and periphery) with information processing, problem-solving and learning.'

Revans, said Lessem, 'placed at the centre of things the "springs of human action". It is one's perception of the problem, he said, one's evaluation of what is to be gained by solving it, and one's estimate of the resources at hand to solve it, that supply these action springs.'

Revans saw the concept as one of great antiquity, citing Buddha as 'an early believer in action learning, teaching others that it is from their own real experiences that the most fundamental truths are most likely to be learned'.

He always took a holistic approach, incorporating some elements of religious belief, to the practice of management. His synthesis of tasks and relationships, personal consciousness and management technique, organizational science and religious faith was distilled into *The Theory of Practice in Management* (1966). This was followed by *Developing Effective Managers* (1971), in which Revans set out a model for achieving managerial objectives, based on three systems – Alpha, Beta and Gamma. System Alpha is concerned with the manager's use of information in designing strategies; System Beta with achieving them by negotiation; and System Gamma with monitoring the learning curve of adapting to experience and change.

Young, fast-track managers have responded to action learning more than the older generation. One of the few leading British industrialists who did recognize its practical value was Sir Arnold (now Lord) Weinstock of GEC. Action learning has been practised in Egypt, Africa and India, and became part of many management training programmes. In February 1988 Sir Douglas Hague wrote: 'We are in a new industrial revolution which requires management trainers to develop "action learning" from real experience within business and industry, rather than getting tied up with theory and academia.'

Revans has been quoted as saying: 'The facts now are that all I have been on about these 50 years is slowly being seen to have been right' (*Makers of Management*, David Clutterbuck and Stuart Crainer, 1990). He remained convinced that action learning was an idea whose time had come – even if his own national peers should be among the last to appreciate it.

Very slowly, this is being corrected. 'The essence of Revans' seminal work on action learning is to empower the learner, not to glorify the teacher,' wrote Mike Levy and Martin Delahoussaye in *Training Journal* ('Reg Revans: a Man of Action', November 2000). The authors quote the British industrialist Sir Peter Parker, former head of British Rail, as saying: 'If I ever wrote a book of heroes, Revans would be there.'

KEY WRITINGS

Revans, R. W. (1966) *The Theory of Practice in Management*, London: Macdonald.
Revans, R. W. (1971) *Developing Effective Managers*, London: Longman.
Revans, R. W. (1980) *Action Learning*, London: Blond and Briggs.

It is indicative of Revans' prophet-without-honour fate that a 1982 symposium of papers on his theories, published under the title *The Origins and Growth of Action Learning*, should have been published under Studentlitteratur in West Germany under the auspices of the Bratt Institut für Neues Lernen and available in an English-language version from a small Bromley firm called Chartwell-Bratt. All Revans' books are difficult to obtain outside libraries. The third edition of *Action Learning in Practice* (Gower, 1997), edited by Mike Pedler, contains an introduction to the subject by Professor Revans and a 1996 interview with him.

45

EDGAR H. SCHEIN

(b. 1928)

The 'psychological contract' between employer and employee

American social psychologist and pioneer of the concept of corporate culture – the commonly held set of assumptions within an organization about its values and practices. His 1985 book *Organizational Culture and Leadership* (second edition 1992) is seminal to studies in this field. Now professor emeritus of management and part-time senior lecturer at MIT's Sloan School of Management, Schein is best known for his theory of the 'psychological contract', the tacit quid-pro-quo expectations that exist between employer and employee, and for that of the 'career anchor', the reasons why people choose to stay with an employer.

After taking a master's degree in psychology at Stanford in 1949 and a PhD in social psychology at Harvard in 1952, Schein served in the US army for four years, carrying out research into leadership and working with other army psychologists on the rehabilitation of POWs after the Korean War. Invited by Douglas McGregor (qv) to join the Sloan School in 1956, he became professor of organizational psychology and management there in 1964, finding many similarities, he later said, between the brainwashing imposed on American POWs by the Communist forces in Korea and the inculcation of corporate values on employees by the likes of GE and IBM.

Britain's Charles Handy (qv) studied at MIT under Schein, Warren Bennis (qv) and Chris Argyris (qv) and has said the experience 'transformed my life'.

Edgar Schein is responsible for two coinages that have entered the language of management thinking – the 'psychological contract' and the 'career anchor'. Both are intimately connected with the analysis of motivation, which is the root of Schein's work.

The first embraces what an employee expects from those who employ him or her, not only in economic terms like pay, conditions, hours and job security, but also how he or she is treated and encouraged to develop abilities and responsibility. Schein believes that many strikes and industrial disputes occur basically because this contract has been broken, even though the flashpoint may appear to be a specific economic grievance. The psychological contract is not one-sided; it also includes a company's expectations about the people who work for it, such as loyalty and diligence. It is essential for both aspects to match or correspond if the 'contract' is to work on a long-term basis.

Allied to this is the career anchor: the perceptions about themselves that individuals hold in a particular organization, and which encourage them to remain in that organization. These relate strongly to self-esteem and satisfaction with the way talents are allowed to develop, and tend to be moulded by experience in the early part of an organizational career.

Schein identified these as typical career anchors: how individuals viewed their technical competence, managerial competence, security and autonomy in the job they were doing. Career anchors can also, he explained, have a narrowing effect on a person's development even within an organization in which he or she seems content: for example, a graduate's view of his technical competence was such that he saw himself doing technical work only instead of expanding in mid-career into managerial responsibility.

The erosion of corporate career structures over the past ten years, and the emergence of the 'Me Inc.' culture – portfolio workers who have either been squeezed out of a company or, like many 'Generation Y' talents, chosen to be a free agent – challenges both these concepts. Schein thinks it is probably healthy that the dominance of the career in a person's life is giving way to a more holistic view. 'Lifestyle has become the increasingly important career anchor,' he said in a 1998 interview.

Of the psychological contract, he has said more recently that the key now is for a business to determine how it wants its people to change in order to make the organization viable. 'Once you are very clear as to what the new behaviour is to be – perhaps you require people to be more responsive or want them to think differently – then you can analyse the culture to determine which cultural elements will help you to get there, and which will hinder . . . The notion of psychological contracts has to be seen as something that management can change, but in doing so it is taking a gamble. If the new way of behaving, the new contract, is an improvement, a new culture will emerge. But if it doesn't work better it will be seen as little more than a management tool, a "programme of the month".'

Other management thinkers, notably Sumantra Ghoshal (qv), have studied what might replace the old-style psychological contract when lifetime careers were the norm. Ghoshal suggests that sustainably successful companies enjoy a sort of 'moral contract' with their people revolving around respect for the individual as a value creator and a responsibility to help him or her develop their full potential.

The assumptions that individuals develop about themselves within their organization are in turn largely shaped by the assumptions those organizations hold about their own values, goals and how things are done, which they pass on in various ways to their employees.

These form a company's culture and may emerge in all kinds of ways, from the sober suits and white shirts that IBM salesmen were traditionally expected to wear to the intellectual clubbiness and sense of belonging that typify many departments within the BBC – always known simply as 'the Corporation' to its career staff. (ICI has a similar 'family' culture, and at one time its historic Mond Division, now subsumed in the restructuring of the late 1980s, had its own culture within ICI based on its leading-edge achievements in scientific innovation.)

Schein says an organization's culture is 'what it has learned as a total social unit over the course of its history'. He defines it as made up of artefacts (dress codes, office lay-outs, the signals a stranger would pick up); values (often enshrined in anecdotes from the founder's time); and underlying assumptions (behaviour within the organization and of the organization in the environment outside).

Consensus on such cultural landmarks among both workforce and management is essential to successful achievement of the organization's goals. Schein outlines five key areas in which this consensus should operate:

- The mission – 'what business are we in, and why?'
- The goals, which should include specific goals for all workers
- The means to accomplish the goals, including reward and incentive systems
- The means of measuring progress, including reporting and feedback
- The strategies for what to do when things go wrong

Schein's belief that the key to successful leadership is managing cultural change in an organization has made him the guru for a rapidly growing band of writers on corporate culture and how it affects, for example, the success or failure of a takeover or merger of two companies with differing cultures, or the diversification of a company into new markets. Schein designed a set of diagnostic steps to help identify such cultural and compatibility problems and suggest ways of solving them.

Diagnostic ability, indeed, is an essential attribute of good management, in Schein's view. His whole work on the roots of motivation began, like that of his mentor Douglas McGregor, by analysing the way managers view the people they manage.

Historically, these models divide into three. There is the 'rational-economic' model held by F. W. Taylor and expressed by McGregor as 'Theory X' – basically, the view that most people have to be coerced into work by economic incentives and require constant management supervision. Then there is the 'social' model, formulated by Mayo and his Hawthorne experiments, which recognized needs other than economic and the importance of a worker's peer groups on performance. The third historical concept, the 'self-actualizing' model, developed the social model further, into understanding the needs of individuals to develop their full potential. Abraham Maslow (qv) with his 'hierarchy of needs'; McGregor with Theory Y; Argyris (qv) and Herzberg (qv) were other influential gurus in this field. To these existing models, Schein added a fourth – the 'complex' model. This argued that in the huge gamut of human needs and motivations, an individual's response will be governed by many variables at different times and in different situations. (More recently, Schein has identified three cultures of management for organizational learning in the 21st century: the 'operator culture', based on the company's operational success; the 'engineering culture', related to the company's technology drivers; and the 'executive culture', driven by senior management. He thinks the latter two have tended to be overlooked because the first generally dominates. The three cultures rarely work well together, he says, but corporate success depends on a balance between them.) Schein also examined how incentives change according to an individual's changing perceptions; for example, why millionaires and other achievers persist in seeking still more millions or in setting themselves new and more difficult goals.

Robert Browning's lines: 'A man's reach should exceed his grasp, Or what's a heaven for?' encapsulate the mystery of motivation which Edgar Schein's work sets out to unravel.

KEY WRITINGS

Schein, E. H. (1978) *Career Dynamics: Matching Individual and Organizational Needs*, Wokingham: Addison-Wesley.
Schein, E. H. (1980) *Organizational Psychology*, New Jersey: Prentice-Hall.
Schein, E. H. (1985, 1992) *Organizational Culture and Leadership*, San Francisco: Jossey-Bass.
Schein, E. H. (1999) *The Corporate Culture Survival Guide*, San Francisco: Jossey-Bass.

46

RICHARD J. SCHONBERGER

(b. 1937)

Each function in a business seen as a 'customer' of the next in the chain

American industrial engineer and now international consultant and lecturer, who is credited with introducing just-in-time and other Japanese manufacturing techniques to the US. After leaving college, he worked for eight years in US defence industries – shipbuilding, aircraft overhaul, army-tank manufacturing. He then took a PhD in business studies at the University of Nebraska, specializing in production management and information systems, subsequently teaching there for 13 years.

At this time, he recalls: 'I was disgusted with manufacturing and thought the future lay with management information systems. I dropped it like a hot potato when manufacturing got exciting again.'

The catalyst in manufacturing happened through his work with computers in industry. Material Requirements Planning (MRP) was, he says, 'the only exciting thing to have happened in manufacturing in 50 years'.

Schonberger's first book, *Japanese Manufacturing Techniques* (1982), has sold over 150,000 copies in nine languages. His second, *World Class Manufacturing* (1986), sold 100,000 copies in eight languages, and together they are the two bestselling books of all time on manufacturing. Each of his five books has grown out of its predecessor, the fourth – *Building a Chain of Customers* (1990) – developing his ultimate theory that 'world-class' excellence in manufacturing and service industries can only be achieved by regarding each function in a business as a 'customer' of the one serving it.

A workaholic lecturer who is now also consultant and trainer to many leading multinational corporations including Hewlett-Packard, IBM, 3M, Ford, Monsanto, DuPont, Philips and Zanussi, Schonberger visits at least one factory a week in the US or Europe. He claims that he never repeats an idea he has previously expounded. 'If I don't have something new to say, I'm not saying it.' Considering that he has published over 100 articles as well as three major books and two 'casebooks', this must make him unique among management gurus.

Asked to distil his life's work into a 'mission statement', Richard Schonberger replies: 'World-class excellence is continual improvement in serving the customer's four basic wants: ever-better quality, ever-lower costs, ever-increasing flexibility and ever-quicker response. And that includes the next process in all the processes in between, all the way to the final customer.'

This is what Schonberger, the evangelist of 'customer-driven performance', means by the title of *Building a Chain of Customers*. In his vividly argued theories, spattered with examples and chatty miniature case studies, the many links between and within the different functions of a business – design, manufacturing, accounting, marketing – form a continuous 'chain of customers' leading directly to those who buy the final product or service. Tom Peters has called the concept 'a bold and meticulously detailed blueprint for redesigning corporations to destroy functional myopia, to live as a whole to serve the customer'.

Schonberger says of the techniques his books expound: 'They are easy to learn, don't cost much and immediately make people feel better about their jobs. Once people begin thinking that way, they cannot define their performance any other way except in the eyes of the "customer" where their work goes next.' With this simplicity, Schonberger argues that it does not take long to train existing people in industry in how to improve rapidly, 'how to love to improve and change, and become customer-focused'.

One of the major themes in his Japanese book, published in 1982, was that the Japanese success was not due to any cultural factors; that anyone could learn the techniques of Total Quality Management and so on. Studying the results as they became practised in hundreds of firms in North America between 1982 and 1986, Schonberger derived the basis of his second book, *World Class Manufacturing*. Hewlett-Packard, which sets forth its operational philosophy in a booklet called *The HP Way*, emerged as the best example anywhere. In 1996, Schonberger carried his research further in *World Class Manufacturing: The Next Decade*, which offered a set of metrics and customer-focused principles gleaned from the world's best manufacturing companies.

Cellular manufacturing is one of Schonberger's keys to the internal customer chain. In this, clusters of people and operations are arranged according to the work flow rather than departmental requirements. He credits its invention to five British industrial pioneers between about 1965 and 1975 – Professors John L. Burbidge and G. A. B. Edwards; consultant Joseph Gombinski; and works managers Gordon Ranson and Charles Allen. (Allen was manager of a Ferranti defence plant in Edinburgh that converted to the cell principle between 1968 and 1971.)

As usual, however, it was left to others to exploit and develop a brilliant British concept and to apply it to industrial practice on the shop floor.

'Toyota took those ideas, polished and perfected them and forced them on first- and second-echelon suppliers,' recalls Schonberger. 'The whole Toyota family of companies recognized itself, moved all its machines into cells and built all its new plants according to the way the product flowed, instead of by departments.

'By and large, we owe a debt of gratitude to the Japanese for showing the power of these ideas, even though there were plenty of other people who were aware of it.'

Schonberger believes his 'customer-driven message' applies to everyone in an organization 'from the CEO to the janitor'. When lecturing for his World Class International consultancy, he often prefers to address the 'up and coming, new blood, next crop of leaders', rather than existing top management.

'I believe the future is in the hands of the doers – the operators, assemblers, clerks, stock handlers, drivers, servers . . . The message – how to become a world-class organization – certainly does not go over anyone's head.

'It won't be a disaster if CEOs and presidents don't read books such as mine; their lieutenants and lower-level managers, and even some of their operators do, and they will run the show right half a generation from now – if not much sooner – with or without the blessings of their high-level bosses.'

Schonberger is encouraged by the growing 'convergence' he perceives in management thinking, by how similar themes of serving the customers and involving the employees are struck in most of the recent path-setting works: he cites Tom Peters' *Thriving on Chaos*, Stanley Davis' *Future Perfect* and Grayson and O'Dell's *American Business: A Two-Minute Warning*. The voices championing the new belief in both controlling the causes of costs and focusing on the customer's primary wants (quality, throughput time, flexibility and cost) are now diverse and international, and Schonberger can claim to be among the pioneers.

KEY WRITINGS

Schonberger, R. J. (1982) *Japanese Manufacturing Techniques*, New York: Free Press.
Schonberger, R. J. (1986) *World Class Manufacturing*, New York: Free Press.
Schonberger, R. J. (1987) *World Class Manufacturing Casebook*, New York: Free Press.
Schonberger, R. J. (1990) *Building a Chain of Customers*, New York: Free Press; London: Business Books.
Schonberger, R. J. (1996) *World Class Manufacturing: The Next Decade*, New York: Free Press.
Schonberger, R. J. (2001) *Let's Fix It: Overcoming the Crisis in Manufacturing*, New York: Free Press.

47

E. F. SCHUMACHER

(1911–1977)

'Small is beautiful': the human scale against corporate 'giantism'

German-born economist who worked for Britain's National Coal Board for 20 years from 1950 and became famous for one idea, encapsulated in a brilliant 'selling' title coined by his publisher for a 1973 book of essays on economics. In *Small Is Beautiful*, subtitled *A Study of Economics As If People Mattered*, Schumacher attacked the contemporary worship of corporate 'giantism' and argued for rethinking the conduct of business, economics and government on a human scale. The phrase 'small is beautiful' entered the language and came to symbolize the revolt against large, impersonal organizations which has grown in strength over the years and is a recognizable ancestor of today's powerful anti-globalization and green movements.

Schumacher not only challenged the corporate addiction to 'economies of scale' but also warned, presciently, of 'impending calamity if rampant consumerism and economic expansionism were not checked by human and environmental considerations'.

Thirty years on, his championing of human-scale units within large organizations has become conventional wisdom, with almost universal acceptance of the power of self-governing teams and cellular structures to promote motivation, innovation and creativity. His daughter

Barbara Wood has written in *Small Is Still Beautiful*, a recent reassessment of Schumacher's ideas, that his deeply religious view of humanity shaped his faith in 'the power of ordinary people to change the world'.

In two or three of his 19 essays Schumacher castigated what he called 'the idolatry of giantism', whether applied to multinational business corporations, megalopolitan urban developments or the size of nations and their internal markets, and noted that the achievement of Alfred Sloan at General Motors was 'to structure this gigantic firm in such a manner that it became, in fact, a federation of fairly reasonably sized firms'.

Surprisingly, perhaps, he also cited his own organization, the National Coal Board, one of the biggest industrial entities in Western Europe, as an example where 'something very similar (to Sloan's approach) was attempted under the chairmanship of Lord Robens; strenuous efforts were made to evolve a structure which would maintain the unity of one big organization and at the same time create the "climate" or feeling of there being a federation of numerous "quasi-firms". The monolith was transformed into a well coordinated assembly of lively, semi-autonomous units, each with its own drive and sense of achievement.

'While many theoreticians – who may not be too closely in touch with real life – are still engaging in the idolatry of large size, with practical people in the actual world there is a tremendous longing and striving to profit, if at all possible, from the convenience, humanity and manageability of smallness.'

Schumacher's prescriptions did not go much beyond such broad-brush statements (indeed, elsewhere in his book he argues quite passionately for the virtues of nationalized industry, not usually associated with the 'small is beautiful' movement), yet his approach – philosophical, influenced by Eastern religions such as Buddhism, and linked to the fulfilment and happiness of human beings in their working and social contexts – struck a resonant chord that reverberated long after the contents of his modest essays were forgotten. He was ahead of his time by about 15 years in advising the recognition of people's need to be involved in decision-making in small units: in the late 1980s Rosabeth Moss Kanter and other gurus would call it 'empowerment' and write whole books about it. Charles Handy says Schumacher has been 'enormously influential in spite of himself', but today it seems incredible that so much fame could have been built on such slender foundations. Even President Jimmy Carter is said to have read and been influenced by Schumacher's book.

As well as his work for the Coal Board, Schumacher set up the International Technology Development Group and became an adviser on economic problems to Third World countries. He always advocated small-scale production techniques and said: 'Organizations should imitate nature, which doesn't allow a single cell to become too large.'

In the late 1990s this became a much-lauded practice in creative firms such as the London advertising agency St Luke's, where projects spawned their own mini-businesses and as soon as the number of people working in them exceeded 35 another 'cell' split off, amoeba-like, to form another business unit.

Small Is Still Beautiful, by Joseph Pearce, a recent (2001) reassessment of Schumacher's importance as a thinker, notes that he was also the first Western expert to perceive that in newly industrializing countries such as India and China, the prime need was for 'low-cost workplaces where capital investment was kept to a minimum so that the manpower and human skills locally available could be used to the full'. It reflects on the continuing relevance of Schumacher's slim book, from the impact of Britain's 'real ale' movement on the massive brewing corporations to the growing global power of the green movement.

KEY WRITINGS

Schumacher, E. F. (1973) *Small Is Beautiful*, London: Blond and Briggs
Recommended reading: *Small Is Still Beautiful*, by Joseph Pearce, London: HarperCollins, 2001.

48

PETER M. SENGE

(b. 1947)

Systems thinking and the learning organization

Senior lecturer on the faculty of Massachusetts Institute of Technology's Sloan School of Management, first director of MIT's Center for Organizational Learning and the world's leading authority on the subject. His 1990 book *The Fifth Discipline* popularized the concept of the 'learning organization' in which individuals at all levels, including management, are enabled to develop their own skills, knowledge and competencies to the greater effectiveness of the whole. In one of Senge's definitions, a learning organization is 'continually expanding its capacity to create its future'.

The term had been coined a little earlier by the British consultant Bob Garratt in *The Learning Organization and the Need for Directors Who Think* (1987). Garratt followed it up in 1990 with a book called *Creating a Learning Organization*, but it was the MIT academic's work the same year, with the powerful resources of a leading US business school behind him, that focused widespread attention on the concept.

Senge's chief contribution was to identify five 'component technologies' or personal-development techniques that go to make up a true learning organization. These were: personal mastery, mental models, shared vision, team learning and systems thinking – the latter, the 'fifth discipline', being the ability to see the whole instead of the parts of an organization and to understand how individual actions can affect it. In 1997 *Harvard Business Review* described *The Fifth Discipline* as one of the seminal management books of the past 75 years.

Senge maintains a low personal profile, unusual among leading gurus, and disseminates little information about himself. He is chairman of the Society of Organizational Learning, a global virtual community of corporations, researchers and consultants dedicated to 'the interdependent development of people and their institutions'. He lectures internationally, holds somewhat 'new age'-style retreats for management (he is said to be a follower of Zen Buddhism) and works as a consultant in education, healthcare and government as well as business organizations. His research centre at MIT is partly sponsored by some of America's leading corporations, including Ford, AT&T and Motorola.

Originally an engineering graduate from Stanford, Senge has been at MIT since 1970 and freely acknowledges his debt to other pioneers in cognitive theory applied to organizations. Among them was Jay Forrester, a computer expert at MIT who got Senge interested in his theory of 'system dynamics' which propel organizations into certain paths of action.

Other powerful influences were Harvard professor Chris Argyris (qv), who originated the concept of single-loop and double-loop learning in his 1978 book, *Organizational Learning*, co-authored with MIT's Donald Schon, and the influential Arie de Geus, former head of planning at Shell, whom Senge credits with being the real progenitor of the learning organization. De Geus is also a seminal figure in the development of scenario planning and knowledge management and the author of one of the most-quoted aphorisms in management writing today: 'The ability to learn faster than your competitor may be the only sustainable competitive advantage.'

Senge was the first to preach that the most successful organizations of the future will be those that encourage learning at all levels and treat the skills, knowledge and experience of their employees as valuable assets – now a generally accepted truism. Managers, including the most senior executives, should regard themselves as stewards, teachers and designers of learning systems rather than top-down leaders. In a sequel to *The Fifth Discipline*, entitled *The Fifth Discipline Fieldbook* (1994), he presents practical tools for applying the principles in companies wanting to create their own learning organization, while his most recent book, *The Dance of Change* (1999), tackles the problem of sustaining learning in organizations over the long term.

Since 1990, the learning organization has become a key building block of change management. The theory has evolved and developed into such revolutionary but now familiar concepts as corporate 'universities', in-house personal-development workshops and knowledge transfer driven by corporate intranets and other information systems.

Senge is founding chair of the Society for Organizational Learning, a global network of corporations, researchers and consultants dedicated to its study and practice.

Peter Senge enjoys a high reputation in a business world that has now adopted many of his teachings even if it remains sceptical as to what a learning organization is and whether it can be created. Increasingly, corporate learning and knowledge are seen as the key to survival, not merely competitiveness. Yet Senge's masterwork requires concentrated application: the reader must plough through a mass of conceptualizing in *The Fifth Discipline* to dig out the nuggets at the core, and there are more accessible and practical later books on the subject such as *The Power of Learning* by Andrew Mayo and Elizabeth Lank (1994), both then working at the British computer group ICL.

Senge's four 'disciplines' which are held together and informed by the fifth, 'systems thinking', are broadly defined as follows:

- Personal mastery – the principle of continuous, lifelong learning by the individual, 'expanding the ability to produce the results we truly want in life'
- Mental models – uncovering and challenging those assumptions and mindsets that govern the individual's attitudes to the world
- Building shared vision – creating 'pictures of the future' that bring people together in pursuit of a common goal
- Team learning – thinking and learning together as a group for more effective performance; this also enables members of the team to develop better than they would individually

Systems thinking is 'a framework for seeing interrelationships rather than linear cause–effect chains, and for seeing processes of change rather than static snapshots'. As an example of a problem in the late 1980s requiring systems thinking, Senge cited the US/USSR arms race, each segment of which connected into a vicious circle fuelling fear and aggression. Systems thinking, by seeing the cycle as a whole, would suggest that it could be run in reverse, by a unilateral move towards arms reductions – and that, Senge asserted, was just beginning to look possible in 1990 with the initiatives of USSR secretary-general Mikhail Gorbachev.

'The practice of systems thinking starts with understanding a simple concept called "feedback" that shows how actions can reinforce or counteract (balance) each other,' Senge writes in *The Fifth Discipline*. 'It builds to learning to recognize types of structures that recur again and again . . . Ultimately, it simplifies life by helping us see the deeper patterns lying behind the events and the details.'

All the disciplines are interrelated: 'If people do not share a common vision, and do not share common "mental models" about the business reality within which they operate, empowering people will only increase organizational stress and the burden of management to maintain coherence and direction.'

Senge's thinking on the mindsets that people hold about their work and organizations was deeply influenced by Chris Argyris' seminal discoveries about the 'defensive routines' that insulate individuals' habits of thought and protect them from upsetting confrontations. Watching Argyris one day conducting an informal workshop at MIT, Senge was struck by the thought that 'with proper training, I could become much more aware of my mental models and how they operated.' The experiences of businessmen with whom he worked at MIT also led Senge to value the importance of openness among work colleagues and to understand the mental models through which people interpret the world – always incompletely.

Argyris' work with Donald Schon on double-loop learning and feedback – learning from others instead of relying on self-perpetuating experience – can also be seen as a key underlying component in Senge's development of systems thinking.

From outlining the development of individual cognitive skills, Senge moved on to redefine the role of management in a learning organization. One element was stewardship – guiding the ideas, core values and mission of the organization. But he also envisioned 'the manager as researcher and designer – researching the organization as a system and the forces, both internal and external, driving change, and designing the learning processes by which other managers throughout the organization come to understand the trends and forces as well'. This would be a key function of leadership in a learning organization, involving mentoring and coaching – a concept now widely accepted in management but radical in 1990.

If guiding the learning processes is not seen as the responsibility of corporate management, Senge warned, 'it will not be done, or it will not be done well. The fact that few of those presently in such positions recognize this role is one of the main reasons that learning organizations are still rare.'

More than a decade on, they are still rare, but pieces of them are beginning to fall into place. Since the publication of *The Fifth Discipline Fieldbook* in 1994, government organizations and companies of the stature of Royal Dutch/Shell, Coca-Cola, Ford and Hewlett-Packard have begun to apply the precepts of organizational learning and systems thinking.

PETER M. SENGE

KEY WRITINGS

Senge, P. (1990) *The Fifth Discipline: The Art and Practice of the Learning Organization*, New York: Doubleday; (1992) London: Century.
Senge, P. (1994) *The Fifth Discipline Fieldbook: Strategies for Building a Learning Organization*, New York: Doubleday; London: Nicholas Brealey.
Senge, P. et al. (1999) *The Dance of Change*, London: Nicholas Brealey.

269

49

ALFRED P. SLOAN

(1875–1966)

Decentralizing big corporations

US industrialist, head of General Motors from the early 1920s to the mid-1950s, and the man who virtually invented the decentralized, multi-divisional corporation of today. Sloan's name crops up more often in the indexes of management books than that of any other individual in industry – Peter Drucker's magisterial *Management: Tasks, Responsibilities, Practices* has over 25 page references to him.

Sloan wrote only one book, and that with assistance from a professional editor on *Fortune*; not usually enough to justify guru status in the management world, but that book, *My Years With General Motors* (1963), has been immensely influential on practising managers and on the study of organizations. James O'Toole, professor of management at the University of Southern California, called it 'the model for how managers should think – indeed, the model for much management education'. Sir John Egan, when he was chairman of Jaguar Cars, wrote in the preface to a new edition: 'I believe that this book should be on the reading list of everyone who can influence, or is influenced by, industrial enterprise.'

What was remarkable about Sloan's achievement in reorganizing the moribund General Motors of 1921 into America's leading automobile company within three years was not only that his innovations succeeded so quickly

270

but that they have stood the test of decades of change and are still models of organizational thinking in a business world unrecognizable from that of 1921.

Twenty-five years after Sloan restructured GM, Henry Ford's grandson applied the same principles at Ford and within five years had regained the company's growth and profit potential. Nearly 30 years after Sloan's revolution, in the early 1950s, General Electric adapted his design and it became, in Peter Drucker's words, 'the standard model worldwide'.

An electrical engineer by training and a graduate of MIT (he later helped finance its Sloan School of Management), Sloan was the general manager of the Hyatt Roller Bearing Company in 1900, when it merged with United Motors. In 1917, United was acquired by General Motors and Sloan, by then United's president, joined the GM board. He became president in 1923, chairman in 1946 and honorary chairman from 1956 until his death ten years later.

Sloan's celebrated design for 'federal decentralization' – autonomous divisions subject to financial and policy controls from a small corporate staff – took him only one month to construct, working with a small committee of top GM executives. Pierre S. Du Pont, head of the chemical company which was a major shareholder in GM, had asked him to help pull GM back from the brink of bankruptcy, and Du Pont himself had earlier restructured his company along decentralized lines between 1915 and 1920; a fact which has led some management writers to assume that Sloan simply borrowed the idea.

In fact, the two firms had been suffering from opposing problems – DuPont being heavily over-centralized, while GM was already untidily decentralized without adequate central control. In working out his own solution, Sloan greatly refined and polished the decentralization principle and, most importantly, developed the first systematic approaches to strategic planning. GM became the first company to change completely, through a planned strategy, the accepted manufacturing and marketing methods of an industry.

Such was the impact of this new approach that within ten years of the outbreak of World War I, the number of US automobile companies fell from over 100 to around a dozen, of which three (Ford, GM and Chrysler) accounted for fully 90 per cent of sales.

Alfred Pritchard Sloan, the Brooklyn-accented son of a New York tea, coffee and cigar wholesaler, was put in charge of General Motors in the midst of the worst slump to hit the infant automobile industry. William S. Durant had put together GM out of eight independent companies, all still run as virtual baronies by their owners, and it was plagued by over-production and wasteful duplication. Ford had 60 per cent of the US market with a single model – the Model T, cheap, standardized and black. General Motors had 12 per cent of the market with eight models, only two of which made a profit.

Sloan's 'federal' plan was designed to do more than rationalize GM's messy structure with centralized financial and policy control and professionally managed divisions each responsible for its own performance. It was to be the mechanism by which he could define and implement a new mission for GM – to produce a car for 'every purse and purpose'.

Up to that time the US auto industry was producing to just two levels of customer demand, the mass market and the class market – i.e. high-volume, low-priced cars, dominated by the Model T, and low-volume, high-priced cars. Sloan perceived much more varied and aspirational possibilities. He devised a five-model range, each overlapping in price and performance with the next, so that the low-income customer could pay a little more than for the Model T and get a car with far better styling and performance (and in other colours than black). At the same time, better-off purchasers could choose to economize with a good-looking low-priced car or pay slightly more and get a near-luxury model. Each of the five cars was designed to be a market leader in its class and competed with the GM car on either side of it, whether Chevrolet, Oldsmobile, Pontiac, Buick or Cadillac.

Sloan also introduced optional extras to stimulate customer interest, and by bringing in a new model every year he virtually invented the used-car market. This killed the changeless, all-alike Model T more quickly than any direct competition could have done. The one-year-old GM car, more stylish and a better performer than the Ford, could now beat it even on price.

The new organization Sloan devised reduced GM's eight car companies into five operating divisions, buttressed by three component divisions. Each division had its own engineering, production and sales departments but was supervised by a central corporate staff responsible for policy and finance. In every other way, each division was truly a business, with its chief executive responsible to Sloan as vice-president. (Sloan also introduced the innovation of taking a lower salary than the high-flyers who reported to him, the career professional.) GM's accessory divisions sold both to the car divisions and to outside customers, including GM's competitors. This was a principle which has retained its value to the present day.

Sloan's ideas, in fact, were very largely based on the functional analysis of management drawn up by Henri Fayol in the previous century. Where Fayol had achieved the organizational solution for the single-product manufacturing business, Sloan accomplished it for the large, complex manufacturing business of the mass-production age.

Sloan introduced a system of checks and balances into the divisional structure that gave engineering, manufacturing and finance equal status. In time, however, his network of committees and policy groups, designed to produce impartial and even-handed decisions, became riddled with factions and the financial arm prevailed. Over-production ensued and GM's market share in the 1980s dropped by 15 per cent. Sloan's design has now had a rebuild, but it had served GM well for nearly 60 years.

Sloan was a firm believer in the impersonal, task-focused concept of management. He was also an early believer in encouraging the sort of creative dissent that Tom Peters (qv) and Richard Pascale (qv) are recommending for keeping companies vigorous and innovative in the 1990s. Peter Drucker and other management writers liked to quote a story about Sloan chairing a meeting at one of GM's top committees. At the end of the discussion, he said: 'Gentlemen, I take it we are all in complete agreement on the decision here.' Everyone round the table nodded. 'Then,' said Sloan, 'I propose we postpone further discussion of this matter until the next meeting to give ourselves time to develop disagreement, and perhaps gain some understanding of what the decision is all about.'

Sloan was almost alone among practising managers before World War II to evolve management theories that have become classics. The other well-known example is Chester Barnard of American Telephone. But Sloan's achievements, though renowned throughout the automobile industry, only became widely known in 1963 when he published *My Years With General Motors*. The book became one of the first bestselling management autobiographies.

By this time, however, Sloan was nearly 90 and the book, it must be said, is no racy read along the lines of an Iacocca or Geneen. It is formal, old-fashioned and sometimes pedantic in style; nevertheless it provides a matchlessly detailed and authentic picture of how US industry was run between the wars. No one else could have produced so authoritative a case study as this man who, born in 1875, had grown up with the automobile and very largely shaped its place in modern American life.

The essentials of Sloan's organizational genius, however, can be more clearly picked out in books by others – Drucker's *Managing for Results*, for example, or his *Concept of the Corporation*. *My Years With General Motors* is best read as a slice of nutritious if sometimes dry industrial and social history.

KEY WRITINGS

Sloan, A. P. (1963, 1966, 1986) *My Years With General Motors*, New York: Doubleday; London: Sidgwick and Jackson; Penguin Books.

50

KAREN STEPHENSON

(b. 1952)

Mapping and managing human networks

Professor of management from 1990 to 2000 at the University of California in Los Angeles (UCLA), computer software entrepreneur and 'corporate anthropologist', Stephenson's speciality is the identification and management of human networks, both in and beyond the world of business organizations. Her methodology of social network analysis (SNA) became a hot topic after the terrorist atrocities of 11 September 2001; in her words 'a monumental moment [when] people realized that human networks could undermine anything'.

A highly independent academic who ploughs her own furrow, she has lectured or held visiting professorships at Harvard's Graduate School of Design, the Sloan School of Management at Massachusetts Institute of Technology and Imperial College, London. Her last known offices, typically enough, were above a rambling second-hand bookstore in New York's Greenwich Village.

She is president of her own Web consultancy, Netform, owning patents on software for analysing human networks, and has been a consultant on change and innovation to leading businesses such as J P Morgan and Hewlett-Packard. Since 9/11, she has also been an adviser to the US Defense Department on counter-terrorism. Her body of research on corporate relationships – she harvests confidential information from at least 80 per cent of individuals in any company she studies – now forms probably the biggest databank of business networks in the world.

A former Texas fine arts and chemistry student who took simultaneous degrees and then moved on to study quantum chemistry at the University of Utah, Stephenson's fascination with molecular patterns led her after three years to switch to anthropology and the study of ancient human trading networks. She earned her master's in anthropology (mathematical modelling) studying with two theorists who invented the field, and her paper won her an invitation to become a doctoral student at Harvard. Her interest in anthropological parallels with business organizations was inspired by the famous Margaret Mead and her work among primitive tribes in Papua New Guinea.

'In many ways the executive working for a large corporation is as exotic a creature to study as the member of a primitive tribe,' Stephenson explained to sceptical colleagues at Harvard. She went on to study primate behaviour and identified human equivalents to the grooming practices that encourage cohesion among groups of chimpanzees. Among corporate employees these would include shared experiences, small talk and gossip around the water cooler or coffee machine.

In a major research project for IBM's Advanced Business Unit, she established her now-famous roles of hubs, gatekeepers and pulsetakers within an organization; respectively, individuals who possess information through influential connections; other individuals with access to those hubs (who sometimes form information bottlenecks); and individuals with an insight into the psychology of the organization through their web of cross-functional relationships.

Overlaying these, Stephenson teaches, are six types of knowledge network governing our lives, between which individuals may move, changing roles from hub in one to pulsetaker in another. Gatekeepers and pulsetakers play a key role when an organization is planning major change

because they can be employed to test the water by respectively spreading word of a new work process and reporting on its reception at ground level.

Stephenson's 'quantum theory of trust' argues that trust is the essential lubrication for an organization's knowledge and information to flow at top efficiency: conversely, undermining trust in hubs, gatekeepers and pulsetakers is a useful weapon for weakening a malign network such as al-Qaeda. In this respect, Karen Stephenson's work could turn out to be more powerful against the global terrorist threat than the blunt instrument of military action.

Social network analysis – identifying and managing the hidden networks within an organization – is now, largely thanks to the work of Karen Stephenson, increasingly recognized as a means of leveraging organizational learning, retaining key workers, planning succession, harvesting innovative ideas and managing both the rate and quality of change. This collective capability, Stephenson argues, depends on trusted relationships between individuals and has more power to influence the success or failure of an organization than any managerial hierarchy.

Stephenson calls this the 'quantum theory of trust'. Among its many benefits, a high-trust organization also lowers transaction costs: when people feel able to speak freely about their work and offer suggestions for improving processes within the business, opportunities multiply and time-frames are shortened. Companies can enhance their competitiveness and power to innovate by cultivating a high-trust organization and by enabling the right people to work in conjunction with each other. It is an idea that other management thinkers have explored from their own perspectives, notably the INSEAD professors Kim (qv) and Mauborgne (qv).

Stephenson works within corporations by interviewing or issuing confidential questionnaires to at least 80 per cent of the employees. Questions include who they work with, from whom they seek career advice or creative collaboration, and who they socialize with. She then feeds this data into her network modelling software and produces a series of maps revealing all kinds of possible networks, each of which has 'an intelligence more than the sum of its parts'.

The idea of key organizational roles such as hub, gatekeeper and pulsetaker was not wholly originated by Stephenson, but she has used mathematical techniques, such as algorithms, to track them more precisely and to suggest how they can be used to improve organizational performance. Her mapping technique uncovers the hidden circulatory system of the organization and enables the effectiveness of individuals in various connected networks to be assessed; a valuable tool for succession planning as well as for solving efficiency problems and pushing forward change.

'If I wanted to increase learning in an organization,' she said in a 2002 interview with the US business writer Art Kleiner,* 'I would take a gatekeeper in an innovation network and put her or him with a pulsetaker in an expert network. That's an algorithm for facilitating the distribution of knowledge.'

She uses her methodology to solve many different corporate problems. At Hewlett-Packard she advised on ways to foster better innovation, at Merrill Lynch to find out why some of its HR managers were more effective than others, at J P Morgan to help in pre-merger work, at IBM to assist in re-engineering processes and at Steelcase, a large US office-equipment manufacturer, to devise a system for designing space for its clients based on good communication flows.

She believes that in any organizational culture there are at least six layers of knowledge, each reflected in a network of people exchanging different kinds of information. The most basic is the work network, involving routine daily contacts and functional talk, the so-called 'resting pulse' of the organization. Then there is the social network, the people both inside and outside work with whom others discuss what is going on. Third comes the innovation network, people who feel they are sufficiently on the same wavelength of trust to try out new ideas on each other and perhaps challenge accepted ways of doing things in

---

* *Strategy+Business* (4th quarter issue).

the organization. Fourth is the expert network, people who have a stored knowledge of the organization and to whom others turn for expertise but not necessarily for support in innovation. Fifth is the career guidance or strategic network, mentors or the people to consult about one's future. Finally, the learning network, people who make improvements by bridging the gap between old (expert knowledge) and new (innovation).

This last network crucially involves those one would trust enough to share sensitive information with. It is important enough to stand alone but works better, Stephenson says, in conjunction with other knowledge networks within a culture or community. It often lies dormant until the organization is faced by the need to change: it is then that the learning network in particular comes into its own as a vehicle for driving change through trusted individuals.

When explaining these hidden roles in a change process, Stephenson likens it to invisible laser beams criss-crossing a high-security room. A person entering the room without knowledge of where the beams are will set off alarms: SNA guides the change-planners through the invisible maze. Mergers, she points out, are another fraught area where skilful use of gatekeepers and pulsetakers can avoid many damaging uncertainties. In such situations, the best people will want to know what the new set-up holds for them; not always in financial terms but also in creative, job-satisfying ones. The networks can tell them more accurately than the architects of the merger, who tend to see the numbers first.[*]

In the wider world of marketing and advertising, the study of individuals as information hubs and communicators has been taken up in recent years by populist writers such as Malcolm Gladwell, whose bestseller, *The Tipping Point*, created a new buzz-word. A 'tipping point' happens when a mysterious process of public-opinion-forming, largely carried by word of mouth, builds up to become an epidemic-like force in anything from shoe sales to political campaigning.

Stephenson's unique contribution is to bring mathematical rigour to this otherwise fuzzy phenomenon of information and

---

[*] *Successful Innovation*, Michel Syrett and Jean Lammiman (Economist Books, 2002).

opinion flows and to capture its workings within organizations. Just possibly, it may also help unravel the world's current worst enemy, al-Qaeda and its unpredictable offshoots. Before September 2001 the fanatical Muslim network's existence was barely known outside intelligence circles: in 2005 it suddenly mutated into a new and even more alarming phenomenon, turning ordinary young British-born men into suicide bombers and mass killers. Al-Qaeda's new 'franchise' operatives, apparently linked only by modern technology and antique religion, will be the toughest challenge yet for the young science of social network analysis.

KEY WRITINGS

Dr Stephenson has contributed to many academic journals, including a co-authored article in the *Journal of Manpower* (1996), 'Managing Workforce Diversity', for which she won an innovation award. But until 2006 her work has been mainly available in the form of videos.

Stephenson, K. (2006) *The Quantum Theory of Trust*, London: Prentice-Hall.

51

F. W. TAYLOR

(1856–1915)

Scientific management and the 'one best way'

The man with a strong claim to being America's first management consultant, Frederick Winslow Taylor was the Quaker engineer who invented scientific management, the forerunner of time and motion study, work study and, to some extent, business process re-engineering. Unlike most of the consultants who followed him, Taylor was at home on the factory floor, and invented a machine tool that revolutionized the steel industry.

He spent his industrial career in steel companies, starting as a humble labourer with the Midvale Steel Works, where he ended as chief engineer, and then moving to the Bethlehem Steel Works of Pittsburgh as a consulting engineer in management. It was here that he carried out his celebrated experiments in breaking down the components of a manual task, timing each movement with a stopwatch. By finding the 'one best way' to perform every action in loading a railway car with pig-iron, he enabled a labourer called Henry Noll to lift his productivity from 12.5 tons to 47 tons a day. When applied to bricklaying, the technique was found to increase performance from 1,000 to 2,700 bricks a day.

Taylor believed that every employee could be trained to be 'first class' at some job, and that it was management's responsibility to identify these possibilities and provide opportunities for improvement.

Even at college, where he was nicknamed 'Speedy', Taylor was obsessed with improving efficiency. He got the rules of baseball changed by proving that over-arm bowling was more effective than under-arm. He was less successful, however, in persuading the tennis authorities that a spoon-shaped racket was more efficient than an oval one.

His revolutionary book, *The Principles of Scientific Management*, was developed out of academic papers published in the *American Magazine* in the spring of 1911. The book that followed was subsequently reissued as *Scientific Management* in 1947. A British army officer, Major Lyndall Urwick, reading Taylor in the trenches of World War I, was inspired to found a movement for scientific management in Britain: he later became the UK's first professional management consultant.

Scientific management had a great vogue in Fascist Italy, the Soviet Union and Nazi Germany, where its methodology may even have influenced the death camps. According to a recent biography of Taylor, one German historian has described Adolf Eichmann as 'a perfect Taylor engineer'.

In the US, Taylor's work was carried forward and developed as time and motion study by the husband-and-wife team Frank and Lillian Gilbreth and other efficiency experts. Japanese industrialists have admired Taylor since 1913 and adopted many of his principles in developing revolutionary production techniques in the 1970s and 1980s: Taiichi Ohno of Toyota, father of the just-in-time system, acknowledged his debt to scientific management. Japan's ready acceptance of the Deming and Juran methods of statistical quality control in the 1950s also owed much to the deep roots Taylorism had already put down in Japanese industrial practices.

Taylor's influence can be strongly detected in business process re-engineering, that dominant management fad of the mid-1990s, and it is interesting to note that, much as re-engineering was initially criticized for de-humanizing work processes, so Taylor in his own day was attacked for stripping jobs of skill and judgement, and for treating workers as machine parts. 'After [Henry] Ford and Taylor got through with them,' notes Taylor's biographer Robert Kanigel, 'most jobs needed less of everything – less brains, less muscle, less independence.'

From management's point of view, Taylorism in its heyday stood for efficiency and the elimination of waste. It powered US production techniques in World War II and its principles can be seen today in any industry based on standardized production and quality, such as the fast-food business.

In 1977 three groups of US historians and managers ranked Taylor first among contributors to American business and management thought – Ford came no higher than sixth. In 1994 the revered Peter Drucker (qv) reasserted his view that Taylor, Darwin and Freud were the makers of the modern world.

For all its flaws, Taylorism remains a powerful, if un-acknowledged force in the insatiable management search, sharpened by the recession of the early 1990s, for doing more with less. For the lasting impact that Taylor's concepts of work measurement and production control have had on industrial practice, he is likely to remain the biggest management influence of the last 100 years.

Frederick W. Taylor believed in one maxim above all, that 'the principal object of management should be to secure the maximum prosperity of each employee.' To this end he preached that management and workforce were interdependent and relied on each other to achieve the common goal of higher prosperity. An early experiment as consultant to a ball-bearing company on raising the quality of their product was conducted on the principle of a modern quality circle with the workers becoming responsible for their own improvement.

Other ideas of his, such as performance measurement – albeit in primitive form in the 1890s – have stood the test of time, but his arrogance in controlling how people worked caused a lasting counter-revolution half a century later, when it became understood that performance was directly linked to motivation, participation and satisfying a worker's sense of self-worth. Taylor deeply antagonized the labour unions by making peak productivity gains (such as Noll's 47 tons) the norm, with penalties for falling short.

His writing exhibited a certain blinkered complacency. 'Under scientific management,' Taylor wrote, 'the initiative of the workmen – that is, their hard work, their good will, their ingenuity – is obtained practically with absolute regularity, while under even the best of the older type of management the initiative is only obtained spasmodically and somewhat irregularly . . . By far the greater gain under scientific management comes from the new, the very great and the extraordinary burdens and duties which are voluntarily assumed by those on the management's side.'*

The Principles of Scientific Management rested on four 'great underlying principles of management'. These were:

1. The development of a science of work to replace the old rule-of-thumb methods by which workmen operated. Fulfilling optimum goals would earn higher wages; failure to do so would result in loss of earnings.
2. Scientific selection and progressive development of the worker: training each to be 'first class' at some task.
3. Bringing together the science of work and the scientifically selected and trained workers for best results.
4. Equal division of work and responsibility between workers and management, cooperating together in close interdependence.

In Taylor's thinking, every task, whether of worker or manager, became discrete and specialized. In its application to management, he described this as 'functional management'. On the worker's side, he saw benefits of increased earnings, by between 30 and 100 per cent.

---

* Taken from *The Theory of Social and Economic Organization*, translated and edited by A. M. Henderson and T. Parsons, New York: Free Press. Quoted in *Organization Theory* (1990) edited by D. S. Pugh, London: Penguin Books.

Taylor and Ford between them set the mould for mass production and the assembly line – although Ford always denied the influence of scientific management on his factories, other car manufacturers were adopting Taylor's methods years before Ford's first assembly line cranked into action in 1913, and reporting substantial cuts in costs and manpower.

'In the past the man was first,' wrote Taylor in *The Principles of Scientific Management*. 'In the future the system will be first.' Although his theories are now ostensibly discredited, they have resilient powers of survival. Robert Waterman, the co-author of *In Search of Excellence* and author of two respected books examining how companies renew themselves and enhance their performance through people management, believes that many managers in the late 1990s are Taylorists at heart.

And, as Peter Drucker acknowledged in his monumental book *Management: Tasks, Responsibilities, Practices* (1974), Taylor was 'the first man in history who did not take work for granted, but looked at it and studied it.'

KEY WRITINGS

Taylor, F. W. (1947) *Scientific Management*, New York: Harper and Row.
Taylor, F. W. with a new introduction (1998) *The Principles of Scientific Management*, New York: Dover Books.
Recommended background reading: *The One Best Way: Frederick Winslow Taylor and the Enigma of Efficiency*, by Robert Kanigel, Viking, New York; John Wiley, London, 1997.

52

ALVIN TOFFLER

(b. 1928)

A world in flux and the rise of the 'prosumer'

Veteran US-born futurologist who virtually invented the genre in 1970 with *Future Shock*, a book of panoramic scope on the 'roaring current of change' that was already engulfing long-established ways of living and doing business. It predicted a post-industrial world of shifting institutions and values in which nothing would ever again seem permanent, a world powered by knowledge and accelerating technology where businesses would need to restructure themselves repeatedly to survive. Toffler and Peter Drucker (qv) heralded the onset of the information economy almost · simultaneously, though Drucker had published his theory a year earlier in *The Age of Discontinuity*, in which he also coined the term 'knowledge worker'.

Toffler went on to publish a big book on seismic social change every ten years for the next two decades, forming a trilogy 'on what happens to people when their entire society abruptly transforms itself into something new and unexpected'. *The Third Wave* (1980) defined the post-industrial society and predicted consumer-oriented 'mass customization' in place of mass production, while *Powershift* (1990) charted how science and technology were changing power relationships between individuals, communities, regions and nations, bringing wealth but also conflict and stress.

Toffler and his wife Heidi, who wrote the books together although she chose not to be credited as co-author, met as liberal-arts students at New York University. Toffler had no natural interest in mathematics or science but he realized that both were going to be crucially important in the postwar world, so he took a course in technology. He then worked in automobile and steel factories, wrote poetry and novels and embarked on a career as a journalist, including a stint as an associate editor on *Fortune* magazine.

In the 1960s, Toffler was asked to write a paper for IBM on the long-term social and organizational implications of the computer, a deeply formative assignment. Working as a newspaper correspondent in Washington, DC, and observing how disconnected the US governmental process was from the social and technological changes going on, he published an article called 'The future as a way of life'. This would become the genesis of *Future Shock*, whose title Toffler likened to the culture shock of suddenly being immersed in another country: only in this case, the shock arrived without moving from home.

The Tofflers have never claimed to predict the future as such. Nobody can, says Toffler: 'What we have constructed is a model of social and historical change.' Much of that change has come about as their books suggested, although some early forecasts failed to materialize – notably a popular revolt against scientists and the death of organizational hierarchies in favour of a fluid 'adhocracy'. The latter became accepted wisdom among a number of management gurus but in reality affected only certain types of business organization.

In *The Third Wave*, however, Toffler accurately foresaw how advanced technologies would proliferate around the world beyond the control of the economies which gave birth to them. He also predicted the future of war as 'electronic terrorism', citing a former US intelligence officer, expert in advanced computing, who told him that with 20 people and $1m he could 'shut America down' by targeting the most vulnerable nodes on the electronic networks.

Despite his non-academic background, his work has brought him scholarly recognition as a visiting professor at Cornell University and a fellow of the American Association for the Advancement of Science.

In their time, the works of Alvin Toffler were said to have significantly influenced contemporary thinking and to have been read by world leaders as diverse as US president Richard Nixon and Mikhail Gorbachev, the last leader of the old Soviet Union.

All three of his big books are massive in scope and detail, drilling down into tiny but telling observations, such as the shortening of attention span that takes place in humans battered by ever faster, bigger assaults of words and images. 'By speeding up change in the outer world, we compel the individual to relearn his environment at every moment. This in itself places a new demand on the nervous system. The people of the past, adapting to comparatively stable environments, maintained longer-lasting ties with their own inner conceptions of "the way things are".'

'Information overload' was one of many phrases to enter the language through *Future Shock*, and Toffler foresaw 30 years ahead of his time the paradoxical stress of decision-making in a consumer world bloated with choice, or 'overchoice' as he described it.

Similarly, he saw the spread of the drugs culture among young people and even of casual violence as probable by-products of the impermanent society with its bewildering complexity of choice, decision-making and disorientation in personal values. In *The Third Wave*, charting civilization's latest shift following its agrarian and industrial economic phases, he predicted that the rapid and fundamental ways in which technology would affect society would bring accelerated stress, uncertainty and trauma: suddenly 'old ways of thinking . . . no matter how cherished or how useful in the past, no longer fit the facts.'

Much of *The Third Wave* was remarkably accurate in its portrayal of the world we live in now: mass production giving way to 'mass customization', with the customer so closely integrated into the transaction process that 'we will find it more and more difficult to tell just who is actually the customer and who the producer.' He called this the rise of the 'prosumer' – consumers who perform tasks for themselves that were formerly done professionally or commercially for them. Online banking and other forms of electronic do-it-yourself have since led to a huge amount of unpaid work being done by the customer rather than the provider, saving the latter £35bn a year in Britain alone in one recent estimate.

Toffler also accurately outlined the flexibility of working time, the growth of homeworking, the fragmentation or 'demassifying' of culture that personal technology would bring and how the new systems would challenge 'all the old executive turfs, the hierarchies, the sexual role divisions, the departmental barriers of the past'. In this he was ahead of later gurus writing about the 'portfolio' future of work and the flattening of hierarchies, although the latter cannot be said to have conquered all of industry yet.

He also foresaw the need for corporations to accept social and environmental responsibilities as well as duties to shareholders, customers and employees, but he was almost comically wrong in suggesting that corporations would become a 'moral force' – a decade later would come the exposure of massive corporate wrongdoing in Enron, Tyco and their ilk, and the need for much closer regulatory controls to curb executive greed.

Powershift has turned out a less significant book, perhaps because it covered much of the same ground, albeit from a different angle – who and what would control the new processes – but it, too, offered early insights into such phenomena as the rise of Islam and the growing urge among fundamentalists to Islamicize the West. Well before the spread of the Internet and the World Wide Web, the book examined the role of the 'subversive media' – how faxes, computers, VCRs and new satellite technology were creating a vast interlinked global media system that would thwart censorship and undermine traditional authority.

Future Shock and *The Third Wave* were exaggerated in many of their extrapolations but they identified a number of business and marketing developments that even today are only just being exploited. One example is the 'psychic component', as Toffler called it; the elusive factor that gives one product more customer fulfilment over another. A prescient paragraph in *Future Shock* runs: 'As more and more of the basic material needs of the consumer are met, it is strongly predictable that even more economic energy will be directed at meeting the consumer's subtle, varied and quite personal needs for beauty, prestige, individuation and sensory delight. The manufacturing sector will channel ever greater resources into the conscious design of psychological distinctions and gratifications. The psychic component of goods production will assume increasing importance.'

That was written nearly 30 years before Shoshana Zuboff and James Maxmin introduced the term 'individuation' in *The Support Economy* (2003), their much-praised study of 21st-century markets, and nearly every brand manager today would take Toffler's analysis as conventional wisdom. The makers of women's anti-ageing creams, to take an obvious example, know all about 'psychic components' in marketing their products.

The Third Wave in particular remains an impressive piece of forward thinking, even though in 1980 Toffler found it necessary to explain to readers what a word processor – 'a smart typewriter' – was all about. In less than five years, Britain's Alan Sugar would be producing the cheap and cheerful Amstrad for home and office and, within the decade, typewriters would virtually disappear.

Inevitably the very pace of change that he was writing about has made huge areas of his books historical documents, but his ability to penetrate through the technological revolution to its deeper effects on human society gives Toffler a more enduring place in management thinking than most of the futurologists, trend-spotters and scenario-planners who have come after him.

KEY WRITINGS

Toffler, A. (1970) *Future Shock*, New York: Bantam Books.
Toffler, A. (1980) *The Third Wave*, New York: Bantam Books.
Toffler, A. (1990) *Powershift*, New York: Bantam Books.

53

FONS TROMPENAARS

(b. 1952)

Managing cultural differences for business success

Along with his Dutch compatriot Geert Hofstede (qv), consultant and academic Fons Trompenaars is the world's leading authority on the study and management of cultural differences between countries.

The son of a Dutch father and a French mother, and cross-culturally educated (a master's in business economics at the University of Amsterdam and a PhD at Wharton, Pennsylvania), Trompenaars joined Royal Dutch/Shell in 1981 and worked for the oil giant in nine countries, gaining hands-on research in managing cultural differences before becoming a consultant for Shell and a roster of multinationals, including Philips, BP, Heineken, Mars, Motorola, GM, Dow Chemical, Merrill Lynch, Johnson and Johnson, and Honeywell. In 1993, he made his name as an original thinker with *Riding the Waves of Culture*, co-authored with Charles Hampden-Turner, which attracted a wide readership among managers for its vivid anecdotal style. It remains a classic in the field.

Trompenaars' approach differs from that of Hofstede, his early inspiration, in being more closely focused on practical management issues. Hofstede looks at the shaping undercurrents of national diversity; Trompenaars at how managers can work with cultural differences and use them to achieve better corporate performance. His message to business – particularly directed at US multi-nationals that believe the American managerial model can be applied anywhere – is to dispel the idea that there is 'one best way' of managing and to promote the concept that cultural differences need to be addressed and reconciled if full potential is to be achieved.

One of his models takes five types of commonly experienced dilemma and examines how they would be resolved in different cultures: universal versus particular, individual versus team, specific or codified versus implicit or diffused knowledge, internal versus external control and top-down versus bottom-up.

Together with the Cambridge-based academic Charles Hampden-Turner (his co-author on several books), Trompenaars founded and runs the Centre for International Business Studies in Amsterdam, a consulting and training organization for international management. He is also visiting professor for the international MBA programme at the Erasmus University/Rotterdam School of Management.

It was after years of doctoral study at Pennsylvania's elite Wharton School of Business that Fons Trompenaars began thinking about the confident American management techniques he had just been taught and wondering how much of it would apply in his home country, the Netherlands, and elsewhere in the world. His subsequent work for Shell in nine countries convinced him that successful management of an international company depended on understanding and respecting the cultural differences of the countries in which that company operated. Beyond that, it required the ability to reconcile problems and dilemmas arising out of cultural differences. Out of this arose his life's work, educating managers in managing across cultures.

One very basic difference between cultures, he explains, is that of universalist versus particularist. A universalist culture implicitly accepts a set of rules that govern behaviour regardless of personal circumstances or relationships. A particularist culture may question or bend these if they conflict with personal loyalties. The US, UK, Germany and Switzerland, with their Protestant-based cultures, are universalist, whereas Catholic or Eastern cultures, such as France, Italy, Latin America – particularly Venezuela – and much of Asia, are particularist, and therefore more prone to look at individual situations in terms of family or friendship ties.

'Culture is a series of rules or methods that a society has evolved to deal with the recurring problems it faces,' he writes. 'They have become so basic that, like breathing, we no longer think about how we approach or resolve them. Every country and every organization faces dilemmas in relationships with people; dilemmas in relationships to time and dilemmas in relations between people and the natural environment.'

In one of his most recent books, *Did the Pedestrian Die?* (2003), Trompenaars illustrates the universal–particular principle with a hypothetical personal dilemma about legal niceties conflicting with friendship. A motorist with a friend in his car is driving too fast and knocks down a pedestrian. When the case comes to court, the driver asks his friend – the only witness – to say he was not speeding. What right has the friend to do this?

A universalist would say none, especially if the injury to the pedestrian was serious. A particularist would take time to weigh up the issues and might well choose friendship over legal obligations. Trompenaars' research in 31 countries revealed that two-thirds of Venezuelans (68 per cent) would lie to help their friend, whereas 93 per cent of Americans and 97 per cent of Swiss would shun the very idea. Switzerland and Venezuela are at the opposite ends of Trompenaars' research spectrum in rule-based versus person-based cultures, with the UK ranking sixth most rule-based after Switzerland, and Russia the third most person-based after Venezuela.

Cultural differences, Trompenaars explains, are not only national; they occur also in different regions of the same country, in large organizations and in professional and other relationships within a society. He identifies five major differences in the way humans deal with each other, and a further two dealing with different attitudes to time (often a critical factor in business dealings) and to the surrounding environment. As well as the universal–particular divide, the other main differences are:

- Individual versus communitarian (do people regard themselves primarily as individuals or group members?)
- Neutral versus emotional (is the expression of emotion culturally acceptable or not?)
- Specific versus diffuse (a business relationship will focus on the terms of the contract rather than on the customer as a person, a typically American approach compared to, say, that of a Japanese)
- Achievement versus ascription (a culture that judges people on what they have achieved in their lives as opposed to their connections in society)

In management terms, a universalist will try to impose uniform procedures on an organization – the 'one best way' – and introduce any change measures in a public manner, treating everyone the same. The particularist works through informal networks, pulling levers privately and treating people in a more subjective way. A contract, for instance, will be 'seen as definitive by the universalist but only as a rough guideline or approximation by the particularist', says Trompenaars. Many a major deal between Eastern and Western companies has foundered on such lack of understanding, when a Japanese use of 'yes', for example, has been taken prematurely as acceptance of a contract instead of a polite staging process towards it.

In *Riding the Waves of Culture*, which deals predominantly with international variations in culture, Trompenaars notes that differences can be strongly marked even between countries of apparent similarity in the same region. 'All the examples show that there is a clear-cut cultural border between the northwest European (analysis, logic, systems and rationality) and the Euro-Latin (more person-related, more use of intuition and sensitivity).'

There are, he notes, even significant differences between Dutch and Belgians – geographical neighbours but totally different in their views of business organizations. The Belgian tradition is of a paternalistic family organization with the head of the family in absolute control, and Belgians think the Dutch are far too democratic, unnecessarily consultative and naturally anti-authority.

Trompenaars quotes the founder of the European Community, Jean Monnet, as saying: 'If I were again facing the challenge to integrate Europe, I would probably start with culture.' Geert Hofstede also sees cultural diversity as one of the biggest challenges to the present EU's survival.

Trompenaars covers some of the same ground as Hofstede in the way he classifies national cultures; for example, Protestant-based individualism versus Catholic-based social consensus. The two are useful to study together because Hofstede is looking at the underlying psychology of national culture as well as how it manifests itself in business or social life. Both theorists also have amassed enormous international databases for their training and consulting programmes.

Trompenaars also classifies corporate cultural structures in a similar way to Charles Handy (qv) and Henry Mintzberg (qv), but with quirkier categories. Along with 'family' (self-evident in its structure), he suggests 'Eiffel Tower' (narrow decision-making area at the top, broad base), 'guided missile' (more egalitarian in the pursuit of a task or project) and 'incubator' (oriented towards ideas and creativity, such as a Silicon Valley start-up).

But the book is at its most useful for managers working in multinationals in suggesting ways of fostering trust and systems that work with the grain of employees' cultures rather than against it, and its simple, anecdotal style has kept it a steady seller over the years. The book was revised in 1997 with new chapters on South Africa's post-apartheid 'rainbow nation' and cultural differences arising from gender and ethnicity, especially in the US.

One surprising revelation in *Riding the Waves of Culture* comes from the charts showing how different nations address the concept of time, especially in forward-planning. These do not necessarily divide along predictably East/West lines, since the Philippines comes out with the shortest time horizons and Hong Kong with the longest. Although the US and UK are notorious for short-termism, in fact Spain of '*mañana*' reputation turns out to be rather more short-term in its time horizons than Britain. The book is full of other such carefully researched findings that overturn conventional wisdom.

Trompenaars' criticism of the one-size-fits-all US management model has incurred predictable opposition among American consultants and management theorists, including Gary Hamel (qv), who has pointed out how many US companies out-perform European competitors in their operations in Asia or Latin America. But Hamel's own authority was damaged by his premature enthusiasm for Enron as a company breaking the boundaries of innovation (including accounting innovation, as it disastrously turned out), while the idea of diversity as desirable within organizations is now so widely accepted that Trompenaars would appear to have the future on his side.

KEY WRITINGS

Trompenaars, F. and Hampden-Turner, C. (1993, 1997) *Riding the Waves of Culture: Understanding Cultural Diversity in Business*, London: Nicholas Brealey Publishing.
Trompenaars, F. and Hampden-Turner, C. (1994) *The Seven Cultures of Capitalism*, London: Piatkus Books.
Trompenaars, F. and Hampden-Turner, C. (2000) *Building Cross-Cultural Competence*, Yale University Press.
Trompenaars, F. and Hampden-Turner, C. (2001) *21 Leaders for the 21st Century*, New York: McGraw-Hill.
Trompenaars, F. (2003) *Did the Pedestrian Die?*, Chichester: John Wiley.

54

MAX WEBER

(1864–1920)

How individuals respond to authority in organizations

German sociologist and political economist, trained as a lawyer, who taught at Berlin University and later became professor of economics at the universities of Freiburg, Heidelberg and Munich. In 1918 he was a member of the committee set up to draft the constitution of the Weimar Republic. His widest-read book was – and remains – *The Protestant Ethic and the Spirit of Capitalism*, a short and stimulating thesis that linked the moral imperatives of puritanical Protestantism, especially Calvinism, with the mainspring of entrepreneurial capitalism, the pursuit of profit and, ultimately, with the 'iron cage' of modern materialism. Weber's chief interest to students of management and organization theory – though now much less influential than it used to be – lies in *The Theory of Social and Economic Organisation*, first published in 1924, four years after his death.

Max Weber was the first writer on management theory to analyse the role of the leader in an organization and to examine how and why individuals respond to various forms of authority. He was probably the first, since the Greeks coined the term, to use 'charisma' in its modern sense of that quality in an individual's personality which effortlessly draws others to follow.

Weber distinguished three types of legitimate authority, as opposed to power, which forces people to obey: the rational, the traditional and the charismatic. The rational, or rational-legal, which he saw as the dominant form of modern institution, rested on a system of rationally thought-out goals and functions designed to maximize the performance of an organization and implemented by certain rules and procedures. Authority here was vested in the office of a person rather than in the individual. It was an impersonal system which he described, with no criticism implied, as a bureaucracy. He held a bureaucracy to be the most efficient form of administration because it worked on a commonly accepted hierarchical basis without personal whims and with a judicious reliance on the appointment of experts.

The traditional form of authority in organizations was seen by Weber as being owed to the person rather than the office; typically, a hereditary system where the leader's writ is established by precedent, as in a family business. It has roots in feudal rights and duties but is not unknown in modern firms where patronage may take the place of inheritance. Weber's concept of tradition may also be detected in the cultures of those companies where the attitude 'we've always done it this way' becomes a self-justification resistant to critical analysis by newcomers.

Charismatic authority, because it relies on the particular qualities of an individual, is unlikely to find a successor in its own mould. Organizations with charismatic founders like Henry Ford or Thomas J. Watson of IBM tend to mutate, either into the traditional (hereditary) mode, with greater or lesser success, or into a succession determined by impersonal factors and hence into a rational, bureaucratic form.

Weber was in no doubt that the latter system was the buttress of efficient administration in whatever kind of institution it operates. 'Precision, speed, unambiguity, knowledge of files, continuity, discretion, unity, strict subordination, reduction of friction and of material and personal costs – these are raised to the optimum point in the strictly bureaucratic administration,' he wrote.

The system's machine-like superiority over other types of

authority rests on its hierarchical form, with each office sub-ordinate to the one above it; every official's role determined by written rules; a regulated right of appeal and the ability to take grievances upwards; and complete separation of the administrative staff from ownership of the means of production or administration, as well as a complete absence of 'rights' to any office by its incumbent.

The purest type of bureaucratic administration, says Weber, exists when its officials conduct the business according to ten criteria:

1. They are personally free, subject only to authority in respect of their impersonal official obligations.
2. They are organized in a clearly defined hierarchy of offices.
3. Each office has a clearly defined sphere of competence in the legal sense.
4. The office is filled by a free, contractual relationship. Thus, in principle, there is free selection.
5. Candidates are selected on the basis of technical qualifications. In the most rational case, this is tested by examination or guaranteed by diplomas certifying technical training, or both. They are appointed, not elected.
6. They are remunerated by fixed salaries in money, for the most part with a right to pensions. Only under certain circumstances does the employing authority, especially in private organizations, have a right to terminate the appointment, but the official is always free to resign. The salary scale is primarily graded according to rank in the hierarchy; but in addition to this criterion, the responsibility of the position and the requirements of the incumbent's social status may be taken into account.
7. The office is treated as the sole, or at least the primary, occupation of the incumbent.
8. It constitutes a career. There is a system of 'promotion' according to seniority or to achievement, or to both. Promotion is dependent on the judgement of superiors.
9. The official works entirely separated from ownership of the means of administration, and without appropriation of his position.

10. He is subject to strict and systematic discipline and control in the conduct of the office.*

Weber's ten criteria are in the process of being dismantled in much contemporary management thinking, such as the work of Charles Handy (qv) and Rosabeth Moss Kanter (qv), who anticipate a sea-change in both the hierarchical nature of organizations and the concept of lifelong bureaucratic careers. But a century ago, Weber was utterly convinced of the superiority of this form of harnessing the corporate effort of individuals, and many an organization in the 1990s testifies to its durability.

'Experience tends universally to show that the purely bureaucratic type of administrative organization – that is, the monocratic variety of bureaucracy – is, from a purely technical point of view, capable of attaining the highest degree of efficiency and is in this sense formally the most rational known means of carrying out imperative control over human beings. It is superior to any other form in precision, in stability, in the stringency of its discipline, and in its reliability. It thus makes possible a particularly high degree of calculability of results for the heads of the organization and for those acting in relation to it. It is finally superior both in intensive efficiency and in the scope of its operations, and is formally capable of application to all kinds of administrative tasks.'*

KEY WRITINGS

Weber, M. (1930) *The Protestant Ethic and the Spirit of Capitalism*, London: Allen and Unwin.
Weber, M. (1947) *The Theory of Social and Economic Organisation*, New York: Free Press.

* Taken from *The Theory of Social and Economic Organisation*, translated and edited by A. M. Henderson and T. Parsons, New York: Free Press. Quoted in *Organization Theory* (1990) edited by D. S. Pugh, London: Penguin Books.

55

JACK WELCH

(b. 1935)

'Maximizing the intellect of the organization'

Charismatic former chairman/CEO of General Electric, judged by *Fortune* as 'the greatest manager of the 20th century' and consistently ranked over many years as the world's most admired businessman. Welch merits a place among management gurus for conceptualizing and implementing such practices as Work-Out (encouraging ideas and problem-solving at all levels of the workforce) and thus making GE the nearest thing to that elusive entity, the learning organization. Since retirement in 2001 he has published his memoirs, *Jack: Straight From the Gut* (for which he received a reputed $10m advance, given to charity), and been appointed executive coach to a number of leading corporations.

In 2005 he published *Winning*, a practical guide to successful management drawn from his own hands-on experience in such areas as hiring the right talent, making change happen and winnowing out non-performers. The book was written with his second wife, the former editor of *Harvard Business Review*, in the wake of a messy divorce which cost him half his $900m fortune and exposed him to damaging publicity about the lavish corporate perks he continued to receive from GE after retirement. However, Welch continues to be in keen demand to impart his wisdom to executive gatherings around the world, and remains the biggest business celebrity of the age, crowned 'manager of the century' by *Fortune* magazine.

The only child of a Boston Irish railroad conductor and a feisty mother who taught him self-confidence and how to both 'hug and kick' people, John F. Welch Jr gained a first degree in chemical engineering at Amherst College, University of Massachusetts, and a master's and doctorate in engineering from the University of Illinois. He entered GE straight from university in 1960 as an engineer in the plastics division and steadily rose in responsibility for various businesses, becoming a vice-president at 36 and the corporation's youngest chairman in 1981, aged 45. Over the next 20 years he turned a successful but unwieldy conglomerate into the world's most valuable company, whose market value soared from $13bn in 1981 to more than $550bn in 2001. In each of those 20 years, GE's share price rose on average by 21 per cent.

Among the keys to Welch's achievement was his initial dictum that each GE business had to be No. 1 or No. 2 in its market, and if not, to 'fix, close or sell'. He conceived and drove four or five key initiatives across the organization: Work-Out (now trademarked) and its offshoot, the Change Acceleration Program; the Six Sigma maximum-quality process; 'boundarylessness', which at a basic level meant cross-fertilizing best practice on a global scale among the businesses; and digitalization. Welch came late personally to e-business although sections of GE had been operating online since 1994: in 1999 he initiated 'destroyyourbusiness.com', which made it mandatory for every GE business to reinvent itself for the digital age.

Welch thinks of himself primarily as a teacher – one of his first acts as CEO was to invest heavily in Crotonville, GE's corporate management academy – and he was quick to perceive that the greatest constraint on the growth of any modern business was not lack of access to capital, but to knowledge and new ideas. He sought best practice from competitors and other industries as well as from within his own businesses, refining Motorola's original 1987 concept of Six Sigma quality and borrowing Wal-Mart's technique of Quick Market Intelligence (QMI), in which salespeople briefed senior managers weekly on the latest customer feedback and consumer trends.

Under Welch, GE was called 'the greatest leadership school in the world', and one of the contenders to succeed him, Bob Nardelli, observed that about 75–80 per cent of GE leadership skills were 'very portable'. Not only has GE furnished many other companies with successful CEOs, but innovations such as Work-Out and Six Sigma have been widely adopted in businesses ranging from engineering to financial services. Less popularly, Welch pioneered the first wave of massive downsizing in corporate America in the early 1980s, leading to his nickname of 'Neutron Jack' (after the neutron bomb, which vaporizes people but leaves buildings standing).

Among the pithy sayings for which Welch is famous are:

- Change before you have to
- Lead rather than manage
- If you don't have a competitive advantage, get out of the game
- Control your destiny, or someone else will

Work-Out, GE's trademarked process of employee innovation, has been called 'one of the biggest planned efforts to alter people's behaviour since Mao's Cultural Revolutions. Unlike China's infamous experiment, however, the ideas-releasing technique that Jack Welch instigated in 1988 has had a wholly positive and energizing effect, and has been copied by scores of other companies. Paolo Fresco, former vice-chairman, explained it in these terms. 'The traditional organization asked maybe 5 per cent of its people to do 95 per cent of its thinking. What we have tried to do is get 100 per cent of the people to do 100 per cent of the thinking.'

The concept was born out of Welch's irritation after a bruising session with his managers in which it became clear that some problems should have been solved lower down the line instead of being dumped on senior executives. He asked Jim Baughman, a Harvard Business School graduate who ran GE's management development academy, Crotonville, to devise a mechanism for forcing accountability and two-way communication between workforce and management. The name Work-Out was chosen to symbolize both problem-solving and making the organization fitter. Crotonville already had a process for making the CEO answerable to his senior managers: Welch told Baughman that he wanted to extend the principle throughout the organization.

It was done initially by holding informal New England-style 'town meetings' for GE's different businesses where groups of employees could discuss problems and solutions among themselves before confronting their managers with proposals for action. The managers had to make decisions on the spot or, in more complex cases, return an answer within one month. The idea was immediately successful and many problems found quick solutions from the people working at the sharp end. It became known at GE as 'picking the low-hanging fruit' – a phrase that has passed into management textbooks to describe easy successes that build confidence, especially in a period of change.

Work-Out was developed into other techniques including 'Action Work-Outs', where brainstorming and exchange of ideas with management happened in the workplace rather than offsite, and the 'Change Acceleration Program', where cross-functional teams were empowered to solve specific problems. The process quickly proved its worth in productivity gains and huge cost savings. At one early Work-Out, a middle-aged employee observed: 'For 25 years you've paid for my hands when you could have had my brains as well – for nothing.'

Welch liked to refer to GE as 'the largest petri dish of business innovation in the world', and to this end he turned every business into a laboratory for ideas. His next big innovation was 'boundarylessness', which involved seeding ideas and best practices in every GE business throughout the organization and beyond it to their suppliers and customers. It was also bound up with the vision of globalization, always a part of Welch's philosophy from his early days as chief executive when he laid down that every GE business should aim to be No. 1 or No. 2

in its global markets. Anything less successful was to be fixed, closed or sold off.

In 1997 came Six Sigma; sometimes described as 'TQM (Total Quality Management) on steroids'. In this complex system of statistically derived performance measurement, the Greek word 'sigma' represents the critical measure of quality and 'six sigma' denotes almost perfect quality, with a target of a mere 3.4 defects for every million operations. The measurements begin with the customer's perception of what is 'critical to quality' in the product or service he or she is buying.

Welch used his clout as chairman and the force of his hands-on personality to drive through these innovations. He was able to do so because he had built the GE corporate centre (run by an executive committee) into a value-adding operation, the reason why GE continues to defy conventional wisdom that conglomerates work less well than focused, one-business companies. With Six Sigma, he imposed mandatory training in the technique for all GE managers, using the martial-arts skills grading of green belt, black belt and master black belt, and linking proficiency to rewards. Attending a course on Six Sigma is written into GE contracts and bonuses are geared to the achievements of targets.

Welch's last big innovative drive was his conversion to digital business in late 1998. Some executives joked that he 'got religion' over it, having previously seemed oblivious to the march of technology, although GE had one of the first industrial websites as early as 1994 and Welch's old division, GE Plastics, was making e-business transactions by 1997. During 1999, Welch imposed his new vision throughout the organization with an initiative called 'destroyyourbusiness.com', designed to push every division of GE into reinventing itself in e-commerce terms before a competitor overtook it. Work-Out and Six Sigma were folded into the digital processes and produced a new IT consultancy business for GE in which customers and providers followed the Work-Out discipline of all-in-a-room brain-storming.

Work-Out has had an impact far beyond GE's borders and in many different industrial and service sectors. Its principle of forcing managers to listen to and act on the ideas of people at the coalface embodies Welch's core conviction that business is about 'maximizing the intellect of the organization'. Without dignifying it with the term, he effectively built a learning organization at GE in which people in different industries and geographies could learn from each other, as well as through Crotonville, ensuring a plentiful supply of high-flyers for succession planning.

He introduced concepts such as 'reverse mentoring', with young and computer-literate staff bringing senior managers up to speed on technology. He believed in 'stretching' promising people, giving them 'runway' to prove their capabilities, and encouraged 'stretch goals' throughout the organization to galvanize performance targets beyond what seemed possible.

If his methods were hard-driving, they were also grounded in a visible adherence to values beyond the bottom line alone. The so-called 'Welch Matrix', in which managers were appraised for their embodiment of corporate values as well as delivering the numbers, was dramatically put into practice in 1992, when Welch fired four high-performing managers who had failed on values. They had, as he put it, forced performance out of their people rather than inspired it. Better financial delivery can be taught, he maintained, but you either have the deeper attributes or you don't.

Jay Conger, professor of leadership at London Business School, has said that one of the keys to Welch's sustained success at GE was 'the ability to spot defining new trends and to remodel the business around them'. His early dictum to 'be No. 1 or No. 2' in markets not only refocused each business and its management but 'weeded out those who were not up to scratch'. He still maintains that every company should get rid of its bottom-performing 10 per cent on a regular basis.

Many of Welch's tools for organizational innovation are now staples of business-school studies. Only one other corporate leader has been seriously compared to him in his passion for communication, ideas, globalization and 'stretch'; Sweden's Percy Barnevik, the former chairman/CEO of engineering conglomerate ABB (Asea Brown Boveri). Barnevik's star faded when he quit executive control of ABB to oversee the Wallenberg dynasty's other investment interests, and ABB, unlike GE, failed to sustain its performance after the master manager left the scene.

KEY WRITINGS

Welch, John F. (2001) *Jack: Straight From the Gut*, New York: Warner, Inc.; London: Headline.

Welch, John F. and Welch, Suzy (2005) *Winning*, London: HarperCollins.

Recommended reading: Tichy, Noel M. and Sherman, Stratford (1993) Control Your Destiny or Someone Else Will, New York: Currency Doubleday; (1995) London: HarperCollins.

Postscript: who will be the next thought leaders?

The world is a different place from what it was 25 years ago, when management gurus were born as a species in the wake of Peters' and Waterman's *In Search of Excellence* with its confident analysis of great corporate performance and eight enduring principles to achieve it. It is a different world even since the millennium, when the dotcom frenzy was in full spate, and a perceptibly more dangerous and volatile place since the terrorist attacks of 11 September 2001 on New York and Washington. The mass destruction of life and property, literally out of a clear blue sky, shook economic confidence around the globe and threw whole industries into crisis.

The gurus of the 1980s issued confident prescriptives for keeping ahead of the competition; those of the 1990s urged the need for radical change and reinventing businesses to capture new markets. The dotcom crash of early 2001 showed that the most inventive new business model cannot substitute for the tested principles of good management, and the impact of 11 September showed that no amount of change-management skills can prepare for the totally unexpected on such a catastrophic scale.

Later came the shocking exposure of Enron's financial conjuring, leading to the world's biggest bankruptcy. The ramifications will be felt for years, with damaging effects on the credibility of accountancy practices as well as of 'virtual'

308

corporations spinning innovative business models out of thin air. Leading business journals and management thinkers as eminent as Gary Hamel (qv) had held Enron up as a shining template of new-economy skills.

Any new generation of gurus, therefore, has to be wary of 'ten steps to heaven' prescriptives: these, along with the lure of the big idea, have tended to fade anyway since the last major management fad, re-engineering, backfired on many companies that looked on it as a handy cost-cutting exercise.

Nevertheless, there are still some interesting thinkers out in the business schools, consultancies and in business itself, looking at the long-term development of the company, the ongoing effects of technology on change and the underlying tides of emotion that govern human behaviour in the workplace and elsewhere.

The following is a brief selection of names, some better known than others, whose work is leading to deeper insights about the nature of individuals and groups engaged in joint enterprises. They are listed in alphabetical order.

ARIE DE GEUS

Dutch economist who joined Royal Dutch/Shell in 1951 and during his 38 years with the group pioneered the use of scenario planning along with colleagues Pierre Wack and Peter Schwartz. Shell's analysis of multiple scenario possibilities is credited with enabling it to weather the OPEC 'oil shocks' of the early 1970s better than its competitors among the big producers, refiners and retailers then known as the 'Seven Sisters'.

De Geus' other major contribution to management thinking is that he has been credited by Peter Senge (qv), the big-idea man of the 'learning organization', with originating that concept. In the 1990s, de Geus turned to studying the nature of long-lived companies as organic communities, lecturing to London's Royal Society of Arts and later publishing an influential book called *The Living Company*.

His argument is that most corporations fail because their managements focus too narrowly on economic activities, forgetting or ignoring the importance of the enterprise as a collective human endeavour. This single book, presenting companies as living communities rather than assets on a balance sheet, has brought de Geus high status as a thinker and lecturer and a key role in the RSA's developing project to define the values of 'tomorrow's company'.

Key book: *The Living Company*, London: Nicholas Brealey, 1999.

ROB GOFFEE

Professor of organizational behaviour at London Business School who has formulated a theory of 'authentic leadership' that breaks some new ground in this much-trodden area and is more likely than other models to be effective in a knowledge economy of non-hierarchical organizations.

A development of what James MacGregor Burns (qv) termed 'transformational' leadership, Goffee's theory is that truly inspirational leaders need to be transparently, authentically themselves, revealing weaknesses as well as strengths in creating a relationship with their followers. Such leaders, he argues, exhibit four key characteristics:

• By exposing some vulnerability they establish approachability and common ground with others.
• They rely heavily on intuition to guide them in their decisions.
• They manage others with 'tough empathy', making it understood that they care intensely but realistically about the work of those they lead.
• They capitalize on what is unique about themselves.

Goffee's latest book, the fruit of 25 years' research with Gareth Jones, a visiting professor at INSEAD, the international business school at Fontainebleau in France, is entitled *Why Should Anyone Be Led by You?*. It argues that those aspiring to a leadership role at whatever level in the organization should be able to answer that question.

Authenticity – or the lack of it – is a pervasive issue today, one of the reasons for widespread public cynicism about politicians, who are rarely perceived as anything other than carefully 'spun' PR constructs. Goffee has identified a convincing theme and his steadily rising reputation makes him a potential addition to the tiny band of British management gurus.

Goffee's other writings have covered such subjects as entrepreneurship, organizational design and corporate culture. At LBS he has directed programmes on executive education and innovation, and he served as deputy dean 2000–2004.

Key book: *Why Should Anyone Be Led by You? The Route to Authentic Leadership* (with Gareth Jones), Boston: Harvard Business School Press, 2005.

DANIEL GOLEMAN

US psychology PhD and former *Wall Street Journal* writer who developed the concept of 'emotional intelligence' or EQ, as opposed to the type of logical/analytical intellect that is measured by conventional IQ testing. Goleman was building on the insights into leadership qualities first presented by Harvard psychologist Howard Gardner in the 1980s and introduced to a wider public in his 1995 book *Leading Minds*. These included a theory of 'multiple intelligences' – covering, for example, linguistic, mathematical and musical aptitudes as well as two personal capabilities: self-knowledge and social skills. Goleman looked deeper into these personal qualities and added three more to define emotional intelligence: self-regulation or the ability to manage one's emotions, motivation and empathy with others. He has built a notable second career out of writing and speaking about his concept, which he theorizes is not only essential to success as a business leader, but more important than IQ in much of life generally.

Key book: *Emotional Intelligence*, London: Bloomsbury, 1995.

RONALD HEIFETZ

US psychiatrist and director of the Leadership Education Project at Harvard's John F. Kennedy School of Government. A powerful influence on Richard Pascale in his studies of nature's own adaptive systems as applied to business, Heifetz has evolved theories of adaptive and non-authority leadership, which he claims are particularly fitted to the digital economy and to a generation in which many talented individuals are no longer willing to be directed from the top down.

Heifetz draws partly on complexity and chaos studies to explore the art of leading through disequilibrium and without relying on traditional authority figures. Historically, he points out, many individuals who have changed the world in fundamental ways had no formal authority – Jesus Christ, the Prophet Mohammed and Mahatma Gandhi among them. The key to exercising such leadership successfully, he argues, is trust.

In 2002, together with a faculty colleague at the Kennedy School called Marty Linsky, he distilled the fruits of his teaching and consulting career into a non-academic book called *Leadership on the Line* (Harvard Business School Press).

Key book: *Leadership Without Easy Answers*, Cambridge, Mass.: Belknap Press, Harvard University, 1994.

JOHN SEELY BROWN

Chief scientist at Xerox Corporation who is now developing a parallel career as an independent director in high-tech industry. Under Seely Brown's hand, Xerox's R&D arm PARC (Palo Alto Research Corporation) famously developed pivotal inventions such as the first PC, the mouse, the laser printer and key software systems like GUI (graphical user interface), only to have the parent corporation fail to exploit them. In the late 1990s he emerged as the principal philosopher and thought leader of the information revolution, taking a healthily sceptical and non-technical view of its impact on the way human beings absorb and process learning.

JSB, as everyone calls him, sees the fault of the early IT revolution as having been obsessed with the technology and insufficiently sensitive to the human users: his key to understanding how people use technology is to study 'communities of practice' – like-minded people with similar work and tastes whose common interests cut across the fact that they may work for competitive organizations. The message of his writings is that only when human habits and interactions are fully understood will the IT revolution reach its full potential.

Key book: *The Social Life of Information*, Cambridge, Mass.: Harvard Business School Press, 2000.

DON TAPSCOTT

Canadian management consultant in the new economy, often called the first 'cyber-guru'. He coined such phrases as the 'Net Generation' and 'paradigm shift' and has redefined the old vertical corporation for the electronic era as communities of business interests tied together by the Internet – 'b-webs' for short. These combine suppliers, distributors, customers and service providers, with the leading partner, differing according to the type of business. These include marketplace businesses such as eBay, middleman retail or wholesale businesses like Wal-Mart, and 'value-chain' operations such as Cisco that tailor services to their customers, knowledge alliances or distributive networks.

Tapscott has also done interesting work on 'human capital' in a world where individuals are increasingly free to sell their talents to the highest bidder. He is the most perceptive thinker and writer on the 'Net Generation' (young people who have grown up with and whose thought processes are shaped by the Internet). At the turn of the millennium he reckoned these to add up to some 88m in North America alone. The human resources industry, Tapscott argues, will have to rethink itself to attract and retain these valuable properties.

Key book: *Digital Capital* (with David Ticoll and Alex Lowy), London: Nicholas Brealey, 2000.

DANAH ZOHAR

US-born physicist and psychologist who works in collaboration with her British psychiatrist husband Ian Marshall in Oxford. Together they have evolved a theory of 'spiritual intelligence' or SQ, which they claim to be the cognitive function in the human brain that deals with big philosophical or intellectual problems such as the meaning of life. Zohar, a graduate of both MIT and Harvard, argues that 20th-century quantum physics should revise our understanding of how the brain works – non-linear and governed by complex 'wiring' but capable of being 'rewired' by unravelling stultified patterns of thought and assumptions. Only by doing this in the corporate context, she argues, can managements come to terms with the kind of change demanded in chaotic 21st-century conditions.

Her studies in neurology have led her to conclude that, while different parts of the brain fulfil different functions of reasoning, some holistic effect is at work beyond the processing of information and images, which results in SQ ability. The word 'spiritual' in this context, she says, has nothing to do with religion but is the part of our intelligence that 'asks why' and which governs the visions and values that make us who we are.

Key book: *SQ – the Ultimate Intelligence*, London: Bloomsbury, 2000.

GLOSSARY OF
MANAGEMENT TERMS

Action learning
A system of management education, invented by the British guru Reg Revans, in which a group of working managers learn by discussing each other's practical problems.

Adhocracy
The opposite of bureaucracy: a term originally coined by Warren Bennis and subsequently adopted by Alvin Toffler, Henry Mintzberg and Robert Waterman to describe small, flexible project teams or groups that operate freely across the departmental boundaries of an organization.

Balanced scorecard
System of measuring an organization's performance, balancing financial and important non-financial areas such as customer satisfaction, cycle-time improvements and learning capabilities. The quadrant design of the scorecard, invented by Harvard professor Robert S. Kaplan and consultant David Norton, enables any business to tailor it to its own needs.

Career anchor
Term coined by Edgar Schein to denote the perceptions that

individuals hold about themselves in their jobs – and which encourage them to stay in those jobs.

Champions
Influential individuals, often in research-based companies, whose backing can ensure that a project or invention gets the chance to prove itself. Peters and Waterman's *In Search of Excellence* found that companies which nurtured champions were more likely to qualify as excellent.

Competitive advantage
The factor that enables a company to gain an edge on its rivals in the marketplace, the result of competitive strategy. Harvard's Michael Porter has worked out a sophisticated formula for determining how companies – and countries – can gain competitive advantage.

Core competencies
What a company does well – the portfolio of skills, technologies and capabilities that give it power to attract customers and a competitive advantage over its market rivals. The term is associated with Gary Hamel and C. K. Prahalad, whose 1994 book *Competing for the Future* stressed the need for managers to think about building core competencies for markets years ahead.

Decentralization
The principle (first recognized in management writing by Alfred D. Chandler but put into practice decades before, in the early 1920s, by Alfred P. Sloan at General Motors) of devolving substantial amounts of managerial power and accountability away from the centre of a large and diverse corporation to semi-autonomous divisions or business units. After Sloan's book was published in 1963, decentralization became the vogue among large industrial conglomerates.

Empowerment
The fashionable managerial buzzword of the early 1990s. In organizations it is usually taken to mean increased participation by employees in the enterprise for which they work, with a view to stimulating initiative and entrepreneurism. It has particular implications for women in eroding the invisible barriers that

tend to keep them in mundane organizational roles. Rosabeth Moss Kanter is the leading exponent of empowerment as an aid to releasing forces for innovation and change within a corporation.

Hierarchy of needs
Motivation model constructed by Abraham Maslow which charts the progression of human needs in the workplace from basic urges of warmth, food and safety to love, esteem and personal fulfilment. Maslow teaches that none of the wants is absolute: that, indeed, a satisfied want ceases to be important.

Job enrichment
Enhancing work by motivational factors that meet employees' aspirations in (usually) non-monetary ways. Frederick Herzberg, who coined the concept, said wryly that it had 'given employment to a hell of a lot of consultants'.

Just-in-time
Revolutionary Japanese low-inventory system for speeding up production, keeping it flexible to customers' requirements and cutting costs. Suppliers supply what is needed *when* it is needed, resulting in faster responses to the market.

Knowledge management
The art of capturing and deploying – through well-managed information technology – the accumulated expertise and experience of the individuals working in an organization to enable it to be shared and maximized for better performance. First promoted by the Swedish financial services group Skandia, the idea became big in the US in the late 1990s with corporations appointing 'chief knowledge officers' or 'chief information officers' – sometimes simply renaming the IT director. Associated with this is 'intellectual capital', an acknowledgement that a company's prime assets reside in the brains of its employees.

Lateral thinking
Defined by the *Oxford English Dictionary* as 'seeking to solve problems by unorthodox or apparently illogical methods'. Inventor

Edward de Bono, who has applied the principle to dozens of challenging situations, including management, describes its purpose as 'the generation of new ideas and the escape from old ones'.

Learning organization

Linked to knowledge management, the learning organization is a coinage variously attributed to former Shell planning director Arie de Geus, British consultant Bob Garratt and MIT's Peter Senge, who made the concept fashionable. The idea is for an organization to enable individual employees to develop their full capabilities and creativity in order to enhance the performance of the whole. Learning is both internal and external – about the company, its competitors, its customers and the environment in which it operates. Whether an entire learning organization exists anywhere is debatable, but successful spin-offs include corporate 'universities' and mechanisms for tapping employees' problem-solving potential such as General Electric's 'Work-Out' sessions.

Management by Objectives

In its heyday in the 1970s, MBO divides corporate goals into objectives that can be assigned to individual managers and measured against performance. Like many other seminal ideas, MBO originated in the fertile mind of Peter Drucker, but was enlarged and developed into a practical methodology in the late 1960s and early 1970s by the British management consultant John Humble.

Managerial hierarchies

The analysis of bureaucratic administration, with each office subordinate to the one above it and every official's role determined by his office, was first undertaken by Max Weber. Alfred Chandler carried it further in his studies of the executive function in great US corporations, arguing that the way an organization's hierarchy operates is determined by its strategic goals. Many of today's gurus, led by Rosabeth Moss Kanter and Charles Handy, predict that the future will see flatter, non-hierarchical management structures in which the 'boss' principle is less important than empowering a wide range of contributory talents.

Mission statement

The distillation of a company's philosophy and corporate goals and values. It can range in length from a sentence to a book (viz. the IBM classic *A Business and Its Beliefs*, by Thomas J. Watson Jr, son of the firm's founder).

Motivational theories

Management theory underwent a sea-change in the 1930s when scientific management, emphasizing measurement of task and performance, gave way to social psychology and human relations, emphasizing the role and motivation of the individual. Elton Mayo, in his seminal work at Western Electric's Hawthorne plant in Chicago in the late 1920s and early 1930s, was the first to identify psychological elements leading to increased productivity. Later theories have included the hierarchy of needs and the psychological contract, but all have stressed the importance of the peer group in job satisfaction and self-esteem.

Portfolio work

Charles Handy's attractive view of the future for many 'knowledge workers', who, as long-term careers in one organization become rarer, will increasingly divide their time into two, three or more discretionary areas of work. Some may be voluntary (e.g. part-time clergy) or otherwise unpaid (e.g. mature student), but have the potential to enhance the quality of the individual's life and personal development.

Psychological contract

Term coined by Edgar Schein to denote what an employee may expect from his or her employer – less in material rewards than in the opportunities to realize potential. It applies also to the employer's expectations of those who work for an organization.

Quality management

How production faults can be eliminated by a management-led philosophy of continuous improvement in every process of planning, production and service. W. Edwards Deming laid down the principle that all processes are vulnerable to loss of quality through variations but that the levels of variation can be managed in order to raise quality consistency. Both Deming and fellow quality guru Joseph Juran insist that quality control starts at the top: Deming believed that 85 per cent of production faults are the responsibility of management.

Re-engineering or business process redesign (BPR)

Described by Michael Hammer, the MIT computer scientist who made it the big idea of the early 1990s, as 'reversing the Industrial Revolution', re-engineering was a mix of techniques from just-in-time back to F. W. Taylor's time and motion study, designed to streamline work processes across departments, take out costs and raise productivity. In practice, it was used by many firms to 'downsize' and ended up cutting muscle as well as fat, leaving companies unable to grow as markets came out of recession. Reaction against its mechanistic nature caused the advocates of re-engineering to look more closely at the human dimension. People rather than processes are now seen as the key to successful change.

'Seven-S' model

The system devised by the then McKinsey team of Richard Pascale, Tom Peters and Robert Waterman to measure the quality of a company's performance: the 'Seven-S' factors divide into three 'hard' – strategy, structure and systems – and four 'soft' – style, shared values, skills and staff. Pascale used the model in *The Art of Japanese Management* in case studies comparing US and Japanese companies; Peters and Waterman employed it for *In Search of Excellence*.

Theory X and Theory Y

The terms coined by Douglas McGregor to epitomize two diametrically opposed sets of management assumptions whose roots go back to Plato and Aristotle. Theory X assumes that most human beings are lazy, dislike work and responsibility, and need to be firmly directed; Theory Y that they actively want to work, achieve and assume responsibility, and should be allowed more self-direction. Before his death in 1964 McGregor was evolving a refined 'Theory Z', but this term was later adopted and adapted by William Ouchi in his book of that title.

Vertical integration

The system favoured by some large corporations for integrating a number of companies down to supplier level to act as an in-house chain of manufacture. Once an established and successful strategy of the US automobile industry, its weaknesses are now more clearly seen as companies have learned that they can't be equally good at a variety of activities. 'Partnering' suppliers rather than integrating them is now the vogue.

RECOMMENDED
GENERAL READING

Pugh, D. S. and Hickson, D. J. eds (1990, 4th edition) *Writers on Organizations*, London: Penguin.

Key readings from the works of gurus who have contributed to the study of organizations, including 17 of the thinkers in *Guide to the Management Gurus*.

Pugh, D. S. ed (1990, 3rd edition) *Organization Theory: Selected Readings*, London: Penguin.

Helpfully chosen tastings from important writings including McGregor's Theory X and Y, Mayo on the Hawthorne experiments and key articles by Mintzberg and R. M. Kanter.

Kennedy, Carol (2001) *The Next Big Idea*, London: Random House Business Books.

A comprehensive analysis of the key management 'big ideas' of the past century and their possible successors from new guru sources, whether research institutes studying the lessons of natural science, industrialists solving problems in the workplace, or the best brains of Silicon Valley.

Micklethwait, J. and Wooldridge, A. (1996) *The Witch Doctors*, London: Heinemann.

Stylish, incisive and entertaining dissection of the management advice industry, including gurus 'on the wild side' such as Stephen Covey, by two leading *Economist* writers.

ACKNOWLEDGEMENTS

Extracts from *The Mind of the Strategist*, by Kenichi Ohmae (McGraw-Hill, 1982) and *The Human Side of Enterprise*, by Douglas McGregor (McGraw-Hill, 1960) reproduced by permission of McGraw-Hill, Inc.

Quotation from *Corporate Strategy*, by H. Igor Ansoff (McGraw-Hill, New York, 1965; Sidgwick and Jackson, London, 1986) reproduced by permission of Dr H. I. Ansoff.

Excerpt from *In Search of Excellence*, by Thomas J. Peters and Robert H. Waterman Jr (Harper and Row, 1982) reproduced by permission of HarperCollins Publishers.

Excerpts from *The Art of Japanese Management*, by Richard Pascale and Anthony Athos (Simon and Schuster, 1981) and *Managing on the Edge*, by Richard Pascale (Simon and Schuster, 1990) reproduced by permission of Simon and Schuster, Inc.

W. E. Deming's 'Fourteen Points' extracted from *The Deming Dimension*, by Henry Neave (SPC Press, 1990) and reproduced by permission of SPC Press, Inc., Knoxville, Tennessee.

Quotations from *The Renewal Factor*, by Robert H. Waterman Jr

Special thanks are due to Peter Starbuck for generously sharing his PhD research and insights into the work of the late Peter Drucker, and for new material relating to John Humble, pioneer of Management by Objectives in the UK.

INDEX

327

balanced scorecard 122, 139, 140–45, 315
Balanced Scorecard, The (Kaplan and Norton)
    140–41
Barnard, Chester xvi, xxv, 19–22, 31, 222,
    274
Barnevik, Percy 82, 83, 306
Barr and Stroud 101
Bartlett, Christopher xxv, 81, 82, 83, 84
Baughman, Jim 304
BBC 254
behavioural patterns 25, 76
behavioural theories xxvii, 112
Belbin, Eunice 23
Belbin, Meredith 23–8
Belbin, Nigel 27
Belbin Associates 24
Bennis, Warren xxii, 27, 29–35, 42, 75,
    104, 108, 165, 180, 185, 222, 253
Beyond Reengineering (Hammer) 100,
    102–3
Biederman, Patricia Ward 33
'blue ocean' strategy xiv, 50, 152, 153, 154
Blue Ocean Strategy (Kim and Mauborgne)
    153, 154
Body Shop, The 95
Boeing Corporation 94
BOP *see* 'bottom of the pyramid' market
Borderless World, The (Ohmae) xxv, 206,
    210
Bossidy, Larry xxvii, 230
Boston Consulting Group 50, 93
'bottom of the pyramid' (BOP) market
    xiv, 240, 242, 243, 244–5
'boundarylessness' 302
BP *see* British Petroleum
brain, right-hand and left-hand sides of
    195, 202
Brandeis, Louis 89
Branson, Sir Richard 149–50
British Airways 169, 171
British Petroleum (BP) 106, 142, 213,
    217, 291
British Telecom 102
Brown, J. A. C. 192
Brown, Wilfred 125
Brunel University 125
Bryn Mawr academy (US) 132

Building a Chain of Customers (Schonberger)
    257–8
Burbidge, John L. 259
bureaucracy, theory of 125–6
bureaucratic organizations 132–3, 200,
    201, 298–300
Burns, James McGregor xiii, xxiv–xv,
    41–4, 310
business organizations and social progress
    19
business process re-engineering (BPR) *see*
    re-engineering
Business Strategy (Ansoff) 6
Butman, John 131
'b-webs' 313

California, University of (Berkeley) xxiii
Campbell, Andrew xxiv
career anchors 253–4, 315–16
career structures, erosion of corporate
    253–4
Carnegie School of Industrial
    Administration 7
Carter, Jimmy 32, 263
Cason, Kathryn 127
Caulkin, Simon xii
cellular manufacturing 259
Cemex 244
centralization 71
Centre for the Study of Thinking (UK)
    37
chain of customers 257, 258
chairman (as team role) 25–6
champions 316
Champy, James 99, 100, 101, 103, 142
Chandler, Alfred D. xxv, 45–8, 222
change
    cultural 255
    and 'knowledge management' 230
    managing 209, 213, 215–17, 221, 222,
        224, 226–7
    resisting 133
    see also defence mechanisms
Change Acceleration Program 302, 304
Change Masters, The (Kanter) 133, 134–5
Changing Culture of a Factory, The (Jaques)
    125